HOOD
WELLNESS

HOOD
WELLNESS

Tales of Communal Care from
People Who Drowned on Dry Land

■

Tamela Julia Gordon

Row House Publishing recognizes that the power of justice-centered storytelling isn't a phenomenon; it is essential for progress. We believe in equity and activism, and that books—and the culture around them—have the potential to transform the universal conversation around what it means to be human.

Part of honoring that conversation is protecting the intellectual property of authors. Reproducing any portion of this book (except for the use of short quotations for review purposes) without the expressed written permission of the copyright owner(s) is strictly prohibited. Submit all requests for usage to rights@rowhousepublishing.com.

Thank you for being an important part of the conversation and holding sacred the critical work of our authors.

Hood Wellness *is a collaborative effort of the author and several contributing essayists. Their stories depict actual events as accurately as their memories allow, with editorial and creative license to recount some events. Some names and identifying characteristics of individuals have been changed to protect their privacy.*

Library of Congress Cataloging-in-Publication Data Available Upon Request

ISBN 978-1-955905-34-3 (TP)
ISBN 978-1-955905-50-3 (eBook)
Printed in the United States
Distributed by Simon & Schuster

Cover illustration by ShinYeon Moon; design by Janay Nachel Frazier
Book design by Pauline Neuwirth, Neuwirth & Associates, Inc.

First edition
10 9 8 7 6 5 4 3 2 1

I dedicate this book to my Self
because I put in that work.

CONTENTS

Foreword by Tanya Denise Fields   1

Introduction   5

SECTION I:
CARE & BODY

My Neck, My Back   13

A Beauty Worth Admiring by Joshua Dixon   26

Can I Hate Your Order?   37

Beg Borrow Heal   48

Care for the Terminally Ill   64

A Road Map for Leaving the Body by Holly Raines   75

Heated   82

Casa de Tami: The Black Fairy Godmother   91

It's My Turn by Simone Gordon   98

Gummy Bitch   103

SECTION II:
CARE & INTERSECTIONALITY

Last Mammy Standing   121

The Stakes Is High   136

Pan(ic)demic   151

Casa de Tami: Kit   164

Girls Just Want to Have Fun (and Code)
    by Kit Fenrir Amreik   168

The South's Got Somethin' to Say   174

The Sweetest Sunday Ever Known: Self-Care Sunday &
   Chattel Slavery   189
Bustin' Nuts in an Antiabortion State   201
For Black Girls Unshifting . . .   214

SECTION III:
CARE, COMMUNITY & ACTIVISM

Casa de Tami: Shevone   223
While I'm Still Here by Shevone Torres   229
Me Too . . . But Who All Gone Be There?   234
Part I: Shout-Out to Claudette Colvin   236
Part II: Me Who?   246
There's More to Me Than HIV by LáDeia Joyce   257
A Drag Deferred   268
Afterword by Dr. Tyffani Monford Dent   278

Acknowledgments   283
Bibliography   286

HOOD
WELLNESS

FOREWORD
by Tanya Denise Fields

■

How do we take care of ourselves beyond surviving another day? How do we surrender our bodies to the extraction of capitalism and all its raggedy symptoms? In the narratives and analyses in the literary tome, there's a thread that weaves through them all. The destructiveness of such systems, yes, but the restoration that community provides us to pivot, to grieve, to celebrate, to unpack, to activate, and to (re)imagine.

This book is long overdue.

The overlooked. The easily dismissed. The victim and survivors of respectability politics. Those of us for whom the conversation of self-care is never broached because we have long been taught and encouraged to hate ourselves. This book is for us.

It's a profitable business; instilling self-loathing and sabotage into "consumers" is one of the pillars of anti-Blackness and misogynoir. Capitalism has kidnapped and commodified the act of self-care while warping the communities and at large the society that facilitates it. Because in capitalism, self-care is a luxury, and the luxuries you have access to determine your worth. Capitalism has long shown cash-poor and working-class Black folx we ain't shit and constructed societies that validate that.

But Black folx, especially queer Black folx, are alchemists, turning pyrite into gold, giving vibrance, life, and culture to a country built on stolen land awash in the blood and bodies of its Indigenous and African captives. And in spite of and because we resist, we shape-shift to somehow create a little bit of what we need, and then we amplify it, not only saving ourselves from the brink but also uttering the strength to pull the rest of the world with us.

I, a dark-skinned, Black, queer mama of six children, was gentrified and displaced out of my childhood neighborhood. I am intimately acquainted with the lack of accessible respite from these systems and how they deregulate our nervous system and negatively impact our quality of life. These systems embed themselves into the minutiae of daily life, disconnecting us from our greatest source of self-care, which is, ironically, community and one another. Ironic because modern-day thought wants us to believe that self-care happens in isolation and in silos, but in fact, it does not, and it cannot.

Acts and rituals of self-care are our inheritance, but somewhere along the way, like everything else we have been so generous in sharing, it no longer belonged to us; we no longer had agency, or we no longer benefited. We found ourselves dog paddling in the proverbial waters, barely staying afloat, while everyone around us felt entitled to our labor, our joy, our trauma, our resilience, our resistance, our words, our fleeting softness, our honey, our speckled, sweet black vanilla paste of sass and beauty. We are fighting against the tide and those who have foisted themselves up by locking their arms around our necks and pushing down.

Hood Wellness sends rescue. It empowers us to know our value beyond productivity and activates the somatic knowledge of rest as a right and the ultimate act of self-preservation. *Hood Wellness* begs us to imagine who we are beyond what someone or something has done to us, and it lays bare the outright lie that self-care and holistic wellness can be sold to you in expensive packaging and slick ads.

My intersection deeply informs how I move. We must all divest from this white, sanitized, commodified version of wellness and find our way back to wellness that challenges systems that not only facilitate healthy environments but also create subversive community-based spaces. Spaces that cradle us in their wombs and unlock our ability to care for ourselves.

As the founder and executive director of the Black Feminist Project, I have spent the better part of the last fifteen years creating soft spaces for Black women, femmes, and children to not only land but to imagine, dream, and care for themselves. We've created a lush urban farm, Black Joy Farm, and anchored in mutual aid and care like the Alice Fields Community Center for Black Women, Girls, and Marginalized Genders. The community center includes a free boutique and children's play area where parents can allow their Black children to fully be children while they rest. I knew our liberation was not going to come in the form of relentless labor, unending frontline activism, or the expectation that we be docile mules for our families and communities with the expectation of nothing in return.

Systems of oppression in a white supremacist and anti-Black world function only to consume us. It cares none for our inherent cosmic value. The only need it has for us is to be a body that can be exploited until it no longer functions to serve the Empire. The bodies most expendable? Cash-poor Black marginalized genders, people living with disabilities, queers, fat people, those who don't wield the capital of desirability, the houseless ones, the ones without husbands and a gaggle of babies, and on and on. I know this all too well.

Voluntary martyrdom has not and will not save or free us.

This book will be yet another tool in our arsenal at the Black Feminist Project to embolden those who enter through our doors looking for relief, rest, respite, and rescue. *Hood Wellness* will strengthen our language and sharpen our praxis. It leans heavily into our ancestral norm of storytelling as bearing witness and documentation. It will serve as another bright light on the path that Black folx are forging toward a liberation that does not consistently require the victimization and sabotage of our bodies and spirit.

Hood Wellness is a literary guide in the spirit of the Underground Railroad; it leads us not only to how we truly care for ourselves but also how we do it with care, grace, tenderness, forgiveness, and compassion for one another.

INTRODUCTION

◼

I'm writing from my spacious New Orleans apartment. It's centrally located in one of the better, more affluent neighborhoods in the city. The kind where white women walk small dogs and white men walk large ones. All my produce is organic, meaning it costs twice as much and lasts half as long. I don't own an expensive-ass Peloton, but it's not because I can't afford it. I prefer to work out in my at-home gym or go for power walks with one of the wealthy divorcées in my neighborhood. Our pools are in the *back*yard, and we open our shutters first thing in the morning.

At forty-one years old, this is the first time in my adult life that I'm living on my own, *outside* the hood. Life has changed drastically for me over the past two years. I always imagined that when I got to this place of privilege, I would finally feel qualified to unpack this mostly legal framework on inclusive and communal care. I believed it needed to be sanitized, perfected, and modeled by my "successful" lifestyle. I was prepared to give the wholesome "manifest yourself to bliss" variation that everyone loves. But a panel discussion I attended here in New Orleans changed all that.

"I wish I would have been braver."

Jarvis DeBerry, author of *Feel to Believe*, said those words. *Feel to Believe* is a collection of his best columns for New Orleans's *The Times-Picayune* publication. It was during a panel discussion of his book, and the crowd was filled with locals who admired and supported him. Jarvis's confession answered the question, "Is there anything you wish you would have done differently in your book?"

I sat in the audience at the Community Book Center, stunned. I found *Feel to Believe* to be raw and unapologetic. For twenty years, DeBerry publicly observed, reviewed, and called out the systems of oppression and the people who uphold them in the Crescent City. He shared details behind the heartbreaking last photo he would take with his dying mother. He shamed local gangs and drug dealers for the grip of violence they held over the city. He called out local and state politicians, by name, for their greed and corruption. Lack of an answer never stopped him from asking questions that mattered, and if Black New Orleanians were living it, he was writing about it.

How is that *not* brave?

The human in me struggled to understand, but as a Black writer I knew exactly what he meant.

One of the greatest challenges of storytelling is getting the reader to, as Jarvis states, "feel to believe." Believe that even though the story you read isn't your own, it still matters to you. In a small, unique way, just by reading it, it's with you now. You can't get anybody to believe anything if you're unwilling to tell the truth. And, for Black writers, this requires us to speak truths that the world has been trying to convince us are lies. It demands that we stroll through the fire and the flames of the very same institutions that keep them rising. You can't spit that kind of storytelling without being brave.

New Orleans may be a progressive city, but it's still located in one of the country's most oppressive states. It's easy to imagine last-minute pivots or "subtle" change requests from higher-ups that would, even slightly, encourage Jarvis to think twice before pushing send on the *whole* truth. His open confession struck a nerve in me that shifted the direction of *Hood Wellness*.

Today my lifestyle is comfortable, but don't get it twisted; I'm for the streets. I'm only a few years removed from my days of hustling back home in New York. Stealing is a gift I'm grateful for, solely because it's kept me fed and clothed when I was without the means to do so legally. I've also resorted to selling drugs so I could make rent . . . and sometimes getting kicked out because, against rule number four of the game, I had a penchant for getting high on my own supply. I'm a high school dropout who spent the first twenty years of my adulthood slinging beers and burgers in the food service industry.

The kind of self-care that got me this far is a long cry from day spas and smelly candles. My wellness can be as tough as Mayweather, but trust, I glow better than people who spend more than twenty-five dollars on face cream.

There are a total of nine voices in *Hood Wellness*, including my own. We're sharing our rock bottoms, breakthroughs, scars, and tough lessons. Each experience is different from the other, but they all share something in common—we went through a major challenge that was unique because of our personal identities, yet, by relying on our desire for more and the strength from our respective communities, we got well, together. For some, it demanded that we become the embodiment of the community we craved. Telling these stories leaves many of us feeling vulnerable, aware that our paths to wellness are roads that are often traveled but rarely celebrated. We tell these stories anyway, to offer reflection and community for the readers who came out the mud like us. We also lend our testimonies because doing so releases us from the grip of societal shame that says we're not supposed to be free in our full, gloriously intersectional identities.

I believe that's the bravery that Jarvis so passionately spoke of. Perhaps it's the kind that can only take place when two or more individuals team up. Even truth needs support in the face of systems of oppression.

There are stories in *Hood Wellness* that are bound to leave you inspired and hopeful. But nobody's here to serve as your cautionary tale. Don't reduce these powerful testimonies to serve as an example of how "grateful" you should be for your life. It's normal to walk away feeling emotional for the lives of those of us drowning on dry land, but these testimonies are not trauma porn. Be inspired, but don't get weird about it.

I'm not a teacher, guru, or authority. *Hood Wellness* isn't a how-to kind of book. It's a reflection of the power of community and an affirmation that, regardless of our intersections and hardships, there is more for us when we walk together. Each testimony holds space for you to figure out how to do this in a way that works best for you.

Ultimately, there's no crystal strong enough to transmute the fluidity of racism. And there is no breathing technique to protect trans and other marginalized genders from the hatred-fueled laws and assaults against their bodies. For those of us who exist within marginalized intersections, our wellness can never be in pursuit despite our identities. Instead, our wellness must always prioritize it. Hood Wellness is centered in an intersectional framework that demands space and support for the most marginalized. It calls for a community that not only "tolerates" but amplifies, centers, and serves those most vulnerable to discrimination, oppression, and other societal hardships.

I hope this book will change your life, motivate you to stay hydrated, and triple the zeros in your bank account. In all honesty, I doubt it. Still, whenever one of us overcomes our challenges by receiving help from our respective communities, it becomes a collective win. And we need all the wins we can get.

Be well,
Tami

Care & Body

■

WHAT'S YOUR CURRENT relationship like with your body? How safe is your body in your home? What about your city and state? Do you need assistance taking care of your body? How mobile are you, physically? Has anything changed over the years? Have you had anything removed? Go numb? Just stop working?

Many of us live with physical disabilities, mental illness, neurodivergence, and/or other conditions that play a significant role in our relationship with our bodies. That's not even factoring in the impact of racism, sexism, poverty, and other societal conditions.

"Care & Body" is dedicated to exploring and unpacking the nuances of wellness with various bodily challenges, experiences, and breakthroughs. As you read these stories and testimonies, consider your relationship with your body, how well it is or isn't received when you step out into the world, and the judgments you make about the bodies of others. Don't be shocked when your ableism or discrimination rears its ugly head—you'll learn from my testimony that before I could genuinely appreciate My Body, I had to stop treating it like an asshole.

MY NECK, MY BACK

■

"There's a funny way that some people interact with those they deem physically unattractive."

—TARANA BURKE, *Unbound: My Story of Liberation and the Birth of the MeToo Movement*

CONTENT WARNING: SEXUAL ASSAULT, SUBSTANCE ABUSE, SUICIDE

A re the handcuffs too tight?" he asked.

"No," I lied.

Scott panted—practically heaved—as he squished his body on top of mine. I lay there, still and unaroused.

Next, the feet. He kissed My Body while wiggling his way down. His lips, thin as paper clips, tickled against my skin.

"Can I suck your feet, baby?" he whispered. I nodded, biting my lower lip to hold back the giggle that rose within me. That part of Scott's little routine underwhelmed me the most. He wanted to be the aggressor and tie me up but then ask to suck my toe, *Mother, May I?* style. Scott was hypocritical in that way. Like, how he loved to rant about the best restaurants in New York City, but he never wanted to venture five miles outside our hometown on Long Island. Even after blessing him with my unconditional submission, which he begged for, he didn't know what to do with it. If he understood how badly My Body craved someone else being in control, he would have put some bass in his tone and stopped playing with my big toes.

I was about to drift into a sea of intrusive thoughts when he made his way back to my face, grabbed me by the chin, and forced eye contact. I tried to focus on his blue eyes, but my gaze wandered to the spot where the deep wrinkles in his forehead surrendered to his receding hairline. *How old was he when he realized that parts of him were disappearing?* I wondered. *How old was I?* Ten years Scott's junior, I spent most of our relationship imagining what he was doing to his body when he was my age.

Next came the blindfold, and I was so relieved. The twenty minutes that followed felt like an eternity as Scott pulled, pinched, choked, and spanked me. He turned My Body around like a rotisserie chicken, locking and unlocking the handcuffs, hoping I'd tell him they were too tight, only for him to torture me more by making them even tighter. My discomfort was palpable, but I was committed to the choreography of it all. His pleasure with My Body was more important to me than how My Body felt.

When the kink wasn't enough to make him cum, I said the things he wanted to hear. I made him believe there were parts of me that only he had access to. I let him think he gave me something I couldn't get anywhere else.

"Daddy, you feel so good." It felt okay.

"Ugh, you're so big! I can't take it!" Lies.

"You make me so wet!" I moaned. That was one of Scott's personal favorites. He didn't realize that, as a twenty-five-year-old hottie who was just waking to her sexual consciousness, everything made me wet. Whispers in my ear in a crowded bar. A lingering stare in the produce aisle. Questions like, "Can I buy you a drink?" and, "Is that your real hair?" The attention made me wet, and it was the one thing Scott was good at giving me.

After he came, he went through the process of uncuffing me. Once my hands were free, I snatched off the blindfold and sat up. I began scooting toward the edge of the bed to make room for Scott to spread out like a starfish, still sweating, panting profusely. A giant human meatball is what he reminded me of. He was an Irish American real estate agent. He had none of the attributes that usually aroused me in a man—he wasn't tall, he wasn't Black, and he wasn't smart. But he liked me, and my yearning to be liked and desired outweighed any of my preferences back then.

While I headed to the kitchen to make him a sandwich, I thought about my time with Scott and what it boiled down to. The original appeal that lured me into his world was more superficial than I'd wished to realize. I thought his Jeep was cool. He was also an Aries, always had good blow, and seemed to like me. Sort of. Still, the more I thought about the unlimited access I'd given him to my life, time, and body, the more it started to sting.

A few weeks later, we parted ways for good. I was bored with his basic-bro, small-town lifestyle, and he was tired of paying my cell phone bill and filling up my gas tank. None of that mattered in the end. After spending my teens as a fat ugly duckling, I had lost weight, learned how to glue in weave tracks properly, and was finally cashing in on the currency of having a young and desirable body. And by currency, I mean privileges.

In the ten years that followed, I used My Body like a chariot, allowing it to whisk me off to places and people that helped me forget everything that had happened to it. I used drugs and alcohol and sex and food and chaos as fuel, taking me from one crisis to the next.

At twenty-seven, I spent two days drinking and getting high with strangers on Fire Island. During that time, I ingested alcohol, cocaine, weed, Vicodin, two packs of cigarettes, and ecstasy. After hours of moaning in a catatonic state, I was told there was "too much" heroin in the ecstasy. My friends held a junkie vigil, taking turns sitting with me throughout the night to make sure I didn't die in my sleep. That would be the first of several wake-up calls that I would snooze through; it was always hard to tell a crisis from a hiccup because My Body wore self-destruction so well.

My Body loved dancing on bar tops in seedy parts of town. Bending over backward for the attention of sleazy men who didn't deserve to drink my bathwater. Back then, My Body was sleek and statuesque — a curvy waist with tits that never needed a bra. Tight Juicy Couture sweatpants and a lace Victoria's Secret thong wrapped around my waist. I once wore a white T-shirt with no bra and won third place in a wet tee contest (I should have won). One night, on a Long Island Railroad train ride home, I lifted my top for all to see, and I yelled, "My Body IS A FUCKING WONDER-LAND!"

Eventually, I got tired of the mundane suburban life offered by my hometown of Bay Shore, Long Island, and took off for Manhattan. I lived there for years, continuing to work as a food server and bartender — a hustle that seemed promising at first. But eventually, my wild ways caught up with me, and I partied harder than I worked.

Society has conditioned us to believe that our bodies are only as valuable as they are "normal" and impressive by white supremacist, patriarchal meathead standards. Not only did I understand this, but I also modeled my life around that fallacy. Being beautiful meant everything to me, mainly because I knew how important it was to everyone else. While I wasn't doted on as beautiful as a child, it was something I gained access to in adulthood, and I took advantage of it thoroughly. Beauty became a drug that I craved and measured my worth against. On the days when I felt pretty, I was kind to myself. And the days I felt ugly, I usually acted like an asshole.

By my mid-thirties, I was a full-blown urban degenerate, and another worrisome binge resulted in losing my wallet and cell phone. I was recovering by cuddling up with my best friend/soulmate, Danny, in the apartment I shared with my asshole roommate. We were listening to Janet Jackson's *Rhythm Nation 1814* when Danny asked a question that changed my life.

"Aren't you tired of this?"

"How can anyone ever get tired of Janet Jackson?" I asked.

"Girl, I'm not talking about Janet. I'm talking about your *life!*" He ran down the series of L's I had taken since living in the city. The impact that late-night partying and one-night stands with losers had on my spirit.

Six weeks later, I moved back home with my parents on Long Island. I decided that Danny was right and gave up sex, alcohol, and substances. This would last several months, until I gradually began drinking and smoking pot in moderation. However, I haven't touched cocaine since, and the celibacy would last for almost eight years.

I also got rid of my extensive collection of waist trainers, tummy teas, lace fronts, faux lashes, and all the other accessories I swore by.

I immediately felt liberated. And ugly.

Over time, My Body began to change. It went from chariot to bulky luggage; instead of getting swept away, I was suddenly grounded in these limbs and human parts that started to bloat and expand. My Body had known no greater appetite suppressant than drugs; without them, my only high came from compulsive eating. And then there was the issue of my teeth. Cocaine stripped them of their enamel while eating away at my gums and bone. Within one year after getting clean, they appeared to look longer and thinner, with an unusual gap appearing between my two front teeth. Within three years, it evolved from a small slit of space to a gaping hole that resembled a two-car garage.

During this transition, I attended a social justice event in upstate New York. I was talking with a Black woman from Detroit named Zora was talking about the misogynoir-fueled violence that had been popping up online—the "Is this Black woman's skirt too short?" and "Is this Black girl dressed too provocative?" memes. Images of Black women doing everyday things but posed with a question that suggests she's not doing it right or righteously. Zora was a petite, slender woman. Deep dark-toned skin with not a single blemish. She was bald, intentionally. And, because of her bone structure, her brows, skin, and shiny head seemed to all work together, making me feel as though there was no other look she should have embodied.

She was pointing out that it's only and always Black marginalized genders who are under the microscope of body ridicule. We're always expected to present ourselves in such a way that there's no question if our skirt is too short. I was certain she was making a good point, but I was also stoned, so I mostly nodded along, agreeing with the general vibe of the conversation. But then she said something that snatched my edges. She said, "You know what it's like being overlooked. I mean, you're a fat, unambiguously Black woman. I *know* you get it!"

Well, damn.

There it was—the sum total of my intersection neatly laid out before me. Fat. Unambiguously Black. Woman. Any single one of those identities is a challenge to navigate, but when combined, I became the antagonist. The words felt so foreign and unsavory paired with my identity. There was no room for beautiful, hypnotic, or even statuesque. Somewhere between slinging drinks near Times Square to serving endless soups and salads in Bay Shore, I transitioned from hot to not; I hated that for me.

I returned home from that event, determined to divest from this pitiful attachment I had with beauty. I understood that I no longer lived in the body that was welcomed on bar tops and adored by men. Not only did I understand, but I accepted, even embraced that. I truly preferred being fat, healthy, and honest instead of thin and strung out, desperate for attention. Still, there was a time when beauty truly felt like a superpower, and I missed having that kind of edge.

The more I reflected on my codependency on needing to be seen as beautiful, I realized how much of my character and identity I compromised for it. One of the lightbulb moments came from owning how I leveraged my Cuban ethnicity to *other* myself out of being recognized as "just Black." Just Black, as in, you are only Black without the additive of another preferred race or ethnicity. While I don't possess a socially-preferred Latina phenotype, I understood that being recognized as "more" than Black American was a loophole that inched me closer to exceptionalism.

"*Mi padre es Cubano, pero mi Español es no bueno,*" I would say to supervisors who wanted to know if I was bilingual or had any other "special" skills. This announcement gave a healthy distance between my identity and the one slapped on a box of Aunt Jemima pancake mix. By announcing that I'm Latina, I get to float under the umbrella of "other," more specifically, "exotic."

The broken-Spanish sentence I've been repeating since childhood comes with another hidden perk; it opens the door for me to reveal that not only do I know my father, but my father is also more than "just Black" and my father is also still married to my mother, which means I come from a two-parent household! That was usually the cherry on top that completed my exceptionally exotic, beautiful, unambiguously Black schtick.

I'm not proud to admit that I leveraged my proximity to anti-Black standards and behaviors for my own personal gain. But I'm not ashamed either. My ethnicity, My Body, my hair, and about every fiber of me had a societal currency attached to it—one that was as interchangeable and conditional as the last. My thinking back then was, *If I can't dismantle my marginalization, why shouldn't I benefit from it any way I can?*

After years of mistreating My Body, living without a single care about the long-term effects of my dangerous lifestyle and reckless decisions, I had made it out alive. I knew more than a few kids who couldn't say the same. Friends who died in their sleep, their hearts finally exhausted from pumping oxycodone. Friends who died in their totaled cars after crashing them into trees during a night of drinking. A few months before I returned home, an old classmate from Bay Shore High, Rianna, died from a fentanyl overdose.

As hard as I tried to shake it, I couldn't ignore the fact that, while I was happy to be alive but resentful that I wasn't beautiful anymore, even in understanding that my desire to be validated as beautiful wouldn't even exist if I weren't on the lower end of societal preference. But it did exist, and to live a life that resembled healthy and good, I was going to have to get over needing to be my old version of beauty and love the skin I was in, or whatever. I was willing to move forward, but accepting this new reality of unprettiness enraged me. So much so that I was angered by anyone who was anywhere near a proximity of external beauty who shrugged it off or failed to acknowledge the privileges that came with it. It was during this time that Glennon Doyle said something that pissed me off in all the right ways.

"I was a really cute kid," Doyle confessed during one of her more popular *We Can Do Hard Things* podcast episodes. She explained her understanding of the currency of beauty at an early age because of how adults embraced and doted on her. However, when she hit her pubescent years, the transition of being treated as regular instead of beautiful took a major toll on her self-image. As the podcast goes on, she unpacks the correlation between beauty and the commentary and societal judgment from it.

It wasn't Glennon's personal experience that got on my nerves. After all, the pressure for girls to present as pretty, adorable, and/or cute is a universal expectation. Girls of every race, ethnicity, and orientation understand what life offers girls who are deemed beautiful and those who are not. The thing that Glennon touched on that pissed me off, in a good way, was the fact that her opinion was so deeply steeped in the master narrative.

The master narrative is what Toni Morrison once described as the default identity society uses to describe as the "norm," be it people, experiences, art, and otherwise. The standard doll is blonde-haired, fair-skinned, and blue-eyed. In romance stories, the couple is white, and the girl next door is the slightly quirky, cute white girl from the average nuclear family. Beauty has always been defined by the master narrative, inflexible in its insistence that white is synonymous with beauty.

When Glennon talks about her proximity to beauty, she speaks of it like a person who was born into it and bore the pressure of maintaining it. Whereas, for a Black girl like me, beauty was the thing outside my proximity, provoking me to reach and attain it constantly.

I was rarely called beautiful as a child, especially not by my mother. I was groomed to look neat and presentable, not pretty. I was a heavyset child, so Mom spent a lot of time telling me in dressing rooms, "You're too big for that." And pretty clothes like dresses and skirts came with the responsibility of keeping my legs closed. I liked to sit the way boys sit, my legs spread open and my feet miles apart. That's not the way you're supposed to sit in dresses and skirts, so I was forced to wear pants—large pants. Never too tight. "You're too big for that."

This isn't to say that Black girls and women aren't beautiful, don't have access to our beauty, or are otherwise unaware of it. Quite the contrary, which is why the act of one Black woman acknowledging the beauty of another is always top-tier flattery. The satisfaction in such recognition is attributed to Black women's fine understanding of natural, pure beauty outside the racist, patriarchal standards of attraction. And, more often than not, the only ones who affirm our beauty are each other.

As a Black woman, I've spent most of my life trying to bend and fold to the master narrative's definition of beauty, one that was intentionally designed to exclude my Black ass. Any chance I have of recognizing my beauty is reliant on other Black women who willingly affirm it. One of the most attractive women in the world, who has consistently exuded nothing but beauty, internally and aesthetic-wise, has always been demeaned, dismissed, misrepresented, and rarely viewed in the light her beauty deserves. It has nothing to do with her looks and everything to do with the fact that she's an unambiguous Black woman. Her name is Serena Williams.

Serena Williams spent her entire lifetime, from youth, studying and perfecting her tennis game, and it showed with every win. Of the 423 tennis matches she played in, she won 367 of them. In 2003 and 2015, the tennis industry used the name Serena Slam to describe the tennis god holding four slam wins at the same time. She's won four Olympic gold medals, matched only by her sister Venus, who has also won four top prizes at the Olympics. She's also shaped like a Coca-Cola bottle with flawless skin, impeccable fashion taste—both on and off court—and a sportsmanship that's steeped in professionalism and integrity. She is just as brilliant and beautiful a person as she is a tennis star. Yet, most commentary about her in media refers to her as aggressive, unprofessional, and even "unladylike."

"No Butts About It," was the headline of a 2006 *National Post* article about Serena Williams's body. The write-up went on to dissect her physical attributes, putting heavy emphasis on the fact that Serena's shape was very on-brand for Black girls, specifically her thick ass. After announcing that she intended on celebrating a recent win by dancing, the article suggested that those who occupied the hotel room below hers "spent the night dodging plaster," a clear dig at her physique and body size.

In a 2009 FOXSports.com write-up, Jason Whitlock's bigheaded ass had the guile to say that Serena Williams was an underachiever: "With a reduction in glut, a little less butt and a smidgen more guts, Serena Williams would easily be as big as Michael Jackson, dwarf Tiger Woods and take a run at Rosa Parks." In that one sentence, Whitlock attacked Williams's body, race, and gender.

People write off the disparaging insults made against Serena Williams as simply sexist commentary. However, there are a litany of women athletes who, while facing various forms of gender discrimination, have never been vulnerable to such vitriol about their actual aesthetic. What makes it different for Serena is the fact that she is both a woman and Black. The overlapping oppression of gender and race too often leads to the cruelest of treatment toward Black women and other marginalized genders.

I grew up hearing a lot of offensive remarks about Serena Williams's body. Apparently, her sheer existence in her natural form was offensive because it didn't fit societal standards of "small" or "feminine."

If that's how they treat one of the greatest athletes in the world, what are they going to say about my flat ass? I often wondered. The hyperawareness that I was deemed lesser than simply for be-

ing Black and a woman was more than enough for me to do anything and everything I could to evade ridicule. Suddenly, beauty
was no longer about a look and had everything to do with a lifestyle.

That whole "Love the skin you're in; beauty is within" crap just
ain't gonna cut it with the levels of misogynoir My Body is exposed to daily. I need to know that I am beautiful and feel my
beauty fully when I leave the house. I know enough to understand
that I'm not going to find it in my makeup bag or the tightest clasp
of my waist trainer, but still, my beauty must be reflected to me
when I look in the mirror. Nothing lifts me up higher than when
a Black woman stops me on the street to say, "I love that color on
you, sis!" or "Okay, curls!" when my wash and go is poppin'.

The more I pour love into myself, the easier it is to see my ex-
terior beauty. My beauty is at its highest decibel[1] when my skin is
moisturized, I'm well-rested, and I lay down my baby hair. I'll always be a sucker for a man who understands that when he's in my
presence, he's with a beauty he doesn't deserve. But it doesn't
move me the way it used to. The attention I seek for my looks is
internal, and it's myself I'm trying to turn on at this point.

This doesn't mean that it doesn't hurt my feelings to be on the
receiving end of misogynoir or witness another Black marginalized gender have to suffer through it. As I write this, I'm actively
trying to bypass what's referred to as "unbig your back" season.
Every few summers, there's a new physical standard that women
are supposed to adhere to. This summer, it's all about losing
enough weight so you don't have a broad back. First, nobody has
time to keep their body aligned with what's trending. And second,
suck my big back dick. I write that with pride, knowing that a few

---

1 The term, "highest decibel" is a nod to EbonyJanice's description of Black
marginalized genders who are deemed exceptionally offensive in their command of space and volume.

years ago, the idea would have been enough for me to double up on gym time and starve myself.

My Body is so over me trying to contort to fit in and have a mass appeal that it wouldn't know how to contort if my life depended on it. I'd love to say that I've reached a level of self-esteem that allows me to divest from fatphobia and misogynoir, but the truth is that I'm just exhausted from it all. Life and beauty have become a lot more simplified since I started actually listening to My Body instead of trying to convince her of what she needed to look like or how to present herself.

Our bodies are not ornaments. They are the only vehicle our spirits have to roam this earthly plane. It doesn't matter how they look, their shape, or what anyone else thinks about them. What matters is that they are ours; our bodies belong to us. They are beautiful and fragile and delicate and hard-working bodies. They deserve to be loved and celebrated. I regret that it took me so long to awaken to the sheer wonder of My Body, but this understanding has saved me from many toxic people, situations, and even my Self.

A BEAUTY WORTH ADMIRING

by Joshua Dixon

■

BLACK AMERICAN MAN – HE/HIM – TWENTY-FOUR YEARS OLD
– CHICAGO, SOUTH SIDE

CONTENT WARNING: ANIMAL VIOLENCE, SUICIDE

*"Radical self-love demands that we see ourselves and others
in the fullness of our complexities and intersections and that we
work to create space for those intersections."*

—SONYA RENEE TAYLOR, *The Body Is Not an Apology:
The Power of Radical Self-Love*

Dad always told us that if one of his two pit bulls ever tried to get out of the yard, make sure to get them back. I came home from school one day, and one tried to run through the gate. When I pulled him back into the yard, he snarled and barked at me. It was a cold December day, and I slid on the ice. That's when it happened. Both dogs attacked me; one was intent on killing me, while the other sacrificed her life to save mine. I was caught in a tug-of-war between both pit bulls. Luckily, I had a leather coat, so the rest of My Body was saved. However, what was exposed, my face and ears, were completely vulnerable during the attack.

My name is Joshua Dixon, and I'm the founder of Admire Wear, an apparel brand that centers wellness and mental health. On December 5, 2007, I survived a pit bull mauling which resulted in losing 80 percent of my face.

The entire attack lasted about two minutes; that's how long it took to change my life. I lost both my upper and lower eyelids on my left eye, both of my ears, and tissue from my cheek, along with severe damage to my nose and left cornea, but it's continuing to heal.

At the time, I didn't understand the severity of my injuries. My dad was so shocked by the carnage of the mauling that I had to answer everything for the paramedics. When I finally got to the hospital, I had my first of sixty-one surgeries which lasted twenty-six hours. I was then put into a medically induced coma because the following surgeries were so intense I wouldn't be able to handle it. The medical team approved the request to wake me up on January 8, one month after the attack, which was also the day of my mother's birthday. That's one memory I will forever cherish—waking up and finding out it was my mom's birthday.

Mom never gave up on me. She held on to hope the entire time, even when others didn't. She had so much faith and always let God have the final say. I had to learn to walk and talk again. She was there for every step, literally and figuratively. She never wanted me to give up. I was fighting battles with life that she could never prepare me for, but that didn't stop her from fighting alongside me, regardless of what it took.

Long before I was released from the hospital, Mom asked me an important question: "Will you be okay returning to that house?" I told her that I never wanted to go back. I couldn't even watch cartoons with dogs. All it took was a dog bark to snap me into painful flashbacks that felt like I was being attacked again. I began seeing a child psychiatrist who did their best to prepare me for the severity of rehabilitation.

The healing process was long and intense. A lot of anger was born from being told that I couldn't do many of the things I used to and that I had to relearn how to walk and talk. The life I once lived was now over, and that depth of grief only enlarged the rage in my heart. When I look at photos of old Josh, I feel like he was a child who died to give birth to who I am now.

An essential part of my treatment has been getting medical balloons, called tissue expanders, inserted into My Body. They expand the skin over a period of time and create tissue that can be used in other parts of the body. I was told they would insert one into my forehead surgically. When I woke up from that operation, I was in so much pain I couldn't eat or walk. Only then was I told that the expanders were placed in my stomach and forehead. By that time, I was in excruciating pain.

I made a fuss and refused medical care until someone explained why the decision had been made without my consent. When my surgeon finally showed up, I told him that if he was going to inflict this pain on My Body, I needed to know. I told him I must be the first person to know, not the last one. From then on, he promised I would participate in that discussion. Every surgery that followed required my signature. That helped me feel more in control. It was also the first time I had really advocated for myself, which helped me do it more as I got older.

CONCRETE ROSE

Having to sacrifice parts of your body to reconstruct the parts taken away is a gift, but it's also painful. When they built my new nose, infections resulted in My Body rejecting it. It happened three times. There have been all kinds of complications—infections, loss of skin, transfusions, long hours, prolonged recovery, and inability to eat. But there's also the gift of having prosthetic ears, which I can wear regularly, allowing me to connect to the feeling of wholeness.

I rarely cried alone. Doctors and nurses cried with me. They were invested in my health, journey, and healing. I was also grateful to spend time with other kids in the children's ward. I would get so excited to see other kids going through the process of having a trachea in their neck or having skin graft surgeries. There's a warm side to hospitals beyond the blue, cold, sterile environment. The medical staff who treated me didn't just give me needles and change my bandages. They cared about me, listened to me, and reminded me that I wasn't alone. Even today, as a grown man, many who nursed me back to health when I was eight are still an important part of my life. They're a significant part of my community and a testament to the compassion required to keep me alive and healthy.

I love to garden. I've been doing it with my mom since I was three. One day after returning home from the hospital, my mom went to the store and said she would be back home soon. I stared out the window at the neighborhood kids playing until she got back. She returned with three rose bushes she had purchased for us to plant together. She said, "These roses will be your friends until you can have friends." She was tired of me sitting in the window watching children play outside, unable to join them.

I had to isolate myself after each surgery to avoid the risk of infection, so I spent that time in the yard with my roses, trimming them, watching them grow, and watching them die. I would talk to those roses. I learned so much about life by caring for them. Roses don't kill or intrude on other roses, and I love that about them.

I noticed that one of the bushes was dying, and the other two were still alive. But, as a few days passed, the other roses started to wilt, and the rose that had been dying began coming alive, looking vibrant again. It almost looked like the two once-strong roses gave their power to the dying rose. This beautiful hybrid rose was red, orange, and white with little roses. I remember thinking, *I'm a rose. I'm resilient. I have my seasons of growth.* We have seasons where we can go one or three years without growing. But, because of the community we have around us and within ourselves, we bounce back and blossom again. It was at this point that I started to gain confidence in who I saw when I looked in the mirror. I saw my own inner flower start to blossom.

Unlike flowers and many other living things, roses give one another space to grow freely and beautifully; they don't interrupt or harm one another's experience. Those roses showed me what true resilience is. By supporting one another, they gained strength. They weren't alone in their pain; it was something they got through together. They taught me that seasons of sadness and despair will happen, but they don't deter from hoping for beautiful, blossoming seasons to come. Learning from them taught me how to build resilience to the pain cast by people who disliked my appearance.

THE REAL, CRUEL WORLD

I didn't know I was considered ugly until people called me cruel names and treated me inhumanely. I thought I was cute until people told me otherwise.

I'm usually pretty open about my injuries and healing journey. I'd rather people be curious than mean. I would even explain the cool side of my care—I've always been able to see the exciting, intriguing side of my experience, even through the pain. I'm fascinated by the medical sciences and technology that helped me in my restorative journey.

I was about thirteen years old with tissue expanders in my face. Mom and I were in the checkout line at Walmart. This curious kid in front of us nudged at his grandma, and she grabbed his head and told him, "Don't talk to him cuz he has Ebola."

Mom was so upset at the older woman that it almost caused a physical conflict. I had to hold her back so she wouldn't hurt anybody. Moments like that hurt both of us. We actually left the store without purchasing anything.

I was the victim of a situation beyond my control, yet there was a lot of hate toward me because of my appearance. Strangers treated me harshly because of two life-altering minutes. For years, I was called countless names like chain face, zombie face, two face, roadkill, Ebola kid, and many others. For too long, I thought it was my fault. The saddest part about our society is that the bulk of the bullying I experienced was by adults.

I went through five years of homeschooling. Each year, I would keep my fingers crossed that I'd get the green light to attend school, but the verdict was always the same: "You're not going because you need to have more surgeries."

Finally, after eighth grade, I tested into a STEM-based selective enrollment in Chicago. That was when I got to step my feet into school for the first time. I was so excited and thrilled. At first, it was awesome. It was such a huge school. My kitchen used to be the classroom, and now I was surrounded by nine hundred students. I learned quickly how parents didn't teach their kids about people who looked different. Poor education about kids who look different, along with diversion and inclusion, became my new problem.

Classes would get disrupted because students couldn't pay attention whenever I was around; instead of learning, they spent their time bullying me. Despite the challenges of adjusting to in-school education, I still wanted to work hard and excel. I wanted to be at the top. I used to be in a special ed class because my test scores were low. My reading skills were weak because of the strain on my right eye and trying to manage the fast-paced demands.

I was bullied so severely in high school I had no choice but to close myself to the world. I didn't have a lot of hope in people. I kept getting judged repeatedly. I would eat my lunch alone and hide around the school during passing periods because most kids wouldn't allow me to sit near them, let alone at the same table. I wore oversized hoodies, regardless of how cold or hot it was. I felt if I could hide my face, I could hide in plain sight like a ghost. I would put my hood over my head to feel safe inside.

I was getting spit on and kicked out of restaurants for how I looked, and I thought, *Will this be my life?* I wanted to have kids, but I saw too many kids cry and yell when they saw me.

In my junior year of high school, I attempted suicide for the first time. Trying to keep up with able-bodied tasks while navigating the isolation and constant bullying without Mom and my medical community was too much. So, I posted a suicide letter on Facebook. Someone from my family contacted my mother. She came at me, livid. She was like, "We're in this together."

I told her, "I've been fighting since I woke up from that coma and still don't feel safe in my skin or body! What's the purpose of all this?"

By this time, I was creating photographic illustrations of myself. I would sit in the corner of my bedroom and create images that reflected my mind's interpretation of My Body. Oftentimes, my parents would be fighting furiously in the background. I tuned them out by putting on my headphones and blasting something like "Never Be Alone" by Shawn Mendes. Creating art was a coping mechanism when I was frustrated and wrestling with suicide ideation.

While Mom talked to me about the Facebook post, her eyes caught my artwork tucked in the corner of the bedroom. "I don't want you to be a modern Van Gogh," she told me.

I had no idea who she was talking about until she explained who Van Gogh was. People thought he was just a crazy old artist dude, but he had a lot of skill. His art reflected the beauty and pain of life, but it didn't save him from his own emotional torment, and he died, suspected by suicide, before he was forty. That's when I started to understand the comparison she was making.

Mom encouraged me to use my voice and art to keep moving further. She forced me to go to counseling, and that helped a lot. It helped me to divest from the weight of toxic masculinity on my identity. My dad had always told my brother and me that we weren't allowed to cry. He would often scream and call us names if we did.

LIFE THROUGH A NEW LENS

There were so many identities and names I attributed to myself. Every time I looked in the mirror, I would bully myself. I kept hearing, *You're a monster. I wish you would have died.* I would stand in front of the mirror for hours and really tear myself down. Counseling taught me how to work through my anger. Now, my thorns repel the cruelty I experience instead of keeping it inside where it hurts the most.

Everyone was on board as I continued to heal and incorporate art into my wellness, including my medical team. They have been family to me for all the years we've been together. They attend my art shows and support me in various ways. Having them as a part of my recovery after my suicide attempt at sixteen was crucial because it helped me prepare for college.

This experience is painful and gruesome, but it's been beautiful because of the ways I've expressed myself through my honesty, energy, and art. Photography became a tool for me to create a bridge, a vessel for people to have deep conversations we as a collective aren't having enough of. It allowed me to express pain that I couldn't always share in words. The photographs I created were a space where a stranger and I could have those safe conversations and learn from each other.

By the time I reached senior year, I stepped outside my hoodie. I learned that I'm my own version of normal, and people wouldn't like it, but I have to learn how to take care of this body that's working for me. I have to be kind to the young Josh, who sacrificed so much so I can be here.

Going away to college introduced me to another societal challenge: racism. I was one of the very few Black students. Every experience that I would share was perceived as the "Black experience." That school wasn't challenging me enough, and they were biased against Black students. I was tired of authority neglecting me and not liking me for who I am. I became very vocal in advocating for myself and other Black students. Participation was required of every student, yet we got very little feedback, and this behavior was normalized. It was also hard to make friends because of the stereotypes that came with being Black from Chicago. Students would ask if I was in a gang and if my injuries were related to gang violence. I realized that I no longer wanted to attend this campus because of being treated differently due to my facial impairment, my wardrobe, and my overall intersection.

One winter Sunday on campus, I went out to catch breakfast with a friend from New York. We had a very similar style and demeanor, and we both happened to be wearing all black. We were laughing and talking, no hoodies, but the entire diner stared at us. The waiter returned and said, "We can't serve you, as our customers seem disturbed by this table. So we are asking you to leave and come back another time. We are sorry for the inconvenience."

They wanted us to take off our hoodies and look less threatening. Because we didn't "comply," we had to leave. We were so upset we took the glasses of water and left. We'd actually gotten kicked out because we were Black.

After that experience, I realized that I wanted more. I'd spent all these years being alive, fighting for a place in this world. I knew I had what it took to get into a top school in photography, and that's what I did. I'm huge on creating memories and taking photos of the healing process. I had a film camera then and took hundreds of photos on the journey. I studied photography, taught myself, and took several online classes to increase my skills and get into a top-four school of photography.

Sophomore year of college, and I was still learning and exceeding. I still wasn't getting feedback on my work, so I critiqued myself. I made an awesome portfolio and decided to apply to the School of Visual Arts and Pratt Institute School of Art in New York, the Rhode Island School of Design, and the School of the Art Institute of Chicago. I started adhering to my current school's standards, even though they wanted to whitewash my work. We worked on the most mundane subjects, like capturing nature and creating abstracts. Nothing about me, My Body, or my race could be involved.

I was accepted into all four schools in March of that year. I decided to go back home and attend the School of the Art Institute of Chicago.

When I returned home to Chicago for school, I was in well-rounded classes where I could integrate my personal views, art, and whole personality into my work. I was in classes with Black professors and teachers.

There's been so much tenderness and intimacy that's come with taking ownership of My Body and taking care of My Body. I understand that if I reside in this body for the rest of my life, I might as well find clothes and a hairstyle that work for me. I might as well take care of myself. After leaving college and surviving two attempts of unaliving myself, I realized I'm not a burden to this world, I add a lot of value, and I need to stop apologizing for my existence.

Being able to help people with my platform by centering wellness and healing is a major part of my wellness. I can't always afford counseling, so I do my best to read books about mental health and illness. I educate myself about high-functioning depression, learn how to talk about PTSD, and navigate life with all these traumas. What gives me purpose is knowing that there are seeds in every tear I cry. The love I get back keeps me going, inspired, and motivated.

I know how much it matters to show up, show out, and give life my all. I live every day as if it's my last, with total effort and compassion, just as I did in my rehabilitation all those years ago. I've come out of my shell, switched up my wardrobe, and made it my mission to promote kindness. I don't fake my smiles anymore. And I learned how to feel the joy that encourages me and inspires others.

I know who I am: Joshua Dixon, a photographer, a survivor, and a human being. I still struggle with self-esteem, body dysmorphia, and ableism, but none of that gets in the way of my blossoming. These struggles affect me, but they don't define me.

Joshua is still based in Chicago, where he continues to run his apparel/wellness brand, Admire Wear. You can follow him on social media via @admirewear_.

CAN I HATE YOUR ORDER?

*"So yes, I'm all about my fucking coin,
and I need you to run me my money."*

—SESALI BOWEN, *Bad Fat Black Girl: Notes from a Trap Feminist*

CONTENT WARNING: SUBSTANCE ABUSE, SEXUAL ASSAULT

What beers do you have on draft?" he yelled. His accent sounded British but could have also been German or Polish. His words landed between my breasts, his warm breath against my cleavage.

"Our beers are pretty basic!" I yelled back, brushing off the suggestion with a wave. I leaned my full lips close to his pink ear. Turned on by my body language, he leaned in too, closer to my breasts. "Tonight's beer special is the best thing on the menu! Much better than draft!" I spoke into his ear. "It's a Belgium ale called Delerium Tremens!" It was also fifteen dollars a bottle. "I love your cologne. You smell *amazing*," I added. I was late for work and rent; I needed to be ambitious with my upselling.

The guy looked over at his two sons, each giving him a thumbs-up of approval.

"We will take three!" he yelled proudly. He stared at my eyes, then my tits, eyes, then tits. Of all the sights this dweeb must have seen in New York City, I would be his climax. The look of satisfaction on his face was one that I recognized from international tourists. There he was—European, dining with his googly white family, about to indulge in Americana fare served by a hot Black woman. He was having the time of his life.

"And what burger should I have?" he asked.

Like stealing candy from a baby, I thought.

I leaned back in. This time, I pressed my left index finger against his back. Subtle enough for his wife not to notice but just enough to get him even hornier. In an instant, his cheeks flushed. He licked his thin lips, his gaze lost in my tits. "Tonight's burger is the house special," I whispered. "Double beef patties with bacon, cheddar cheese, jalapeños, mushrooms, and a fried egg." If he smelled the remains of Hennessy on my breath I downed while getting ready for work, it only aroused him more.

The way I cranked up the heat on this trick, it's hard to believe that a slice of my pussy wasn't slathered somewhere between the brioche bun and organic beef patty. Also, there's no such thing as a house special. Totaling twenty-four dollars, double the cost of a regular cheeseburger (fries and beverage sold separately), my co-workers and I had affectionately called it the *rent burger*.

"That sounds absolutely amazing," he whimpered. "We are all getting house burgers!" Everyone looked amused except his wife.

I didn't love working that hard for a sale, but I clocked in (late) on a mission: to get paid and lit. There was no way I could walk past my roommate without my total share of the rent, and I was dangerously low on weed.

It was 2015, and I was in my third year working as a food server and bartender at Blane's Beef and Libation. Blane's was a hip eatery located a stone's throw from Times Square, and the location was a definitive upgrade to my résumé. Like many restaurants, it was fueled by sales. These sales determine everything from how many hours a week you'll be scheduled, how profitable of a section you'll get assigned for your shift, and even how well you'll do in tips. On that night, I was assigned as a first cut in a shitty section. This meant that not only did I have a lesser number of tables than other servers, but I would also be the first chosen to go home when the manager made cuts.

According to indeed.com, New York City food servers make an average of sixteen dollars per hour, adding up to $33K per year. I averaged thirty-five dollars, sometimes as high as fifty dollars an hour during busy seasons. I was earning more than I ever had. This would have been perfect if not for lofty expenses, like over-priced rent for an apartment with a roommate who I was certain was plotting my demise, the costs of living in the city, and my pesky and expensive cocaine habit.

I started punching in drink orders quickly before I forgot.

"Table seventy-four is mine, not yours, Tamela!" Carol yelled. Her long blonde hair was pulled into a too-tight ponytail at the back of her head, and her forehead and neck veins bulged. Unlike me, she wore her white blouse buttoned up to the top, looking like she was about to hand out pop quizzes. I fucking hated Carol.

"No, it isn't." I lied. I was aware that table seventy-four was, in fact, Carol's when I approached them. But it was a six-top, and I needed it to compensate for my musty-ass section. Getting assigned to the aisle section was punishment for clocking in late again—allegedly. Charges I planned on refuting, even though I was not the wrongly accused. "I have tables seventy-one, seventy-two, seventy-three, *and* seventy-four."

"Table seventy-four is mine!" Carol whined. She even slightly stomped one of her feet. I cut her off by putting a finger in her face to continue ringing my order. I only looked up at her when I was finished, and even then, I gave her an expression of annoyance.

"I already rang them in." I shrugged.

"Tami Wami!"

I turned to see Rob, the shift manager, approaching. He was wearing his favorite red pants. I knew they were his favorite because whenever a table complimented him on them while walking by, he squealed, "Oh my God, thank you! These are my favorite!" He paired it with a black buttoned-down shirt and a brown blazer. I liked the look and made a mental note to compliment him on it when we clocked out and headed to the bar. "I was going to wring your neck for coming in late, but I just walked past table seventy-four. Wow! They *really* love you!"

"Yeah, the dad totally wants to fuck me." I grinned. "And why does everyone keep saying I'm late?" This is the first level of the lie—deflection. Next, I'd start pretending that I was actually on time.

"Rob, Tamela stole my table. Again!" Carol stammered.

"Rob—one, since when does the aisle section not get table seventy-four? And two, Carol, how often do you accuse people *like me* of stealing?" I was reaching, but at this point, my patience was wearing about as thin as Carol's wispy edges. In the three years I'd worked at Blane's, the aisle section had always been exclusively two-tops, meant for parties of two. This was referred to as a training section for new servers still working up to waiting on bigger parties. After years of being a high-ranking server and bartender, I knew nothing about such small sections. I was a big-top girl. My personality was meant for groups of co-workers celebrating a retirement or white girls from New Jersey celebrating a bachelorette party. Just two Saturdays ago, when Blane's hosted the *Saturday Night Live* after-party with Lady Gaga, I was one of only two servers from our store chosen to work. I was the go-to server/bartender assigned to work at other locations within the Blane franchise, and when I walked through the door, management was always pleased with what they saw. I was quick, I could remember an order for a table of ten without writing it down, and I always looked good doing it. Late (allegedly) or not, a woman of my stature had no business in the aisle section.

"Yeah, right! The aisle never gets table seventy-four!" Carol was outraged, but it was deeper than me beating her to that six-top. She was painfully aware that the social hierarchy she'd known her entire life, which placed her at a level of importance and priority far higher than mine, had no value in establishments like Blane's. The three qualities that Blane's valued were the ones that Carol lacked: good looks, high sales, and skills. Carol wasn't ugly by any stretch of means. But on a busy dinner shift, when the lights dimmed, the drinks started flowing, and the DJ started cranking up the jams, she was easily lost in the crowd. And while she could take food orders and deliver drinks properly, she lacked the finesse that encouraged her tables to order more and tip higher, benefiting the staff and management.

To be fair, I was no supermodel—at least not by the patriarchal, European phenotypical standard. However, I was curvy and always knew the right half-wigs to wear to look natural and accentuate my perfect bone structure. Paired with a face card that never declines and tits shoved up to my throat, you would want to hold your man tighter when I walked up to take your order.

Hotness is not an actual requirement for many positions in the food service industry. However, a well-kept secret is that the more exclusive the establishment, the higher the expectation of having your front-of-house employees (e.g., hosts, food servers, management, and even bussers) easy on the eye.

In a 2021 *Newsweek* article, a bartender who worked in an establishment for four years talked about the lack of respect—and tips—she received after gaining weight. Cassidy Tweedt, who was a bartender at the time the article was published, admitted that her "whole life changed," in the service industry after gaining weight while undergoing treatment for an eating disorder. "People don't even look you in the eye anymore, they're not nice to you, especially men."

Cassidy's experience reflects an unfair reality in the service industry, including retail—physical desirability can play as big a part, sometimes even more, than actual skills and experience. Of course, beauty is subjective. What got me favored in a midtown burger bar wouldn't work at a more snobby eatery. Still, my looks, "well-spoken" demeanor, and charisma usually got me whatever job I auditioned for. I use the word *audition* with intention; interviewing for a food service position in New York City requires pageantry. Back then, the ideal résumé had a small head-shot-like photo in one of its corners and read like a press kit bio.

"I must say, we thought our mind was made, but then we saw your résumé . . . Impressive." I had worked everywhere, from four-star restaurants to local eateries on Main Street, but variety wasn't my appeal. Because of my writing skills, I could curate a résumé that embellished any task I ever got paid to carry out. For example, when I worked at Cookies & Cream back home on Long Island, my responsibilities for working lunch shifts were pretty basic. Aside from waiting tables, my job was to turn over the chairs, warm up coffee, and confirm the menu with the cook. But my résumé said, *I was the head coordinator in front-of-house lunch shifts, responsible for opening and arranging the restaurant, as well as co-partnering with the chef in curating an innovative and popular menu.*

And, when it came to skill, it took much more than a cute face and nice pair of tits to earn a living. "Nobody pays their rent off hamburgers and fries!" was a constant statement at Blane's, chanted by everyone from kitchen staff all the way up to regional supervisors. This was their way of conditioning employees to upsell! Upsell! Upsell! To keep a restaurant running and fully employed, you must have enough customers to pay a decent chef, waitstaff, hosts, bussers, etc. Having learned this years ago while working at a chain restaurant back home on Long Island, up-selling has become a skill for me, often keeping me in the good graces of employers who had a say on who was scheduled to work. I could ring in an order, convince a guest to get something three times more expensive and extravagant, and keep them laughing while they waited. All the while, keeping the cold drinks flowing to the hot and often thirsty kitchen staff. A gift that Carol couldn't pull off on her most congenial day.

"Well . . . ," Rob began, "when we open up all the sections on a slow weeknight like tonight, we sometimes give table seventy-four to the aisle section."

I was impressed that Rob could quickly develop a lie from scratch. That was usually my style.

"Then, why is the table written in my section on the floor plan?" Carol was plain indignant. "I mean, come on! The aisle section doesn't get a center table! There's a reason it's called the *aisle* section!" She flailed her arm at my sad, tiny section. Just then, two Black women who were sat in the aisle looked up at us. We all smiled broadly and waved. I held up an index finger and mouthed, *One moment.* They smiled and gave a thumbs-up.

"Carol, look," I began, still sporting my fake smile. "Why don't you just take table seventy-two in my section? I can tell they're cool ladies."

She looked at the two Black women and then back at me. "I'll wait until you're done with my table."

"Actually, Carol, you are going to take table seventy-two," Rob told her. "Please go and greet them."

After an exasperated huff, Carol trotted her little ass over to the two Black patrons.

Without saying a word, I looked at Rob, one hand placed on my hip, the other extended toward Carol's direction, presenting my voilà moment. Rob said nothing but shook his head from side to side. He knew as well as I did why Carol didn't want to serve table seventy-two.

Though petty, those kinds of wins were highly satisfying to my ego. For all of Carol's societal privilege, she could never reach the favor I had accrued at Blane's. Love me or hate me, it could never be denied that I exceeded my position and did a good job of making myself look like a team player. Carol may have only been a server for the summer, but I'd been a Black girl my whole life. If there's one thing society had taught me, it was how to leverage every nook and cranny of favor I could get my hands on.

At thirty-four years old, I had a strong command of my attributes and how to leverage them. Aside from being a babe, I spoke Caucasian fluently. Paired with a hyper understanding of power dynamics and how they could complicate or compliment my intersection, I was showing up to win, no matter how late I clocked in.

By the end of the shift, my cash and credit tip totaled $380 ($560, if you include the blow I sold to staff—a little side hustle to help ends meet). I could have saved a killing, but because I dismissed Biggie's advice and always got high on my own supply, my take-home was little over $225.

After hiking up the fourth-floor walk-up into my apartment, I went through the routine of peeling out of my ranch-soaked uniform. As I put my hand on the door handle, the note loosely tacked to my door slid down the floor, landing on my toes.

I need that rent, my nigga.

I closed the door behind me and pulled out $800 from under my mattress and $200 from what I'd made that night. I took the $1000, wrapped it inside the note, walked down the hallway, and slid it under her door.

Bitch, I mumbled to myself, heading back to my room.

It was then that I realized there was a downtrodden feeling within myself. It confused me. I hopped in the shower, hoping that would help, but instead, I started sobbing. *What the fuck is wrong with me?* I wondered. It had been a decent day. I'd made good money, and I'd paid my rent. Yet, a deep dissatisfaction that I couldn't shake off smothered me.

After drying off, I slipped into my jammies and bonnet and curled into bed. My heart raced from the cocaine, and my legs throbbed from running around all night. *I'm tired*, I realized. And not just physical tiredness. Not tired in a way that I was simply exhausted and needed rest. I was weary in my soul, in my heart. Tired of everything.

I'd spent two decades working my ass off in the food service industry, and I had nothing to show for it but aches and pains.

If the food service industry were Las Vegas, then restaurants would be the house. And, just as the saying goes in Sin City, "The house always wins." This meant that it never mattered how good-looking or well-liked I was. Room for advancement was slim and only desirable if hospitality was truly a calling. For me, it had never been more than a hustle, no more or less important than selling grams of weed or charging people to revise their résumés. Thanks to living much of my adult life in survival mode, I never had time to consider what life would look like for me later down the road.

I had been thrown in the ring for a dead-end hustle and was getting TKO'd. I felt like a fraud. Humor and charisma were character attributes I exuded naturally, but working in white spaces like Blane's meant I had to crank up the dial on my appeal so as not to come across as angry or uneducated, labels which, often enough, seemed to find me anyway.

I was a rising star when I first got hired at Blane's. My charm and can-do attitude made me a hit with everyone, from fellow servers and hosts to managers, cooks, and even the cleaning crew. My sentiment was authentic, but my behavior had to do with the fact that I understood the system I was a part of and how important it was to bob and weave it with assimilation. But, as time passed, I began resenting the very schtick I had mastered. I no longer wanted to grab drinks after work and go to the holiday parties and staff baby showers. I hated these people, and the sad truth was that I felt satisfaction in knowing they hated me too.

I began to think about what would happen if I were to show up to work the next shift and be my pure, unhappy, unsmiley Self. What section would they assign me then? How many shifts would I lose?

They say that if you can make it in New York, then you can make it anywhere. But no one defines what "making it" should look like. I was making a living, but barely and not much else. I was too busy to entertain love, too broke to plan for the future, and too tired to take real care of My Body. No matter how hard I tried to find success and joy in New York, the city rejected me like a bad kidney. I didn't have the income or good credit to qualify for my own apartment.

In a 2014 *Today* article written by Ben Popkin, he shared a startling statistic revealed by Restaurant Opportunities Centers United: 80 percent of women and 70 percent of men admitted to being a victim of sexual violence at one point. This statistic speaks to me on a deeply personal level, having navigated sexual assault situations that ranged from minor to life-changing. In the twenty years I was employed in the food service industry, I had my kitty cat groped, my ass smacked, my breasts pinched, and was yelled at and publicly berated—by management, a cook, a busser, and even patrons. "This industry is crazy!" was often the response whenever another employee or myself would confess to being physically and sexually violated.

The patriarchal-dominated restaurant industry is prime breeding ground for sexual misconduct, verbal abuse, and sometimes physical abuse as well. For all the showmanship that takes place in front of guests on "the floor" or in the "front of house," there's a dark world that exists behind those swinging doors—the "back of house": the kitchen, manager's office, locker room, dry storage, etc. It is often in these spaces where predatorial behavior takes place.

With the constant flow of alcohol, dim light settings, and questionable behavior that would never fly in a cubicle office, I had come to expect degradation and sexual violence. I often laughed it off, brushed it off, tried my best to pretend as though I was thick-skinned enough to tolerate the abuse. What I didn't realize was that I wasn't, and that I was trying to disassociate the horrible hours, excruciating physical labor, and sexual and verbal violence with a bad attitude, drugs, and Hennessy.

The industry was killing me.

I yearned to manifest my way out of my shitty life and couldn't figure out how I hadn't found a way yet. My bedroom walls had become littered with vision boards of dreams ranging from global travel to designer clothes, a size-six figure, and a full-time writing career that would finally take me off my feet and onto a bookshelf.

I did everything that the law of attraction insists will bring on a good life. I practiced hot yoga classes twice a week, chugged water by the gallon, meditated, and constantly visualized a life filled with ease and writing. And, of course, the drugs and promiscuous sex.

I knew I was swirling in a downward spiral of self-destruction, but I was convinced there was no way out. *What's going to happen to me?* I wondered.

BEG BORROW HEAL

■

"My weary body asked my weary mind:
'Was this all you needed, then?'"

—ELIZABETH GILBERT, *Eat Pray Love*

Society constantly reminds us that our opportunities are as marginalized as our intersections. The more we navigate life within our restricted confines, the more we become conditioned to believe it. Think about how many times you said:

I can't go because I can't afford it.
I can't do that because I don't have the qualifications.
I can't complete this because I don't have the capacity.
I can't participate because I don't have the time.

Now think about the proximity of that *can't* and your intersection. Money, meritocracy, the ability to "hustle" or high function, and time are privileges many of us lack (and some don't even want). Too often, the impact of that lack leaves us with a slim selection of access to our most basic needs: housing, money, and affordable healthcare.

Rather than addressing these issues head-on, the wellness industry takes a fluffier, toxic approach, using spiritual bypassing to dismiss the harm. *Cleanses, yoga retreats, and bubble baths will heal something in you. Focus on the positive, and high vibe your way to greener pastures.* It's a great concept—for white, able-bodied, financially secure, and neurotypical people. But . . . what about the rest of us?

It was 2018, and I had been living at home with my parents for about three years. Daddy had repurposed my old bedroom as his "closet," which consisted of books, out-of-date electronic devices he'd never gotten the hang of, and more books. I was left to the back room, which was once the bedroom that both my brothers, Terrell and Tyrone, shared.

I was thirty-six years old. I had not become a successful author, performer, or journalist. I was not married, was not well-traveled, and had nothing to look forward to.

After I crashed and burned in New York City, I took Danny's advice and moved back home. At first, it felt like the best decision in the world. I didn't have to pretend to be anyone else. I didn't have to be sexy or charismatic. I didn't have to worry about making everyone comfortable around me. I was back to being just Tami, the baby in the Gordon family.

Within weeks of returning home, I was working at the same local chain restaurant I worked in before I left. A long cry from the fast-paced shifts and serving A-list celebrities, I was now running around delivering extra ranch and stale french fries to old classmates. I began to loathe serving tables so much that I convinced myself it was time to "climb the ladder," meaning, get promoted to a management position. I was able to pull it off within six months.

Management sucked balls. For starters, I only got paid twice a month. The bimonthly pay was a serious cramp in my style. As a server and bartender, I was promised cash money to take home every shift. I was convinced that was a big reason I always had what I needed or wanted but rarely had any savings. It was the romanticized idea that getting paid on a bi-weekly basis would make the money stretch longer. However, it barely covered my monthly bills, expenses, and toiletries. Sometime between that interim, I would find myself needing a loan from one of my parents, or even Terrell. By the time the next payday came around, the same amount as the week before would feel like less because I owed more.

There was also the fact that I was never built for a management position. My personality is tailor cut for after-hours, not ready for primetime audiences. The action was on the floor, and that's where I shined brightest. I loved talking with people, entertaining them during their dining experience to the point where they had no choice but to tip me 25 percent.

I'm often described by others as "eccentric" and "theatrical," which is ideal in an industry that often requires its waitstaff to sing embarrassing variations of "Happy Birthday" while wearing a dozen goofy pins on our suspenders. Management position demanded me to show up in a serious, authoritative manner. I was supposed to reprimand employees who were late and fire the ones who stole. Because I spent most of my years in food service as a table-stealing thief who was always late, these requirements were tough for me.

I wouldn't have to battle my disdain for management for long. After three months, a disturbing discourse with my manager became the straw that broke my corporate American back. I quit that job, only to hop over to another shitty chain, this time applying as a server.

"Impressive résumé," the supervisor said at my interview. I watched as she recited the names of notable establishments I had listed.

Yeah lady, I know. I'm overqualified. I watered down all expectation that the next gig could "lead to something" and was looking forward to working at a place where I could get by doing the barest of minimums. Plus, the restaurant offered dental care, which I seriously needed. Toothaches were beginning to wake me up at night, and I no longer had confidence that I could take a bite into an apple without losing a filling or chipping a tooth.

Within a week, I was in uniform of that restaurant, wrapping up an intense five-day training session. It felt good to be working, but I missed the fast-paced intensity that came with serving in the city. Without the free flowing of alcohol and drugs under dim fluorescent lights, the mundane manual labor was boring and desperately uncool. Worst of all was that I was no longer a standout, other than the fact that I was, by far, the oldest person on the floor. Instead of the actors and dancers I once shared space with, I was now working beside college kids and housewives who were in need of part-time work. No one clocked in and treated their job as a career.

Add to the fact that I was making peanuts in comparison to what I made back in the city, and it was clear that I'd be working to stay poor indefinitely. This made me feel stuck, like I was progressing at a snail's pace. Worse, I had lost all sense of adventure. As someone who used to travel on a whim and cancel all plans for last-minute adventures, I perpetually worked to pay bills and wondered, "How do I get out of this rut?" These feelings of stagnancy brought me back to the one book that always seemed to motivate me and reignite my dreams.

BEG

One day, I found my old copy of *Eat Pray Love*. Ha! I laughed to myself. You couldn't tear that book out of my hands back in 2009. I unpeeled the pages, trying to keep them intact. Memories came flooding back of my older sister shoving the book in my hands during one of our regular brunch-and-book-shopping Sundays. Now ten years older, that beaten book had survived rush hours on a packed D train, hot beach days on Fire Island, and squished middle seats on long flights. I read it everywhere.

Eat Pray Love is a 2006 memoir centered on writer Elizabeth Gilbert's emotional journey through divorce, depression, and self-discovery. After realizing she no longer desires the life she once yearned for, she commits to a year of travel to find herself. Even though her story and background didn't correspond to mine, I found so much of who I was becoming in those pages when I read it for the first time at age twenty-five. Like Liz, I was a young woman ready to admit that the direction I'd first chosen for myself was no longer leading me to the place I wanted to be. I dreamed of spending months in Cuba off the grid, learning how to make *arroz con frijoles* like my abuela, then hopping to Hawaii and doing nothing but eat fresh pineapples and fuck surfers. Just thinking about it would excite me to the point of practicing my Spanish and shopping for a perfect bodysuit. I would get so hyped that I'd be convinced it was all going to happen until I remembered the sad fact that I'd yet to escape New York.

My reality was very different from Liz's. For starters, I may have been a writer, but not the kind that gets comped for high-end trips and lives on their own in Manhattan. I was the kind of writer who had to tell bill collectors, "Oh, Tamela's not here right now" when I answered the phone. The kind of writer who cashed her checks at the check cashing place where I reloaded my prepaid credit card. The type who must use self-checkout at the grocery store with earbuds plugged in, so she could pretend to be too distracted to notice she was stealing two-thirds of her groceries.

I barely got halfway through Elizabeth's excursions through Italy before I shoved the book in the back of my collection. Liz and I were on totally opposite missions.

I felt humiliated thinking of the years I'd lost, prancing around like the flowers I was shitting would always blossom. *Why didn't I travel sooner? Should I have gone to college after all? Was quitting food service a bad idea? What the hell was I thinking all these years?*

I became furious at Elizabeth Gilbert and *Eat Pray Love*. I felt disgusted that, unlike cigarettes and booze, there was no warning on the back of the book that said: *WARNING: THIS IS NOT A BOOK INTENDED FOR CASH POOR, FAT, BLACK WOMEN WHO LIVE WITH THEIR PARENTS AND DON'T OWN PASSPORTS. IF YOU ARE SAID WOMAN, READING THIS BOOK MAY ENDANGER YOU INTO THINKING THAT THERE ARE OPTIONS FOR YOU THAT ACTUALLY DO NOT EXIST. YOU'RE STUCK, BITCH. GO PUT THIS BOOK DOWN AND FIND YOU SOME IYANLA.*

For Liz, the awakening of her discontent brought her to her knees on her cold bathroom floor. I, too, would be grounded in my deep despair; only I sought solace at my altar. Another difference between Liz and me—she had to hunt and gather to form the kind of spiritual grounding I had been born into.

My father didn't pass along a lot of Cuban traditions or customs to me or my three siblings, except for Santeria. Daddy, along with his parents, were always clear that the religion had been in our bloodline for generations, and it wouldn't stop with us. Even Mom was involved, taking precious care of her altar, making sure the water offerings never got cloudy. I had my first altar at four years old. It was simple, really—one glass of water, a white votive candle, and an old prayer card of my maternal great-grandmother's. They sat atop a small card table covered with a white pillowcase.

"What am I supposed to do?" I whispered to my mother. We were the only ones in my bedroom, but I could tell from the theatrics of it all—the white clothes both Mom and I were wearing and the bottle of Florida water she doused me with—that something serious was taking place.

"Kneel down and pray," she whispered back. I plopped down on the floor with my legs wide open.

"Girl, close your legs!" Mom snapped through gritted teeth. "I said kneel. *Kneel.*"

I got in proper formation, pushing my feet behind. "Now what?" I whispered.

"Pray."

I would spend the better part of my childhood privately embarrassed by my family's Indigenous religious practices. Whenever friends visited and wanted to know why there were so many pots strategically placed about or the meaning of religious statues, I would lie and say they got it from vacation or an auction sale. Only when I matured did I begin to take interest in my relationship with santos, Spirit, and my ancestors. My appreciation for a connection outside myself, outside other humans, anchored me in adulthood. I began studying hoodoo and the power of moon cycles, incorporating that into my spiritual practices as well.

I often sit before my altar with purpose, knowing exactly what it is that I'm asking, desiring, or giving thanks for. However, that night, miserable in my brothers' old bedroom, I felt clueless. Much like my last days in the city, I had a hyperawareness that I needed more and better, but I had no idea what that actually looked like.

"I am so lost," I softly sobbed. As tiny bubbles rose to the top of water glasses, I gave them as an offering, and the flame of a single white votive flickered rapidly, I knew that I was in the presence of Spirit. "I know that there's more out there for me. Please help me get to it. Please help me get out of my way. Show me how good it can get!"

I couldn't stop crying, but I continued to pray. I prayed like a church elder on Easter Sunday. I gave thanks for the lessons and the blessings, for all the times my life had been spared. I prayed for everyone I knew. The tears poured out of me as I sobbed with an unfamiliar intensity until I eventually pulled a cord in my throat. Even then, I continued to cry. The ugly cry. I felt it all, I lived it, I survived it. Now, I was ready to grow forward.

BORROW

"Healing is ugly, my nigga!" Those words were spoken loudly by my friend and mentor, Tanya Denise Fields. She was recording a Facebook Live, talking about her journey to healing herself. While the conversation was rather delicate, she held back no emotion, yelling much of the time, clapping her hands, some-times laughing but also crying. "You know the shit I had to hear from my kids in our last family therapy session? And, you know what? They were right! I got mad work to do! That's why I'm not playing about my healing." Tears streamed down my cheeks while I lay clutching my phone, watching her as though my life de-pended on it.

The more I meditated on Liz's experiences abroad and Tanya's journey with therapy, the more I understood the life I was desper-ate to conjure: a chapter of selfish, private, unapologetic, ugly healing. Not just the regular weeping-through-therapy-and-stuffing-my-house-with-candles-and-plants healing (though that would come with time). A kind of healing that would allow me to transition from struggling and getting to a place of comfort. The healing that addressed the immediate needs that mattered to me, not just trendy self-care shit that did little to fill my emotional cup. *But wait . . . What the hell are my needs?*

I took out a notebook and began jotting down everything I needed to jump-start my personal healing journey. Even though I was knee-deep in a place of scarcity, I didn't let thoughts of what I didn't have or why I didn't have it get in the way of writing it down. If I couldn't afford it, attain it, or acquire it in any way, I still had to identify it:

Access to good dental care

A home—a stable home with no roommates that do not require a decent credit score

A full-time writing career that keeps my rent and bills paid

Access to the beach

Proximity to an affordable gym (preferably Planet Fitness or Blink)

A neighborhood where people mind their business and I'm relatively safe (emphasis on relatively, of course, but it's got to be better than the corner of 155th and Frederick Douglass Blvd. at four a.m.)

Out of everything on that list, there wasn't a single thing I could afford or a solitary reason to think I could get it. But it didn't matter because it was what I needed. I may have been pushing it with the beach access, but it was the one place in the world where I felt truly free and beautiful. I'm a firm believer that heat makes humans at least 30 percent more attractive than temperatures below 76 degrees. I also believe that the weightlessness of bobbing around in the ocean is a physically euphoric experience that does wonders for mental illness and low self-esteem. So yes, I needed that form of water therapy in my life.

With my sister, whom I affectionately call Sissy, already living in Miami, I knew that was the right city for me. Maybe I wouldn't fuck surfers in Hawaii or spend a season in Cuba. But maybe I could satisfy my craving for exotic life and water therapy in Miami. I had no idea how I would get there, but I was convinced that I was on my way. I went to bed feeling oddly inspired that night.

BORROW

Days later, I rummaged throughout the house in search of magazines, glue, and cardboard. The urge to create a vision board of what I wanted my life to look like in Miami took hold of me. I spent hours, and I mean hours, feverishly cutting through old *Essence* and *House & Garden* magazines. I found images of the styles I wanted to embody, the foods I wanted to eat, the luggage I wanted to use, the bedroom decor, etc. I found images of beautiful beaches and pasted them. I also cut out specific words so I could spell out, *I Love my OWN Home*. There were moments when I laughed at myself, thinking how absurd I must look from the outside, a grown woman imagining her future with glue sticks and cardboard. But I quickly shrugged those thoughts off and remembered that my job wasn't to focus on my looks, my doubt, or my insecurities. My job was to focus on what I needed to begin this intense healing process.

I was exhausted when I finished but also aroused by the finished product. This wasn't my first time creating a vision board, but it was the first time I captured such a deeply suppressed version of myself, which I had never met before. I was excited to live the life I'd cut and pasted.

I didn't know if it was the angst of all the life and adventure I was preparing to welcome in or the presence of the Divine itself, but I felt so deeply spiritual at that moment that I knew I was not in that room alone. *Thank you,* I found myself repeating. I was grateful because, for the first time in a very long time, I no longer felt stuck. I was no longer willing to surrender to the idea that I was the sum total of my intersection. Yes, I was aware of how hard life had been for me, and I knew that life would continue to be hard for me, but I also knew that it should be good too. And I knew that the most radical thing I could do was get my shit together and get to where I deserved to be.

From that moment on, I continued to go through the motions of everyday life. I worked at the shitty restaurant part-time and even got bold enough to start blogging again. At the time, my social media platforms were beginning to gain traction due to my hot takes on white supremacy and intersectionality. Random musings about current events gained me lots of followers. So much so that by 2018, I was occasionally asked to guest on podcasts and speaking engagements. It was through these platforms that I was able to reinvent myself as a writer—one who gave intriguing hot takes on pop culture, politics, and intersectionality.

I really think you should start a Patreon page, a follower once suggested via direct message. I had only heard of the website, but I wasn't fluent with it. It was my understanding that Patreon was a professional website that allowed creators to monetize their work by charging subscribers monthly. Talking shit on the internet didn't qualify me as a "creator." Or did it?

For Black people, to be a participant in any digital arena is to understand that every morsel of our intellectual property is susceptible to theft, outside of cat memes and Tabitha Brown reels. Over the years, I witnessed the ways in which my own content was repurposed, sometimes word for word. Even though I needed to get paid, the idea of being able to create and have full autonomy of my artistry, from what I wrote to the style I wrote it in, was enough for me. I created a Patreon page, and within several months, I was generating five hundred dollars per month in subscriptions. It wasn't enough to quit my shitty job, but it affirmed my dream of working as a writer full-time.

When I wasn't waiting tables or building my online base, I was deeply invested in self-improvement. I continued to read my way through my self-discovery journey. While I no longer held contempt toward Elizabeth Gilbert, the wounds of exclusion were too fresh to read the white lit I had grown up on. Instead, I turned to Black literature, which helped me gain a much better understanding of where I was in life and how I'd gotten there.

I also found cathartic healing by submersing myself in online and offline Black-centered spaces. I spent as much time as possible with other Black marginalized genders, sharing our stories of survival and our plans to live a liberated life, fully divested from white norms, expectations, and misogynoir.

I never forgot about my dream of living in Miami, but I didn't obsess over it either. For every new opportunity or personal win, I would think, *You're one step closer to the beach life!* The only thing I had going for me was faith in knowing that I hadn't gotten that far just to get that far. I allowed that belief to carry me through insecurities, discouraging situations, and a lack of affirmation from the universe that things would work out as I desired.

Nearly a year after I created my vision board, Sissy's daughter, Somalia, called to tell me she was relocating from New York to Miami. Unlike me, she had a job and apartment lined up. The only thing she lacked was childcare for my grandniece, Bella. I eagerly offered my services.

And, just like that, in the summer of 2019, I was on a one-way flight to Miami.

For the first three months, I slept on Somalia's sofa, caring for Bella after daycare and on the weekends while Somalia worked.

While we got along well, there was no denying that her cozy one-bedroom apartment was not big enough for three people. Living out of my suitcase was challenging, and sleeping on Somalia's stiff sofa was the pits. In the fall of that year, I expressed these woes to a friend, Vanessa, an activist and community organizer known for raising money for Black marginalized genders in need.

"We can have the money to get you your own spot fundraised by the end of the week!" Vanessa assured me. I knew it was true, but I never considered that an option. At that point, I assisted and/or led many digital fundraisers for Black marginalized genders. A digital fundraiser (also referred to as direct giving or digital philanthropy) is simply a person using their social media platform to raise funds for various needs. I had held fundraisers for myself before, but it was for things like book wish lists, tickets to a writing conference, and community-organizing feats. I had never considered a fundraiser to get my life together.

Initially, I didn't feel my need for housing was as immediate as someone with a more vulnerable intersection or someone more destitute than I. What changed my mind were the words Tanya said to me when I told her that my whole mission was based on her Facebook Live from earlier that year: "Housing is a need. An immediate need. The only reason why you're identifying your need as 'not as important' is because it's *your* need. Treat yourself the way you treat others, and get that money up."

Vanessa was right. Within a week, more than $5,000 were raised on my behalf. Three months after arriving in Miami, I signed my first lease. It was a shitty apartment in a rough neighborhood, but I wouldn't have wanted it any other way. I yearned for my own so deeply, I never bothered to manifest something nice; I wanted to manifest something *now*. So, *now* looked like a small four-hundred-square-foot studio in the heart of Little Havana, a historical, traditional neighborhood in downtown Miami. At the time, my monthly income was between $700 and $900, and my rent was $1,000, not including utilities and monthly expenses. For the first six months, The Black Fairy Godmother organization sent me everything from money for groceries and bills, to linens, kitchen appliances, and home decor.

HEAL

Mornings came early in Little Havana. This was because of the roosters that roamed the pavement on Southwest 9th Street where I lived.

I would rise, meditate, and ease into my day. After breakfast I would stop by one of the coffee stands on Calle Ocho and indulge in a cafecito, sipping shoulder-to-shoulder with other mamitas and older men. Together, we would sip, go over the news of the morning, and talk about how hot it was. Sometimes I would explain, "Mi Español es no bueno," and they would smile and continue talking in Spanish.

The heat from the sun, not a single cloud to hide behind, beat down on every inch of My Body. I would dab off the small puddle of sweat above my upper lip and smile. I got to a point where the heat no longer stirred me into a fit of anxiety; rather it would surrender all my nerves and uneasiness. My Body reacted to heat and sweat, fabric gathering itself in the crevices of my rolls and mascara dripping down my cheek. Anxiety would spike as small droplets of sweat would fall from the side of my face onto my blouse, a brown-tinted stain remaining from my concealer. Eventually, I had to surrender to the fact that My Body sweats in heat, that sweat is a human reaction, and that I'm still pretty when I sweat. I repeated those thoughts on a regular basis until I finally believed them, or at least, got so tired of being hot that I couldn't care less about sweating. I learned to be grateful for the fact that I live in a body that's so alive, it reacts to its surroundings.

I no longer cared about what my rolls did with my clothes, and I rarely wore makeup anymore. I didn't wear much at all. SPF and confidence became my go-to look, and I wore it pretty well.

When I got back home after my coffee break, I wrote for a few hours. Afterward, I prepared lunch, which consisted of fresh avocado salad mixed with tomatoes, red onions, and cilantro. At around two-ish, I slipped into one of my bathing suits, ordered an Uber, and headed down to Ocean Drive. I spent the remainder of the day on the beach, swimming, smoking pot, and listening to my "Love My Life" playlist.

By the time I got back home, the day was winding down. The most magnificent sunset fell over the city. Colors—pink, orange, blue, and purple—practically screamed through my window. The entire apartment complex smelled of sofrito and Sazón.

I shook off the sand and prepared a hot bath. I ran the water as hot as it could get, and I dumped in Dead Sea salt, Florida water, and some fresh rose petals I plucked off my altar. I surrounded the tub with candles, rose quartz, and amethyst crystals. I slipped into the bath and let every inch of My Body unclench. I giggled a little, thinking about how much fun I had in the ocean, remembering the fish I saw and a little kid whose dad was teaching him how to swim. And then, I started to get choked up.

That simple day was the best I'd had in my adult life.

Little Havana became the place I learned how to slow down, center my peace, and really, truly take care of myself. I ate mindfully and slept well. I also lost many friends who were either uninterested in this version of my Self or simply bothered by it.

I was grateful for that moment in life, what I looked at as a second chance at adulting. I felt that, with such a huge blessing, I had no choice but to do right by those who invested in me, literally and figuratively. I worked hard to stabilize my income so I could take care of myself on my own, and I helped to facilitate and amplify as many fundraisers as possible for other Black marginalized genders who needed a leg up like I did.

Ultimately, my version of *Eat Pray Love* was a lot less elaborate than Liz Gilbert's, but it was no less important or purposeful. In the end, I stopped blaming her for providing me with a version of self-exploration that doesn't leave enough wiggle room for cash-poor Black girls like me. After all, without her memoir I may not have ever had the idea of finding places in the world where I could run off and get some ugly healing done. Still, attempting to live a life of luxury with a low income and a lot of bills isn't easy. As I continued transitioning into living on my own, I'd experience that not only was my healing ugly, but so was my struggle.

CARE FOR THE TERMINALLY ILL

■

"Thank your body for being so giving!"

—HOLLY RAINES

CONTENT WARNING: ASSISTED UNALIVING

I was so afraid I wouldn't get to see you before I go! Holly texted.

I read the words repeatedly, my heart always stopping at *go.*
Holly was alive and well, but her body was dying.

It was January in 2022 when she was planning to visit me in
New Orleans. She was a small-framed Vietnamese woman from
San Diego. Married to Marco, a white Brazilian, the two of them
raised their preteen son, Dylan, and their two dogs, Bob and Jan.
They lived a simple, modest life in Southern California, one that
included late-night shows to see Marco play with his band and
wandering around mountains during weeklong hiking trips.

Like many important relationships I've developed, I met Holly
on social media. It was during the Trump era when your contact
list became a weird Twilight Zone of racists and queer and trans
antagonists. Unlike non-Black people who distance themselves
from anti-Black white supremacy and discrimination, Holly used
her platform to promote anti-racism. She even joined one of those
anti-racist infinity groups on Facebook—the kind where all the

members are non-Black and all the admins are Black, and members pay dues, reparations, and provide various resources. Holly gave tirelessly, even though many of us later learned that she and Marco worked with a very humble financial situation.

As the political climate grew more violent, Holly dug deeper into anti-racism, often finding reflections of discrimination inked in her childhood. *I have a lifetime of experiencing this dynamic where I could never quite speak out like white girls that were my peers growing up,* she once confessed in a vulnerable Facebook post. *They were brave, I was angry.*

She was tough and never afraid to speak her mind, but she was also human. Holly lived with depression, anxiety, and ADHD. Shortly before publicly sharing the recurrence of her cancer, we talked about the importance of taking care of our mental health by refraining from social media.

"I know," she agreed. "I really don't need this right now. I honestly have some serious health problems, and I do not need this kind of stress." She compared her experience with that online anti-racism group with the cult NXIVM, pointing out that so much of the harm experienced in those spaces is due to the readiness of white women who were "willing to pounce for 'power' over other women."

A survivor of toxic transcultural adoption, she was raised by two super-white evangelicals who deprived her of all knowledge of her Vietnamese family, culture, and heritage. Because of this, Holly grew up feeling pretty lost. The more she tried to find herself, the more her family pushed back. By the time she entered adulthood, she completely cut them out of her life. Only then did she find the freedom to express, explore, and love.

Not only did she start her own family, but she would eventually be reunited with her birth mother and several siblings and extended family members. Sadly, as these relationships began to deepen, Holly learned that the cervical cancer she thought she had beaten years ago returned, and this time it was terminal.

"I've got it from here," she told doctors after they broke the news. She longed to live a full lifetime, but she wanted to remain grounded in her quality of life rather than the quantity of days and years. Determined to spare both herself and her family from the pain of medically-induced deterioration, she opted out of experimental treatments.

Instead of spending her last days dreading her diagnosis, she, Marco, Dylan, and the dogs took off for a cross-country road trip. Her goal? Spending the rest of her time making memories with her family. Her care? Traveling the country with her family and visiting her most precious loved ones for a final time.

She set up a GoFundMe and raised money to cover the expenses of food, gas, and lodging. This "last lap," as she called it, was about saying goodbye. She chose me, of all people, places, and things, to meet before making her final earthly transition. Holly decided to see me before she had to go.

It was and remains the most beautiful, liberating act of wellness I've ever witnessed.

The night before we were set to meet, I lay in bed, scrolling through old text messages and DMs Holly and I had shared over the years. It was bittersweet realizing how often she had hit me up just to say *Hey*, to let me know that she was thinking of me. I often took days, sometimes weeks, to respond. I tried to give myself grace, but the lost time I willingly passed on ate at my conscience. I lay there sobbing, realizing that I had cheated myself out of a deeper connection with someone who truly cared for me. Though I couldn't get those moments back, I made a vow to cherish every single second I was about to spend with Holly and her family. I wouldn't cut her off mid-sentence, play with my phone, or allow my mind to wander while she spoke.

I only lived a few minutes from the hotel, but Holly insisted that she and Marco rent me a room so that traveling would be "easier" for me.

Please, allow us this small token of appreciation to you, she texted.

I wanted to convince her that commuting from my own apartment was simpler, but I figured too much protesting would seem rude. I swallowed my reservations and responded, *Okay, thank you!*

You never really know what it will be like to meet an internet friend. Online characters known for swallowing up space in your newsfeed can present as rather underwhelming face-to-face. And the quieter ones who come across as more reserved online can be obnoxious in person. But the sweet, kind, and vulnerable Holly I'd instantly loved on Facebook was the same person who knocked on the hotel room door.

She sat in her wheelchair wearing black pants, a black lace camisole, and a chunky black sweater. Her face was beat, and she was wearing a light-blue wig—very on-brand for the French Quarter and one I'd seen her wear in various selfies.

Marco stood behind her wheelchair, tightly holding on to its handles. His sandy blond hair hung down to his shoulders, his crown covered by a baseball cap. Beside him was Dylan, who was wearing dark pants and a black T-shirt. I want to say that he was tall for an eleven-year-old, but the truth is that I don't know how tall eleven-year-olds are supposed to be. He had a short, shaggy haircut with thick strands of dark hair resting on his forehead but not touching his brows. He said hello, but he didn't smile. And, as soon as I said it back, he broke eye contact and stared at the artwork and fixtures on the walls of the hotel hallway.

"Hello!" I greeted them. I smiled as hard as I could to conceal my heartbreak. It never dawned on me that Holly would be using a wheelchair. In my mind, I imagined her walking with full mobility. I realized that, even though I had seen her in a wheelchair in some photos, I had somehow dismissed them in favor of the other images of Holly who hiked and climbed mountains.

"I'm so sorry we're late," she apologized. We'd agreed to meet at seven thirty, and it was a little before nine, but I didn't mind at all. She, slowly, stood up and hobbled two steps toward me, giving me a delicate embrace. "We had to change my stoma bag so I could enjoy dinner."

"Girl, don't be sorry to me!" I said, waving a hand at her. "I was comfy in my hotel room." I smiled broadly, swallowing the lump in my throat. I remembered a post Holly made on Facebook about being devastated for having a stoma bag placed in her abdomen shortly after the return of her cancer.

The hotel where we stayed was only one block from my favorite restaurant, Creole House, so we decided to eat there. Over the course of two hours, the four of us bonded over oysters, fried green tomatoes, and alligator bites.

After complimenting me on a necklace I was wearing with a chunky amethyst stone, Dylan talked to me about crystals. He was once a huge collector, he told me, and had accumulated dozens of them over the years. I told him that I wanted them all and that I was willing to order in bulk and pay for the shipping.

Holly explained that for Dylan, the appeal of crystals was deeper than aesthetic. "My baby is a very spiritual child," she said with a smile. She told me about his interest in mindfulness and spiritual self-care, from meditation by the beach to receiving reiki regularly when he was about seven. Holly was certain that their eternal connection would only strengthen after she transitioned. "He knows that, even when I die, I'm not really going anywhere," she said, pressing a hand to her heart.

For the most part, Marco was silent, allowing Holly and me to get to know each other. Sometimes, he threw in a funny joke or added detail to Holly's story.

Like all married couples, Marco and Holly had seen their fair share of good times and bad times over the course of their ten-year marriage. But all the small issues of yesteryear were thrown out the window from the moment of her diagnosis. From that moment on, the two of them were inseparable. It was important for Marco to show up as not only a spouse, but a solid source of support for Holly. And it was clear by observing their love language of deep eye contact, gentle smiles, and soft whispers that cancer had no impact on their passion for each other.

Holly and I got lost in conversation, giggling about past exchanges with random weirdos online. We also got serious, and she opened up about her life and the loose ends she was trying to tie up before she *goes*. I knew that Holly's adoptive parents were emotionally abusive. However, her birth mother was a sweet woman whose only sin was living with mental illness.

"They took me away from her because they thought she didn't have the capacity to care for me." When she used the word *capacity*, the hairs on the back of my neck stood up, alert to the hidden meaning of the coded word. Capacity is a term that many use, including myself, to gauge the person's ability to complete, engage, or otherwise exert mental, emotional, and physical energy. But too often, "Do you have the capacity" is code for "Can you handle it?" Holly's mother would go on to raise her half sister without incident. However, it was the state of California that decided she didn't have the capacity to also raise Holly.

My adoptive parents purposely kept me away from my biological family as much as they were legally allowed to, she wrote in a Facebook post. Like a lot of the challenges in her life she faced head-on, she was open with sharing the beautiful relationship she later developed with her biological mother. She felt strongly about educating people about the dark side of transracial adoption because of what happened to her and her adoptive parents.

By the end of our meal, we were holding hands. It felt like the most beautiful date I'd ever had. There were moments when I wanted to say, "I wish we did this sooner!" but I held back. *Sooner* is only a reminder of time, of which Holly was already hyper-aware. There was no need to remind her. Still, I didn't want it to end. So, when Marco explained that after checking out of their hotel the following morning they would be heading to their next stop, Texas, I couldn't stop myself from asking, "Why not come to my place and chill between checkout and hitting the road again?" I wasn't ready for Holly to *go*. There was still so much I wanted to discuss with her. I wanted to hear her stories, I wanted to laugh more, and I wanted to be with her.

"We would love that!"

The second they agreed, I remembered the twenty-seven stairs that led up to my apartment. I lived in a beautiful home on Magazine Street, between The Irish Channel and affluent District Garden neighborhoods. My house was like many of the others, beautiful to look at with amazing architecture. And far from handicapped accessible.

The first five steps, which bridge the concrete with our fifteen-foot-high porch, are the steepest. Despite being relatively agile and having no problem jumping up and down stairs, even I must climb the first five monster stairs slowly, one step at a time, while holding on to the rail. Even after surviving the first steep round, Holly would still have to walk through our spacious-though-crammed foyer and up the remaining two flights and twenty-two hardwood stairs leading up to my apartment.

"That's okay." Holly shrugged. "Marco will carry me if he has to."

Wow, I thought. I wasn't blown away by the extensive assistance Holly needed to get around but rather by the much-deserved assistance she had access to. *Who would carry me?* I wondered, imagining myself in a state where my mobility was compromised and I would have to go up twenty-seven stairs alone.

After Marco paid the bill, the four of us walked out of the restaurant, appreciating Louisiana's balmy January sweater weather.

"Where to next?" Holly asked. "Should we check out Bourbon Street?"

I was shocked, though I shouldn't have been. It's only natural to want to take in the most popular sites, and in New Orleans, Bourbon Street is often stop one. Even I had found myself wandering through the tourist trap my first two visits to the city. However, after a year of living in New Orleans, I was as over Bourbon Street as I was Times Square. What many mistake as the heart of the city is nothing more than a capitalist pit with overpriced restaurants and cheesy bars.

"Let's!" I said with enthusiasm.

The moment we turned the corner to Bourbon Street from Canal, the stench of trash and vomit smacked us in the face. The street was dark, illuminated by the neon signs that blared through small bars with oversized and overpriced daiquiris. People staggered all over the narrow street, walking through couples who held hands, bumping into strollers, and of course, cutting off wheelchairs. Tourists shoved without saying excuse me and grunted their teeth from behind us as they hurried around to get in front of us. They were impatient, oblivious, and unkind. And the cracked, uneven sidewalk did us no favors. Marco at times had to push the wheelchair with extra muscle to move through unforeseen cracks in the road, sidewalks that were sometimes so thin that only one person could walk in any one direction at a time. And, of course, the vomit.

We made it down to the end of the block and decided to walk back to the hotel through Royal Street, only one block away and far less congested and obnoxious than Bourbon Street.

"That was a lot!" Holly gasped as we made our way up the cleaner, calmer sidewalk.

"Yeah, and sometimes it smelled really bad too," Dylan chimed in. We laughed and then fell silent as their San Diego eyes soaked up the images of the city.

When I got back to my hotel room, I threw myself on the bed and sobbed, disappointed in the ableist end to what could have been a beautiful evening. *Why didn't I warn them about how shitty Bourbon Street can be?* I wondered. It was a Saturday evening after ten p.m. Of course the street was going to be filled with wasted, disrespectful tourists. And why didn't I think of going to other places that were wheelchair accessible? Just when I would begin to let go of my guilt, images of Marco breaking a sweat while he carried Holly up my twenty-seven stairs would break my heart, and I'd start all over again. Maybe I couldn't build a ramp in time, but at least I could make sure it was spanking clean and have coffee and cake. I convinced myself that I would compensate for my stairs by being an extra-gracious host.

I woke up early—4:45 a.m. on the dot—and took an Uber back to my apartment. Once I got there, I cleaned from top to bottom like *Home & Garden* was coming over for an interior design shoot. I scrubbed every nook and cranny of every room, sparing no expense with Fabulosa and Comet.

Later, I reconvened with Holly and co. in front of their hotel room. We went for brunch, and this time I was just quick enough to beat Holly and Marco for the bill. Afterward, we checked out of the hotel and headed to my apartment. It was rainy that day, adding a chill that hadn't been present the night before. I sat in the passenger seat, talking aimlessly, trying to fill up the car with so much noise that we would all forget about the stairs. It was possible that I was the only one who was sweating it, the only one who cared at all. For the most part, Holly, Marco, and Dylan just pointed at random houses and oak trees that stood out.

"It's a lot nicer around here," Dylan said from the back, only a few blocks away from my home.

"I know, right?" I snickered. A twinge of guilt swept over me because my neighborhood was in fact much nicer than many parts of New Orleans. A long cry from the violent streets that spread throughout various wards through the city, my neighborhood was not the kind featured on *The First 48*. It came with its own security service with guards who patrolled the neighborhood twenty-four seven. My neighborhood rarely smelled like shit because it was prioritized by the sanitation department. I wasn't and likely will never be as wealthy as my neighbors, but just by existing within proximity to them, I got many of the community perks. It was nicer, but the reason gave me a little bit of ick.

As we pulled up to the house, Marco and Dylan sprang into action. Marco began by taking out the wheelchair and preparing to lift Holly out, while Dylan hopped out and grabbed Holly's stuff. I made my way to the porch and unlocked the door.

Though Marco was willing to carry her, Holly insisted on walking with his assistance. She gripped both hands on the stair rail and walked sideways, one slow step at a time. Marco stood behind her, gently placing a hand on her shoulder, prepared to catch her should she stumble. Holly didn't mask the pain each step took out of her, often having to take a break to regain strength and composure. It took a solid ten minutes, but we eventually made it upstairs to my apartment.

Dylan settled in my office area, spinning around in my $200 chair. *Why don't I do that more often?* I thought.

After a few moments, Marco and Dylan decided to check out the neighborhood while taking the dogs for a walk. Holly and I fell into a deep conversation alone, just us girls. She scooted over to me on the sofa, pressing her tiny head on my chest. I wrapped my arms around her, and she reciprocated the embrace. She didn't know that I hadn't been held, truly held, for several months and how grateful I felt for the warm contact.

When the boys returned, they brought Marco's electric guitar from their truck. Once they got plugged in, the two sat across from each other, Dylan still in the chair and Marco now perched at the edge of the sofa. Marco took the guitar first and played some chords. He then passed it to Dylan, who tried to imitate his father's notes. The morning drizzle unfolded into full-fledged rain, pounding on the roof and puddling on the balcony. The light tapping of rain, paired with Marco and Dylan's jam session, made for the perfect background noise to my soft sob session with Holly.

"I want you to share everything, Tam." Shortly after she volunteered to include our time together in this book, those were her words. "If my experience can help any person in any way—especially a Black or Brown person—then this is a gift. I want them to know my story."

A ROAD MAP FOR LEAVING THE BODY

by Holly Raines

■

VIETNAMESE WOMAN – MOTHER – SHE/HER
– SAN DIEGO, CALIFORNIA

In December 2018, I had a hysterectomy. The cancer was caught so early that they said, "You're cured. There's no sign of cancer anywhere else." So, I would go to all my checkups, and after a couple years, I stopped going and didn't come back. During 2020 and early 2021, I would have these moments when going to the bathroom felt worse than having a baby. But it would go away. I've always had upset tummy issues growing up. I always ate spicy food. All I ate was Hot Cheetos when I was a kid, ya know? But one day, there was this pain, and it almost felt like I was constipated, but it didn't go away for a couple weeks. It hurt to the point where I was walking weirdly so I wouldn't feel the pain.

I went to my primary care and told them something hardcore was happening. My doctor is an amazingly beautiful person who cares about her patients. She was the one who was adamant with me about getting a pap smear. She was like, "I know how you are; you're going to take forever to schedule it, so let's just get it done now." So, she was the one who caught the cancer for the first time.

So, in March 2021, she was on it when I told her about these issues. She called me and said, "Holly, there's an enormous mass down there. It's got veins and blood flow. Usually, when there's a mass like that, it's a tumor." Of course, I set up everything with oncology. On April 1st, I had surgery. April Fool's Day. Like, is this a joke?

They removed most of the cancer but couldn't remove it all because it was wrapped around an artery. They removed what they could, and I went through a bunch of chemo. It worked really well. The remaining cancer shrank so small that it couldn't be detected by scanning. But the cancer mutated and became smarter than the treatment. So, the cancer grew again. Like, it blew up.

Overall, I was still really healthy. The chemo weakened me, but I could still run five miles, take Dylan on road trips, and go camping. So, the day my oncologist told me my cancer was incurable, I was sad, but it didn't mean anything. I felt fine, aside from the side effects. But then, months later, we went camping. I already had issues with feeling constipated and bloaty, but I got these terrible cramps the first night of camping. The following two days, it only got worse. I'd start feeling it, and we'd have to stop, but it would go away, and I'd say, "Okay, let's keep going!" But, one night, we returned to the campsite, and I got the worst cramps. I finally went to the bathroom, but then I started puking.

So, it's me, Dylan, and my friends, and we're eight hours away from home, and I just didn't want to mess up the trip. But eventually, I told my friend I didn't think I would make it, so we went to an emergency room in Utah. The doctors there said that I had an obstruction in my abdomen. They offered to treat me but suggested I go home because they didn't know how long I'd be hospitalized. That was great advice because I was hospitalized for two and a half months when I got home. I had major surgery. I didn't think I was going to make it through that; I thought I was going to die.

Even in the last few months, I have felt very close to death. There's something about the way my mind works—I can almost smell and process things differently. I can feel that My Body is dying. I can feel it. It's weird. Both times I almost died, I could feel and process things differently. My Body picks up on things differently because it's dying.

There was a 5 percent chance that I was supposed to get cancer again. At every turn, they were confident they could take care of it, but they couldn't. So, nobody knows how much time I have. It depends on which way the cancer grows. But I'm already in so much pain with the way it's growing. I can feel My Body, just . . . It's tired. It's just tired. Honestly, if it gets to a point where they can't help me figure out the pain part, I told Marco I'm just going to do the medically assisted death. I don't want to be miserable. I don't want my son to remember me being weak and sick. I want Dylan to remember me living. I'm not trying to survive life in this kind of pain. So, you know, we've talked about how there will be a day when I just take those pills and nap. That's why we're trying to get all this stuff in because it might be sooner than later. At my last scan, everything had doubled. And, within the time it doubled, all this pain started coming on, super intense. This past Christmas, when I had to go to the ER, it was the first time they couldn't do anything to help the pain go away.

We've tried everything, but at this point, the only options left are sketchy. I don't really trust any of those experimental drugs and trials. Black and Brown women are the most likely to get cervical cancer, yet Black and Brown women are the least likely to get treatment. I asked, "Do you pay my family for participating

in this trial?" They said, "No, the payment is you get this treatment." So, you're using My Body for data and information, and
my family gets nothing? For some expensive medicine that's not
going to be accessible to people like me after the fact? No, I don't
want you using My Body for that shit. If you're going to use My
Body, pay up. It's My Body, my life. I'm not a lab rat. I would love
it if they could use My Body to help other people, but the way
cancer works, it will only help people who can afford it. So, no.

Why would I want to be the first human to try? What if the side
effects are awful? I don't want to ruin the last few months I have.
I'm not desperate to stay alive, I'm desperate to live a full life. I
really could just stay alive forever and deal with pain. Slowly de-
teriorate and get stuck on drugs. But that's not what I want. If I'm
not going to live a full life . . . I don't need to just be alive — I need
to live.

This trip, one of the last things I get to do, is wonderful because
I get to see the people I choose to see. But at the same time, it's
hard because there are so many other people I would love to see.
I didn't consider how hard the goodbye parts would be on this trip.
When Dylan and I have taken road trips before, we've seen our
friends and loved ones around the country. When we leave, we
say, "Goodbye, we'll see you next time!" Now it's like, "I love you.
Thank you for being who you were in my life, and I don't think I
will see you again." I'm so lucky I get to do that, but at the same
time, I didn't think about how that was going to hit. When I said
goodbye to my friend Tara, her daughter, and her husband in
Florida, I didn't think about how sad that would be.

The time in the car with Marco and Dylan, listening to music,
seeing parts of the country . . . The middle of America is not very
exciting, but Marco had never driven through it! So now he can
say that. I think that's the cool part about Dylan and me — our

family has never had a lot of money, so flying wasn't an option, regardless. But these road trips allow us to physically see and be with the people we love and care about.

I'm a little worried I won't make it to Hawaii. I was scared I wouldn't make it through this road trip. It's been really painful and tiring. It sucks, I'm here, and I want to have fun with my friends. But I'm tired. I'm in too much pain. The pain is ruining everything. Most people would be excited to walk around, but My Body is wrecked. I hate that I don't even care about missing out on anything anymore because I'm so tired.

When I think about what we do, we didn't have money, but we had time. We didn't have much money, but we had enough money to put gas in the car and go, and we had the time to hit the road. I'm lucky that Marco is here to drive me around. This trip was really the goal for Dylan and me. Dylan and I have touched every single one of the forty-eight states. Even if we just touched a corner, we did it. Our goal is still fifty. Every state wasn't the goal, but it just evolved into it. We get to go to Hawaii next. I'm hoping Hawaii works out. I'm hoping My Body carries me through that. I'm hoping to go to Alaska after that if I can make it through.

Food is really important to me. A lot of gatherings are around food. A lot of the way my (chosen) grandma expresses love is through food. For Christmas, her present is tamales, which is her gift to us. She feeds us, and that's her present to the family. That's a gift of love; that's real love. I love cooking. We do a lot of sushi and fish dishes because Marco works in the fish industry. I love going into a restaurant and replicating a dish that I like. Specifically, I'm a soup/stew person. I love pho. I've been trying to keep this journal where I write notes in it, and I keep pictures of what I see and write memories or even notes of encouragement or things that I want him to know so he can read it when I'm gone and he's sad. I haven't been doing a good job of it, though. I think I can write well and have things to say, but it doesn't hit when I sit down to write it. It doesn't hit. It doesn't come out the same.

One of the things I left in that book is his favorite dinner he's always loved from sushi night, so I wrote down all the things I use and how I make the rice. So he knows how to make it when I'm not here. Even our chocolate cookie recipe. It's nothing special — I ripped it off Pinterest. But he likes it, so now he can have it. Same with brownies. I know there are going to be times when he feels it. Just like a teenager, he'll feel sad and lonely. I want him to read words of encouragement. I want him to hear what I'd say if I were there. Even the lectures.

I'm not too worried about him because he's empathetic. Dylan is the responsible one. Sometimes he's even more responsible than me. You know, there are things I'm probably not very aware of. For instance, I rarely pay attention to the gas tank. There have been a few times I've run out of gas, and as a result of that trauma, Dylan is very aware of the gas tank. This kid is never not going to worry about the gas!

The trip has been enjoyable. We went to West Virginia. My favorite part was learning about Bill Withers from there. We were listening to Bill Withers while we were driving. I told Marco that finding a musician who sings about something positive without sounding cheesy is so hard. We all identify with angst, but happy songs don't come often. But, when "A Lovely Day" goes on, you believe it! It really is gonna be a lovely day! Not to be dark or morbid, but I've already decided that will be one of the songs on my "Time to Go" playlist. It's gonna be a lovely day, ya know? Because I want that to be a lovely day for me. I know it won't be as lovely for Marco and Dylan, but I want it to be something lovely, so they understand I'll be better off. I'll be in a lovelier place than where My Body is now. It's a lesson in letting go. Sometimes you want to hold on, and it's not meant to hold on anymore.

In March of 2023, two months after her visit to New Orleans, Holly Raines transitioned. Prevent your risk of cervical cancer by getting tested regularly, as well as getting vaccinated against HPV. For more information, please visit mayoclinic.org.

HEATED

∎

"Dreaming is a form of radical resistance because it calls us to a conscious stillness, which manifests itself as ease in the body."

—EBONYJANICE, *All the Black Girls are Activists:*
A Fourth Wave Womanist Pursuit of Dreams as Radical Resistance

The first three months living in Little Havana were brutal financially. I'd lived on my own before, but it was always under the living arrangement of at least one roommate—often two, sometimes three or more. Rent and utilities were always divided among us. Now, on my own, I was balancing rent, electricity, Wi-Fi, food, toiletries, etc. And with a very compromised budget. Without help from The Black Fairy Godmother's organization, I would have been on the street. Simone, the founder and my friend, would ask if I needed help with bills or groceries each month. Sometimes I would admit I did, and she would fundraise to cover necessary expenses. Other times I would lie, too embarrassed to keep taking help, a clear indication that I still couldn't take care of myself at thirty-eight years old.

Fortunately, food was easy to come by in Little Havana. Huge avocados, bigger than a fist, were only eighty-nine cents. And you could get a massive bag of tomatoes for less than three dollars. Breakfast and lunch looked like half an avocado with sliced red onions, tomatoes, and cilantro. Sometimes I would add a fried egg or roasted mushrooms. My diet was suddenly very fruit and veggie heavy, and I couldn't help but notice the shift in my attitude and energy level.

I enjoyed the benefits of clean eating, but sometimes I craved red meat, chicken, and prepackaged food. Those were cravings that required me to do the thing I hated most: steal.

To be fair, I never just stole; I would pay for some stuff. My go-to strategy was to hop in the self-checkout, plug in my earbuds but keep my phone on silent, and not actually listen to music. Instead, I would bop my head, pretending to be so enthralled by what I was listening to that, "I'm sorry, I didn't notice that the sixteen-dollar salmon fillet did not beep when I pretended to swipe it." Sometimes I would be so in character that I would go as far as singing lyrics out loud to a random song, giving it all I'd got. And, no, I cannot sing well.

Without my connections and networks in New York, my hustling took place online. The days of making cold hard PayPal cash from long Facebook posts about racism were long gone. It seemed my platform had become victim to the racist algorithm, restricting me from the kind of traction that my content normally got. And my Patreon membership was stagnant, mainly because the stress of surviving made it difficult to read, let alone write a review about what I read. I would get random freelance work from someone needing help with their book proposal or manuscript. It usually came just in time, like when a bill was heading into final notice, or the only food in my fridge were condiments.

While standing in my little kitchen, not more than six feet long and so narrow that only one person can pass at a time, I sobbed while preparing breakfast. I watched tears fall from my eyes and splatter onto the smooth, juicy avocado slices. *I'm scared*, I realized. The awareness of fear brought on a fit of panic that I didn't see coming. My hands began shaking so much I had to put down the knife. I left the kitchen, plopped down on the blue convertible futon, and tried to catch my breath. While I was where I wanted to be, I still had no idea where I was actually going. I needed so much help to keep myself afloat that I couldn't help but wonder, *How long can I last like this?*

Afraid of where my thoughts would take me if I sat inside all day, I quickly ordered an Uber and headed to South Beach, just a few minutes away from my apartment. When I got there, I lay on a blanket on the sand, doing my best to pay attention to nothing but the crashing of waves and the beat of my heart. The fear had yet to subside, but the feeling of assurance was also coming over me. *This is par for the course, girl,* I assured myself. *You're going to be okay.* I let the voice within affirm me, and when it sounded faint, I nudged it with gratitude. *So many people love me and are ensuring I'm going to be okay! Look at how far I've come!* The tears kept falling, but this time they were tears of progression rather than fear. Even through anxiety and panic, my faith that I would make it was unwavering. I didn't know how to make it, but I was. Knowing that was enough to keep me encouraged and focused.

A deep growl roared in my roared in my belly. That's when I realized I had left the avocadoes and tomatoes half-prepared on the kitchen counter. I checked the time on my phone, and it was 12:06 p.m. Then I checked my PayPal and saw that I had just enough funds to get me home and afford cafecitos for the remainder of the week. *I wish I had enough cash to eat out,* I thought. Instead of dwelling, I shrugged and thought about where I'd take myself when I had the money. I began Googling restaurants along Ocean Drive until one caught my eye. It was called Harrat's, and it was on Washington Avenue, only a few blocks away from Ocean Drive. They had a decent happy hour menu and steamed mussels and garlic bread for only twelve dollars. I quickly Google Image searched menu items, my mouth watering as I stared at a massive bowl of mussels swimming in butter and two huge slices of garlic bread beside it. I put my phone away and lay back down, the sun growing stronger as beads of sweat popped out of my pores.

Exhausted from hunger and anxiety, I drifted off to sleep in between the sun and the sand. I woke up half an hour later, and it was hot! Much hotter than it was when I first got to the beach. It was one p.m. I considered packing up my things and heading back home to see if I could salvage that avocado when I noticed a few people swimming in the ocean. This surprised me because the water was too chilly when I tried to dip the week before. Even though I figured it would be too cold to swim, thankfully, I still wore a bathing suit. *Fuck that avocado!* I stripped down to my two-piece and ran into the ocean.

The water was cold but tolerable, a welcome chill from the heat. I took turns swimming against the waves and surrendering to them, allowing the ocean to toss, splash, and flip My Body. It felt so good to be weightless. All I felt at that moment was good. Good to be alive and swallowed by an ocean that knew what to do with My Body. It was as though it sucked the fear out of me.

The laughter of strangers reminded me that I didn't have the entire ocean to myself. I looked around and saw people of all races and nationalities having as much fun as I was. I lived in one of the most prominent tourist destinations in the country. People from all over the world saved and dreamed about being in the place I called home. This was a highlight of their year for them, but for me, it was just Monday.

When I was done splashing around, I returned to my beach blanket, plopped down, and let the sun and breeze dry me off. *That panic attack had a purpose*, popped into my brain. It was such an odd, random thought that it threw me off. But the more

I thought about it, the more sense it made. Because the panic attack was brought on by this fear that I had been suppressing—one that played on my shame about taking care of myself.

The ocean was the reminder I needed of how intentional my journey was and how much work I put into manifesting it. Sure, it was hard, but making it is never really easy. And, even though I'd been on my own before, I had never had to balance as much responsibility as I did while doing it in a new city with a new career. I needed to give myself grace and props for having made it as far as I did and believing in myself enough to trust the process and keep it going. *What do I need to do again?* I thought. I remembered a task on my mind before my nap, but it lost me. As I tried to think, an image of the half-sliced avocado and tomato popped into my brain. *Eat! I gotta eat.*

Just then, my favorite sound, *cha-ching*, came from my phone, alerting me of PayPal activity. I saw that a woman named Debbie made a $250 deposit in my account. I was confused. The name was unfamiliar, and I couldn't think of any invoices I'd sent. I was just about to use Facebook to search for the person's name when I received an email with the subject: *Thank you. I wish I could give more.*

Debbie was a white cisgender woman from Portland, Oregon, and said she read an article I wrote back in 2017 about white feminism. Debbie said it opened her eyes to so much that she had never considered, and she was grateful for what she'd learned from me. The article moved her so much that she looked for me online and followed me on all the socials. She loved everything I posted, specifically my hot takes on wellness and self-care. Debbie said that because of my dedication to my healing, she was setting off on her journey, taking her to New York. As far as she was concerned, that was all because of me, and the money she gave was her way of saying thank you.

I immediately replied, thanking Debbie. I let her know that she was helping me in ways I couldn't express and that I was grateful for her support and generosity. Then, I logged on to my electricity account and paid my bill. Once the payment went through, I packed my stuff and went to Harrat's.

Within half an hour, a massive bowl of mussels with Italian bread was placed in front of me. It looked so much better than the photograph I'd Googled. The mussels were humongous, and I was convinced that if I asked for extra bread, this would be enough to hold me over for both lunch and dinner. I took my time plucking each one out of its shell, letting them plop into the garlic sauce and marinate a little longer.

What started with anxiety and fear quickly evolved into bliss and good fortune. I was so amazed by the twist of events that I sat over my mussels, going through a play-by-play of the day.

In some areas, I did my part to shift the energy of my day. I could have stayed home and been swallowed alive by the intrusive thoughts and worst-case scenarios. But instead, I chose to seek healing at the beach. And I could have complained about not being able to eat what I desired, but I chose to excite myself with visions of what my next dining out would be. Those were conscious decisions I made to improve my mood and perspective. I did that. But Debbie came out of the clear blue sky. Or did she? My desire for those mussels was so real my mouth watered at their imaginary taste. And I definitely hit a peak state of bliss when I was dipping and diving in the ocean.

I'm not normally the type to take photos of my food, but I whipped out my phone, took a shot, and posted it to Facebook with the simple caption: *Thank you, Debbie.* I savored every bite I took, often holding back tears of gratitude.

I think about Debbie and the words of appreciation she showered on me. Specifically, the part about how my journey to a new city inspired her to take a trip, much like how Elizabeth Gilbert's journey in *Eat Pray Love* inspired me to move to Little Havana. Debbie may have found me because of my content on racism, but ultimately it was my life, my story that moved her enough to pay me.

As blissed out as I was, I still knew I was going to have to find a better way to sustain myself, and quick. Since monetizing my online platforms, I'd gained traction and clientele by discussing race, intersectionality, and Black literature. I'd also gained heaping portions of anxiety from constantly defending my work and resentment for having a portfolio filled with "anti-racism teaching" content. Like many other brilliant Black writers and creators, I fell into the lucrative-yet-creatively-stifling community within the anti-racism industry. Built off a concept of "dismantling" white supremacy, it was, at best, a performance kink for faux progressive white women with a lot of money to burn and a new reason to show up as a savior. The ick factor peaked when I moved to Miami and began sharing the nuances of my independence and self-discovery. Most followers were supportive, but there were the "allies" who would shamelessly comment or DM, *I miss your teachings.*

A rebranding was in order, but I couldn't figure out what that looked like for me. The book club was a great platform that facilitated discussion on Black literature without being performative. Still, many of the members were heterosexual cisgender white women who identified as intersectional feminists, which is as ridiculous as me identifying as a Kardashian.

I am the brand. Period. The words hit me, just like that. I looked around to see if anyone else had heard it. *What the hell does that mean?* When I thought about brands, I thought about perfectly curated content and adventurous lifestyles worth documenting.

My day in the sun was cute but not necessarily worthy of a You-Tube video or Instagram post. Or was it? Apparently, it was to Debbie. *How many more Debbies are out there?*

I was still wired from excitement over the day's events when I got home. I knew something was brewing, shifting me into a new direction, but I couldn't tell what or where. Either way, it was the kind of day that deserved to be celebrated. Feeling smug that I still had some cash to spare, I headed back out in search of a treat. Maybe a sundress or a new book. Something to mark the day so I remembered my magic every time I saw it.

I window-shopped up and down Calle Ocho, almost feeling like a tourist. I stumbled upon a botanica—one I hadn't noticed before. When I walked in, I was surprised by how scarcely stocked it was. There were religious candles, but only white, red, and black. And a skim selection of Florida water and baths. I was underwhelmed, seeing how Little Havana is the Santeria capital of the country.

"What you want, miss?" the man behind the counter asked. He was light-brown-skinned and short. He stared at me without even a suggestion of a smile. I was about to ask him if there was another, *better* selection of candles when a small basket of crystals sitting beside the register caught my eye. I rushed over and picked up the one that shined the brightest, a silver-dollar-size rose quartz. It was smooth and fit perfectly in the palm of my hand.

"How much is this?" I asked.

"That's a pretty one, right?" He smirked. "*Veinticinco, mami.*" I rolled my eyes.

Ain't nobody paying twenty-five dollars for no quarter-size crystal, I thought. I had never bought a crystal for myself before but had received several of them as gifts. I liked the idea of having a little extra juju in my back pocket, purse, or bra. And, as much as

I wanted a memento for my special day, twenty-five dollars could have gotten me a week's worth of produce and a bottle of wine.

"You very pretty, miss." His compliment distracted my inner deliberating.

"Thank you," I said. I went back to checking out crystals but couldn't help but notice that he wouldn't stop staring.

"You got boyfriend? Or girlfriend?" The thick coat of sleaze in his gaze was stuck on my breasts.

"I have a boyfriend," I lied.

"Aww, that's too bad," he said. "I like Black girls. *Big* Black girls."

"What that gotta do with me, *papi*?" I snapped. "And why you overchargin' these little crystals?" I held up the allegedly twenty-five-dollar rose quartz in the air, staring at it and then at him.

"I give it to you, but you gotta show me something, baby." He licked his lips, continuing to look at my breasts. I wanted to smack the shit out of that pervert. I was about to give him a mean tongue-lashing, but a phone ringing behind the counter robbed me of such an opportunity. Instead, I took that chip and shoved it in my bra. Not a second sooner, he hung up the phone and returned his attention to me. "So? What we gonna do?"

I smiled coyly and leaned over the counter, my breasts pressed against each other. He smiled widely and leaned in to them. And then I whispered, "I'm going to find another botanica with better crystals and no nasty creeps, you degenerate."

He started telling me off in Spanish, and I laughed myself out of his dusty botanica.

CASA DE TAMI:
THE BLACK FAIRY GODMOTHER

The Black Fairy Godmother Foundation is a New Jersey–based nonprofit that centers in providing financial aid and resources for people in extreme conditions that compromise their safety, health, and quality of life. Since its inception in 2018, thousands of people across the country have had their lives saved by the organization. I'm one of them.

After about a year and a half of solidifying a stable income, I was able to pay forward the blessing of a home that was publicly funded by my cyber community. Wanting to share the benefits of good self-care, I invited several Black marginalized genders to fly down to my home in Little Havana, where I would submerge them in three days of intensive, sporadic self-care.

Sometimes guests covered their own airfare and ground transportation. However, there were several guests who were fully fundraised for, their only expenses being their cute fits and souvenirs. Even when I relocated to New Orleans in the fall of 2022, the tradition continued. All in all, there were a total of ten guests.

They all were special, and none was more important than the other. However, there is one guest who, if not for her, no other would have been possible. Her name is Simone Gordon.

"Where you trying to take me, Tam?" I was grocery shopping in Publix while on the phone with Simone, stocking up on snacks, cheese, and wine. Simone was home in New Jersey, ensuring I had covered all big and small details. Two days before her arrival, sis was dealing with severe cold feet.

"Relax," I said, dashing down the wine aisle to grab several bottles of Cupcake prosecco. "The beach. Downtown. Dinner. Shopping!"

"You know I can't take long walks, right?" Of course I knew this. Simone checked the "limited physical mobility" box of the Casa de Tami intake form I requested all guests to fill out before proceeding with plans. It was something I had made up to ensure that their physical, mental, and emotional needs would be taken care of during their stay. When each guest arrived, I knew their allergies, sleeping preferences, mobility challenges, and medical conditions. I understood that she had to book a flight that could accommodate two seats for her body, we could only eat at restaurants with chairs that could accommodate her, and because of her chronic illness, PCOS, there were times when she would need to slow down and rest.

Simone's anxiousness was beyond valid. At thirty-five, she had only flown once. Her stay at Casa de Tami was her first legitimate vacation. The two things that had always prevented Simone from traveling in the past were her body size and leaving her then eleven-year-old nonverbal autistic son, Jarvis, in the care of someone.

We had been friends for years. The kind of good girlfriends who went to comedy shows together and got messy over giant sticky wings at Dallas BBQ. We never had issues with each other, but the tension between us grew as the days until her arrival at Casa de Tami came near. Simone's worries about leaving Jarvis behind in New Jersey heightened her anxiety, and her patience with me wore thin. Trust between us had never been an issue, but now that the power dynamic had shifted and she wasn't in control, she struggled to believe that I properly took care of all the loose ends of her travel and stay in Miami.

When we met in 2017, she was already solidified as The Black Fairy Godmother, known for raising obscene amounts of money for marginalized people nationwide, specifically Black mothers. From young parents needing immediate shelter and survivors of domestic violence, to the pregnant person needing baby clothes and food, The Black Fairy Godmother was the one to call. I watched Simone do this work for years, from sunup until sundown. As her efforts intensified, her social media platforms soared. When she agreed to stay at Casa de Tami, she was already blue checked on Facebook and Instagram and had more than 45,000 combined followers and friends.

"I want somebody to care about me the way I care for everybody else," she would say during our late-night conversations. I understood where she was coming from all too well. Unlike me, Simone couldn't just throw caution to the wind and move to a white-hot city not known for its handicap accessibility. Everything and everyone she took care of, from her family and home to her education and philanthropic efforts, she did solo. For all the good she was doing, it was taking a major toll on her health and overall well-being. She was often sick and stressed out, juggling a multitude of crises at any given moment. It was common to call Simone and try to talk about something important while she was in the middle of a class or feeding Jarvis or getting ready for work.

Taking care of her was my only goal, and I took it seriously. There would be no Casa de Tami without a casa *for* Tami. No matter the legions of women across the country who sang their gratitude for what Simone and The Black Fairy Godmother Foundation had done for their lives, I wanted to be one of the recipients who could give back the bounty of blessings the organization had given. I had everything planned out, from her arrival to her departure. I was certain that, with a few days without worrying about the labor and stress that came with community organizing and presenting as head of the household, Simone would realize that her magic was best served taking care of herself.

The day Simone arrived, I met her in the lobby of my apartment building. She was wearing a floor-length blue floral skirt with a matching sleeveless top. She wore a medium-brown, shoulder-length wig with a bob cut. She looked beautiful.

"Hey, sexy!" I said, taking her luggage out of her hand and giving her a big hug.

"I don't know how you do this!" she gagged. She explained that her legs hurt and cramped from the three-hour flight. I carried her large suitcases and we walked up the stairs to my second-floor apartment.

"You get used to it," I lied.

She didn't have to say she was referring to the heat in order for me to understand. It was mid-May when Florida's humidity is at the cusp of "don't even bother going outside unless you're okay with melting." I was used to it, but I'd learned early on that I was an anomaly. Even die-hard Floridians complain about waking up to heat so severe the chocolate sitting on top of the fridge melts into a puddle, oozing out of the crevices of its wrapper.

After getting settled, we sat down in my bedroom, and I began to go over the itinerary. Day one is usually jam-packed so that we can maximize their stay. However, I went down the list of beaching it up, getting Cuban food on Calle Ocho, and possibly clubbing. I watched as Simone's eyes slowly slid behind her head.

"Girl! I need a nap." She sighed.

"Of course!"

As she settled in bed, I headed into my living room and read. It was two p.m. At three p.m., bored, I quickly ran to Publix and picked up some more fresh fruit, seeing as their selection was slim the day before. When I returned at three thirty p.m., Simone was still asleep. At four, I got hungry and decided to make an avocado salad. By the time I was done eating, it was a quarter to five. Simone was still asleep. Rest was what her body and spirit needed most, but as a community organizer and parent to a special needs child, rest was the last thing afforded to her. When she awoke shortly after five thirty p.m., she was a new woman.

On day two, I made Simone breakfast in bed. Afterward, we began the Casa de Tami morning mindfulness routine—ten minutes of meditation, a few moments of deep breathing, and body movement. Afterward, I turned on some Solange, handed Simone a new journal, and left her with a twenty-minute journal prompt to write about what she wished to experience and fulfill for herself that upcoming summer.

"Nothing work-related, nothing Black Fairy Godmother–related," I instructed. "Think about what you need and what you want to do." I imagined her elaborating on a new love, new home, and other goals we'd discussed for years. Only, instead of speaking about them as though they were just dreams, this time I wanted her to imagine what it would be like to achieve them honestly.

I went to the kitchen to fix myself breakfast. By the time I returned, Solange was just belting out "Cranes in the Sky." Simone had put the notebook down and was scrolling through a GoFundMe page, likely checking to see if more funds had been raised since her departure.

"This is journal time, babe!" I said.

"Yeah, but I have work to do."

"I know," I said. I picked up the notebook and pen and handed them back to her. "*You* are the work." It was evident by the look on her face that she was neither inspired nor amused. But I stood there, notebook and pen in hand, waiting for her to take it. I wasn't playing either. I knew not to push Simone too hard, but I also understood that it would take her a long time to get comfortable putting herself before her nonprofit and her family; there was no other way. After a moment of teeth-sucking and eye-rolling, she finally caved, put down her phone, and went back to journaling.

Later in the day, we headed for pedicures and shopping at Trader Joe's (because we're among the Black women who love us some Trader Joe's), and then lunch. Over frozen blue drinks and crab legs, we talked about how good it felt to exist without the burden of labor.

"You knew what you were doing when you came here," she told me between sips.

I simply smiled and looked off into the ocean. *I did, didn't I?* I thought. The truth was that I was totally winging it, hoping that an awareness of each guest's comfort, paired with what I'd learned about care on my own, would be a framework solid enough to share with others.

We spent the last day on South Beach, soaking up the sun and having brunch on Ocean Drive. We went shopping in midtown, and I took her to House of Intuition for candles, crystals, and other metaphysical stuff.

"You still mad at me for bossing you around?" I asked with a smirk.

"You were getting on my nerves, but I'ma let you have it." We both laughed, an acknowledgment that, as annoying as I may have been at times, it was worth it.

Ultimately, Simone indulged in enough inclusive self-care to put together her regime. Journaling didn't cut it, but she was a big fan of morning meditation and deep breathing throughout the day. The sundresses and halter tops she rocked during her stay reminded her of how good it felt when her flesh directly touched the sun, air, and life.

"I want this for all of us," Simone said, digging her toes in the sand.

"Same." I sighed.

IT'S MY TURN

by Simone Gordon

BLACK AMERICAN WOMAN – SHE/HER – THIRTY-FIVE YEARS OLD
– NEW JERSEY

I'm a caregiver to my son. I wake up at four a.m. every morning. While I'm getting him prepared during the day, I'm also corresponding with people who have been trying to get ahold of me, people who are in desperate situations. And when I say desperate situations, I mean their water and lights have been cut off, and they have no money or resources to get them cut back on. Their refrigerators are empty. I'm talking about mothers who need two dollars to ride the bus to work. I'm talking about those kinds of situations.

I have never been away from my son since he left my stomach. Leaving Jarvis behind was not easy. My son is glued to my hip. He goes to school, but I'm always his primary provider; I'm there to provide everything he needs and make sure he's living a good life. When I wake up, he's beside me because we sleep in the same bed. He requires twenty-four-hour care. But I knew if I made it to Casa de Tami, it would at least lower my blood pressure for a weekend. Plus, I wanted to see some sunshine. I have never been on vacation a day in my life. I'd only flown once before, but that was to visit my mentor. My first vacation was in Miami at thirty-five. People think the cost of a flight is no big deal, but for me and mine, it is. I pay medical expenses for me and my child. I pay for childcare. Alone. I fill up my fridge. On my own. The little dollars I make go straight to keeping me and mine taken care of. That's my reality.

When people talk about The Fairy Godmother like I'm not a living, breathing human being, they make me sound rich, like I got my whole life together. But most of the time, I did this work as a college student. Head of household, looking after my son and my parents. I have thyroid disease, PCOS, and I suffer from depression.

I didn't tell anybody this until I got to the airport, but I had leg issues that made walking hard. And, I don't have the kind of healthcare that would cover the surgery and treatment required to treat my pain. I got on the plane, and they had to get two seat belts to buckle me. I was embarrassed because even with two seat belts, it wouldn't fit. They had to get two attendants to help me put it on. My legs started getting numb and stayed like that for two hours. But I just kept thinking about that sun, that beach, and that peace. Two hours later, I landed in Miami and was not the Black Fairy Godmother. I was Simone Gordon.

I had never seen something so beautiful when I got into that Lyft. I was stuck in the New Jersey, Brick City state of mind. I was always going to trains and subways in New York City. I didn't know anything outside that. So when I was in the Lyft, I saw palm trees, rocks, and sunshine. I could smell some of the Spanish food through the breeze. I could smell cigars! When I got to Casa de Tami, I was greeted with a bowl of fresh fruit. I don't eat breakfast because I never have the time. That fresh fruit meant a lot to me. Mangos, berries, and grapes.

Tami put me on that Trader Joe's peppermint body wash. I always ensure I have some, and I use it when I'm going through my anxiety. I can't soak in a tub because I don't fit. I can't have candles around a tub because my son will knock them over. But that peppermint calms my nerves.

People think hiring a babysitter or a nurse is so easy, but it's not. There are services, but every household is different, and so is every child. When you have a child who requires twenty-four-hour care, you have to make sure they don't run out of the house, they're not choking, and nobody calls the police on them if they can't stay "quiet."

The pandemic was a challenge. Everything was virtual, meaning I had to help Jarvis with his classes while still maintaining the Black Fairy Godmother and going to college. So, where's the time for me to eat?

The difference between Simone Gordon 2023 and Simone Gordon who stayed at Casa de Tami is that this version of myself has boundaries, time management, and self-care. I'm not saying things are perfect, but I was so stuck on being the Black Fairy Godmother, and they are not the same. Simone Gordon is a mother, student, daughter, sister, and friend. Black Fairy is a philanthropist, activist, and advocate. There's a separation between the two, and I put being a human and mother before all those other labels. I deserve true love. I deserve a house. I deserve a career. Black Fairy gives those things to people, but Simone Gordon has to give that to herself.

I have not been in a relationship in years because of the emotional abuse I experienced from Jarvis's father. I'm now able to have someone who loves me for me: my eczema, my cellulite, my chronic illness, and my son.

God made me go through everything so I can enjoy this moment. Because even though I've been through all these things, I have to love myself first. Once I love myself first, all the energy of love will come back to me.

I'm not a bitch; I'm bitch-like. I say "no thank you" to negativity, "no thank you" to gossiping, "no thank you" to comparing my life to anybody else's, because nobody can be me. And no more accepting verbal disrespect from anybody else. I make it my business to stay in good health, live my best, and enjoy all the love extended to me.

I'm going to take my degree, and I want to go into public health and open up home health agencies. I want to go into public health because there are many people with disabilities, HIV, and heart conditions who are not getting the help they deserve.

Black Fairy has stabilized Black and Brown families for ten years. We have two women, one with a hair salon and one with a nail salon. The one with the nail salon came to me when she was about to get evicted during the pandemic. There was a white woman who was retiring, and she had property. She said, "If this young woman wants to be a nail technician, I'll let her be on my strip." And she did just that. It's just one example of going even deeper than fundraising in the name of reparations and really providing tangible redistributed resources as needed. Today, this young woman does nails for celebrities, their children, everybody.

Storm is a Black woman sleeping in the car with her two kids and husband, who has a physical disability. After helping her get on her feet, she became a welder who runs her own business.

When I returned to Jersey, it was still hard for me. Sometimes we change, but the world and the people around us stay the same. I continued juggling my education, family, and organization, but I understood that I would have to make changes. It wasn't overnight, but over time I learned how to use boundaries to ensure my needs were met and my love tank was full. I started saying "no" more often and didn't always feel pressure to answer every request. That's really how it began. My road to healing. My road to recovery. My road to self-love.

You can support Simone Gordon's organization by donating at theblackfairygodmother.org.

GUMMY BITCH

"And also, I ask you this: What is normal?"

—JENNIFER PASTILOFF, *On Being Human: A Memoir of Waking Up, Living Real, and Listening Hard*

Mornings are almost normal. I wake up and count my blessings. *I am grateful to be alive. I am grateful that I can breathe, feel, and think.* Whether the day ahead is good or bad, there are bound to be moments that remind me how shitty life can be. Acknowledgment of what's going right, I have learned, is one of the few weapons I have against this reality. It isn't until I slip my legs out of bed that I remember I don't have any teeth in my mouth.

I press my fingers deep into my cheeks, poking at the vacancy between my jaw and gums. I pee, pressuring myself to take a good look at my face in the mirror when I wash my hands. That first look is the most critical vision of myself I'll have throughout the day. Avoiding my image without teeth confirms that I am not okay, not presentable—*worthless.* I do not want that for me. And so, while rubbing my hands under the faucet, I lock eyes with my reflection staring at me in the mirror. I see it all—the heat bumps from frolicking in the sun without wearing enough sunblock. The specks of gold in my brown eyes always give off an air of flirtation. I see the tightness of my lips as they collapse into each other. The faded pucker of what remains in the loss of bone and gum tissue. The luster in a perfect deep caramel complexion. I see it all.

What does it look like to see your beauty in times of profound loss—specifically, the kind of loss that can never be genuinely replaced? Like a limb or one of our senses? How do we continue to love and see the value in ourselves when we lose what we believe is most valuable?

"Full extractions," Dr. Esteban, my new periodontist, told me. She was a small-framed, light-skinned Cuban woman. No taller than five feet, her eyelashes were incredibly long. Each time she blinked, they slapped five with her perfectly arched brows. Like most Miamians, Dr. Esteban looked like a model.

"We will create a beautiful set of false teeth for you. Don't worry. The only ones who are going to know you're wearing dentures are me and you. You'll see. We're going to make a temporary first—after the extractions. And, after your gums heal, we'll make you a permanent set that will fit your gums."

Dentures? Permanent? Fit my gums?

"But I don't even have dental insurance!" I sobbed. She gave me a few napkins for the tears and waited until I was consolable.

"Don't worry," she said softly. She waved her hand as though that was the least of my concerns. "Someone is going to walk you through getting a medical loan."

"Okay."

"I know this is a lot," Dr. Esteban said, patting my shoulder. "But it's going to be okay. Focus on your needs and take it one step at a time."

The year was 2021 and, whether I liked it or not, I was about to lose all my teeth. I returned to my studio in Little Havana with a nearly $9,000 loan to CareCredit, cosigned by my mother. I was also down six teeth. Dr. Esteban removed six molars on my right side—three on top and three on the bottom. I was told they would take the other four molars from my top left side when I returned in two weeks. They were going to work their way to the middle like a Tootsie Pop. Halfway through, they would begin measuring and molding for prosthetic teeth.

"What the fuck is going to happen to me?" I cried to my swollen, droopy reflection in the mirror. I had been home for hours. The Novocain was wearing off, but the shock would not budge. I kept thinking about how Dr. Esteban said, "Focus on what you're going to need." Prioritizing my needs worked to get me many things I'd needed and desired in the past, but I *wanted* those things! I didn't want this. I didn't want it to happen, and I didn't want it to happen *to me*.

I kept thinking, *Everyone is going to judge me, they're going to laugh at me, and they're going to be so happy that they aren't me. For the rest of my entire life, when I fall in love, when someone wants to know why I don't eat apples or corn on the cob or suck dick anymore, I'm going to have to tell them that I'm a gummy bitch who will never have natural teeth again. HOW AWFUL FOR ME! I WANT TO DIE!*

My immediate coping mechanism was to comb the internet in search of people like me. Every resource I found was targeted at older people. It only added to the feeling that I would soon be aged decades because of this prognosis.

There was also the influx of worrisome facts I kept stumbling upon. Like, people with false teeth have a life expectancy that's ten years shorter than those with natural teeth. This is because dietary restrictions take healthy yet hard-to-chew foods off the menu. Also, a variety of unexpected speech impediments accompany getting used to false teeth: an airy whistle that appears with words that have soft s's, slurring, and an overall sound of someone talking like they have marbles in their mouth. Many wind up feeling like they must learn how to speak all over again.

I lay in the dark, the right side of my mouth still packed with gauze, the harsh light from my phone illuminating my worst fears. Me, dead at fifty, even though I'll look like I'm eighty because I survived on nothing but mashed potatoes and ice cream.

I sobbed myself to sleep like a neglected newborn every night for one month.

I needed a hand to hold, a voice to soothe me, a friend to make me laugh. As much as everyone loved me, worried about me, and rooted for me, none of them could really "get" what I was going through, myself included. I knew there was a space of people who had already been where I was headed. Those were my people, and I needed to find them.

Like everything else, most of the support groups I found were online on Facebook. I joined the first one that stood out, surprised by their entry questions:

When is your e-day?

I had to Google the word to find out it was the term for extraction day. The awareness that I was entering a world with its own lingo was heartbreaking and exciting.

Answer: *Unsure. I just got the news that I needed to have full extractions a few days ago. Plus, I was told that my procedure would take place over the course of several visits.*

Do you/will you have dentures or implants?

I was so not at peace with the word "dentures." I couldn't hear it without my chin and lower lip quivering. Every visual I could imagine seemed like a prop for a prank or an elderly person. I hated that the thing that was going to make me extra different from everyone else was *dentures*. I hated that every time I had a sleepover or tender piece of meat I would need to be concerned about my *dentures*.

Answer: *At first, I will have to wear false teeth. But eventually, I'd like to get permanent implants.*

Why do you want to join this group?

I wrote, through deep sobs: *Because I just got the news about needing full extractions a few days ago. And even though it's not a surprise, I'm still so sad and scared about it. And lonely! I'm very lonely going through this because I don't know anyone else who has. This experience is mortifying, and I don't think I can get through it without community.*

After pressing send, I shut my laptop and rolled off the sofa to the floor, sobbing into my teal shag rug. Unanswered questions continued to hound me. *Who's going to love me after this? How am I going to take all that pain? What are my new teeth going to look like? How will it affect my speech? Will people be able to tell I'm wearing false teeth when I talk? What about podcasting? Who's going to love me? What do I do during sex? Can I still give head? Everyone's going to talk about me. Everyone's going to laugh. Who's going to love me? What if I just . . . don't do it?*

For the first time, I questioned if I would be strong enough to make it through to the other side of this experience.

In addition to joining a support group, I also upped my therapy game. With additional earnings I was bringing in from freelance work and Patreon subscribers, I could afford actual therapy— nothing fancy, a therapist on betterhelp.com that charged a fraction of what I was paying through in-person sessions. I found a woman, West Indian, named Claire.

During our first video session, I let it rip. "Like, I always knew that the only way I could get implants was by getting . . . dentures;

by the way, I *hate* that word! Anyway, I had no idea it would be this expensive, this soon, this painful, and this long! And during a pandemic. We're going through a pandemic, and I'm in this hot-ass city all alone! I don't have a single hand to hold or person to check on me and bring me soup, and I hate that for me, and I feel like it's not fair!" The only time I paused was for air. I used up so much of it through talking and sobbing that, like a whale, I had to take intentional breaks to breathe. Claire sat there, eyes wide and head bobbing up and down. "I feel like a failure," I sobbed.

Claire mostly just listened in that first session. When she did say something, it was often to remind me that every feeling and fear I had was valid and that I should be proud of taking the proper steps for my health, even if it meant everything changing.

"Your body's check engine light is flashing, Tamela," she said. "There are a lot of people who would be too scared to address it; they would keep driving. But you're making the right decision for your body! You're pulling over and doing the right thing."

The reminder that I was doing the right thing for My Body was much needed. When I first chose Miami as my destination spot for healing, dental work was on top of the list, right beside financial independence and water therapy. Love it or hate it, I was on track with my path to ugly healing, both physically and otherwise.

I was approved to join the false teeth group a few days after I requested. I spent most of that day scrolling down the group's timeline, trying to gain as much access to vital information and resources as possible.

I'm so freaking happy I did this! one woman's caption read. Homegirl took her photo immediately after her false teeth were placed. Her left eye looked bruised, her lips were swollen, and blood was still on her chin. Under normal circumstances, I would have been mortified. But she was smiling so hard, so pleased with her new, perfect set of teeth, I couldn't help but smile at her.

I've never been a fan of my teeth. I'd been living with shitty teeth for so long that I was convinced I would have to get used to it for the rest of my life. But seeing this bloodied and slightly disoriented woman and her new set of grills gave me a perk of excitement. Not big enough to stop crying throughout the day, but enough to make me smile at the thought of me smiling.

I logged on to Facebook for days, making a beeline to the tooth club. I learned the importance of stocking up on things like good pillows and sheets since I'd spend a lot of time resting in bed. I learned I would need plenty of Ensure to get me through the oral surgery days when I couldn't chew. I learned that most people couldn't eat corn on the cob, which upset me even though I don't even enjoy corn in its cobbed state. However, many false teeth wearers can eat most foods with time.

Finally, after one week in the club, I felt safe enough to share the following:

Hello all!

I am sooooo scared of this process, but I'll do anything to get back to good oral health. I have concerns about having enough bone for dental options, but I'm trying not to get too worked up. I am so grateful to this group and each of you for being vulnerable and open with your journeys! 🙏

I let out a different kind of cry after hitting the send button. Instead of feeling woeful, I was relieved to get such heavy fears off my chest to people who understood. I felt so good that I wasn't even concerned with how many likes or comments I got. But, in a group that got modest traction, I was grateful to have received twenty comments. Some of them spoke directly to my fears:

> *Sharon: I admire you too . . . I have to admit I'm nervous too. But it's now or never for me.*
>
> *Randall: It will be worth it in the end.* 👫
>
> *Janet: If you have significant bone loss, hopefully you are a candidate for bone grafts. An oral surgeon best does that type of work.*

Within a week, I was feeling comfortable sharing and asking all the questions I was too bashful to ask Dr. Esteban:

> *Me: I'm not trying to be vulgar or suggestive in any way, but I have a very practical question to ask. How do you still engage . . . sexually? Like, I know, for the most part, it's the same, but also, there are a few things I currently practice with natural teeth, and I'm wondering what that will be like with false teeth.*
>
> *Donna: If you're talking about giving head, it's better to take it out. All that sucking is going to shift them out of place. Plus, they love gummy heads.*

I died.

> *Eric: My girlfriend and I have false teeth. It's not a problem when I'm going down on her, but she takes out her teeth when she goes down on me. So much better.* 😊 *I think she's still a little hung up about it, but I totally don't mind.*
>
> *Tanisha: I don't give them, period.*

Tonya: Take them out, and they'll have the experience of their lives.

Me: How long do you wait before telling your partner about your false teeth? And how do you handle rejection because of your teeth?

Gregory: I try to slip it in there as soon as possible. It gives them the choice to make their own vain decision and takes a load of anxiety off my back.

Sarah: Ugh, I've been dating a guy for three months, and he has NO idea, and I have NO clue when to tell him smh.

Bethenny: Rejection sucks, but you know what? Anyone rejecting you because of your health is a piece of shit. Would you want to be with a guy like that anyway?

I felt some real, tangible hope for the first time. Maybe I would survive this. Possibly, just maybe, I would be okay.

SURRENDER

I woke up the morning after my fifth round of extractions, unable to recognize the face that stared back at me in the mirror. A large, deep purple bruise sat under my left eye, the same side where the extractions occurred. Also, that side of my face was incredibly swollen, so much so that my eye looked like it was closing. The gap between my two front teeth was at least twice as wide as when I first visited Dr. Esteban. It was so wide that, for a moment, I wondered if a tooth had actually fallen out. And my lips. My perfectly shaped lips were now ballooned in size, my upper lip practically poking inside my nostrils.

For each round of extractions, there would be a noticeable difference to my face — more often than not only noticeable to me, but a difference all the same. I would find my face becoming more withdrawn, my cheekbones more refined by the loss of teeth. The pucker in my lips faded into my mouth's vacancy, looking tighter and pressed. I had been warned that the healing process could be brutal, but the image staring back at me in the mirror was mortifying.

"What's happening to me?" I mumbled to Dr. Esteban after rushing in for an emergency visit. I was braless and still wearing my jammie pants, a sign that I had left the key to my common sense back at my studio apartment.

"This is normal, Tamela," she assured me. She explained that the bruise under my eye was from the necessary pressure applied from extracting my canines and remaining molars. The swelling was more intense than usual because My Body was catching on to the reality that it would have to work harder to fight off infection. The swelling in my lips was a reaction to the antibiotics I'd taken over the past several months. And the reason why the gaps were widening was because as more teeth were removed from my gums, weak from the trauma of multiple extractions, they'd loosened, causing my remaining teeth to spread.

"This is temporary," she said softly.

"I don't think I can do this anymore!" I whimpered. My Body was rejecting the process like a kidney transplant gone wrong.

"We're going to be done soon, Tamela. It's going to be okay." And then she said something about my experience that had nothing to do with my teeth or gums. "Your body is doing the best it can, but Tamela, this is a serious trauma it's taking on. You mustn't get an infection or bigger health issues right now. You must avoid as much stress as possible and care for yourself."

I sat in the chair and began to cry—the ugly cry I usually reserve for myself in private. I didn't care if anyone in the neighboring rooms could hear me. I just needed to release that feeling of pain. Dr. Esteban walked across the room, grabbed a box of tissues, and returned to her seat beside me. I lifted my hand for one, but she took a tissue and gently wiped the tears from my face.

"When this is over," she whispered, "you will be so happy that you did this. I promise your quality of life, how you feel about yourself—it's going to get better. You're almost there."

Dr. Esteban knew very little about who I was at that time. She didn't know that I was a struggling writer, that I was surviving through the pandemic and a racial uprising on my own, that I had to fight to love myself, my *Self*, harder than I ever had before. All she knew was that I was her human patient and needed more than dental treatment. In those moments, my dentist became an integral part of my community. Not just the person who extracted and stitched me up, but one concerned for my mental and physical health.

"Today is awful."

Later that night, I went through my usual routine of eating my edible-laced mashed potatoes, then falling asleep to affirmations on YouTube. I lay in bed repeating the mantras that have often saved me from intrusive thoughts and impulsive behavior. *In this moment, everything is okay. In this moment, I am safe, loved, and have everything I need.* I said those words repeatedly, and they did me no good. Frustrated, I sat up and walked to my altar, submersing myself in prayer. Nothing. The pain that had overcome me that morning and followed me to Dr. Esteban's office was still within me. Despite how hard I was trying to get through this experience with grace and optimism, there was still a huge chunk of me in the most profound despair. I wanted to be angry about it, enraged, but I couldn't get past the fear.

I got off my knees to head to the bathroom. I did not make it. I pressed my back against my bedroom wall and slid to the floor. A primal scream found its way from my gut through my mouth, rattling the loose teeth that remained. This wail that came from My Body was something I'd never heard or felt before.

I wanted to identify this feeling as anxiety and write it off as another panic attack. But there was something so still yet visceral about it. It was an ache, an awareness I had avoided for too long.

This fear inside me had a name, and it was *worthless*.

I was still hooked on the external validation of being seen as beautiful. Without it, by my own conditioned belief, I was worth *less*. I was worthless. I thought that if I could surround myself with as much love and light as possible, focus on the good parts, the trauma would fade into the background. I was very wrong. I had been so desperate to prepare myself, half-cup-full my way through this experience, that I almost convinced myself that I wouldn't have to feel it.

I had such a fucked-up relationship with beauty and My Body, and my oral health journey amplified that. As deeply as I wanted to overdose on acts of self-love and self-care, my self-worth didn't have the capacity to receive those actions. Before I could reach for a better state of mind, I would have to accept that my state was pretty shitty.

"Not okay," was my response when Sissy asked how I was doing the next day. I admitted my feelings of low self-worth and disappointment with my prognosis. My honesty was abrasive, and I was rather unapologetic about it. Sissy, who knows me better than anyone, was jarred by my response.

"This, too, will pass," she said.

"I know," I agreed. "And, when it does, I'll go from being a miserable bitch to a gummy bitch." The laughter that came between us was as unexpected as it was welcomed. It was the first time I was able to make a joke about it, talk about it without breaking into sobs. We laughed so hard that we had to wrap it up with the honorary "Whew, chile!" and long, high-pitched sighs of exasperation.

Sissy was right; as much as that moment sucked, it would soon be over. The pain, the anxiety, the dread. In some ways, I felt like I was dragging it, feeling overly sorry about something that really wasn't that uncommon. Nearly forty-one million Americans wear dentures. I'm just one of them.

After five months, eleven dentist visits, and twenty-nine extractions, it was finally over.

It took a whole week before the trauma of the procedure subsided, two months to relearn how to speak, and three months before I was comfortable eating in public again.

Speaking has been the greatest challenge. My *s*'s are too hissy, and my *ch*'s are too soft. It used to take three or four cocktails before I noticed anything that sounded like slurred speech. Now, with dentures, it's more like a drink and a half.

Sex is normal. If I'm feeling frisky with someone with a dick, I may give a simple optical illusion of head—heavy on the licking and jerking, light on actual suction. I apply some excellent advice from a good friend: "You're trying to be cute, not win a dick-sucking contest."

On the good days, I walk around with the confidence that exceeds that of a mediocre white man, which is exceptional. I look at people in the eye when I speak to them, and I don't bother covering my mouth when I laugh—at least, not as much as I used to.

I'm very kind to myself on the good days. I congratulate myself for that tough time I got through. I stare at my beauty in nearly every reflection I pass, and I give thanks that I can still see it. I eat what I want, give big smiles to anyone who seems worthy, and live well.

The bad days are tough. Those are the days when the feelings of inadequacy haunt me, and I keep thinking My Body is less than. Less than it should be, less than it was, less than what's considered a good body. The old me would allow those feelings to consume me and leave imprints on my behavior and decision-making. But, even on the bad days, this version of me has learned to be kind to myself. So, instead of self-loathing, I reach out to a friend. With their consent, I vent through the emotions of my bad day, letting the sharp thorns from within come out so they can't hurt me. My favorite friend to do this with is Jennifer Pastiloff. She's got a beautiful mouth full of teeth. She lives with severe hearing impairment, often having to rely on reading lips as well as her hearing aids. I'm a gummy bitch; Jenn is a deaf bitch.

"I feel like such a fucking loser," I once sobbed to Jenn over the phone. "I failed at the whole taking-care-of-myself thing. I did a bad fucking job! And now I'm everyone's worst-case scenario."

These feelings were triggered by a brief interaction with an acquaintance. An online friend messaged me to share that they'd booked a visit with their dentist after reading a post I wrote about adjusting to dentures. *Girl, I thought about you and was like, Let me go ahead to the dentist while I still have my teeth!* I imagine she told me this to let me know I inspired her. But the way it came out was like, *Baby, I'd rather be anybody but your toothless ass!* I tried to take the comment on the chin, but inside, I shriveled up and died. I was the walking reminder of the importance of flossing and brushing your teeth daily. The reality of that gutted me.

"I hate being everyone's cautionary tale," I admitted to Jenn.

"Fuck that; we're all somebody's cautionary tale about something!" she snapped. She was right. Western humans are wired to reference people who experience extreme challenges for their own benefit, whether to prove a point or make themselves feel better, knowing that somebody out there has it worse. It's why trauma porn is at an all-time high, and the only time parents care about kids in Africa is when they're trying to convince their own kids to eat all their food.

"I hate this for me," I whined.

"I know. It sucks. It fucking sucks," she confirmed. The tears fell again, but this time they were tears of acknowledgment because someone was seeing me. "But you know what?" Jenn continued, "You don't have to be anybody's anything. You don't have to be anybody's cautionary tale. By living your best and truest life, you're a living, breathing best-case scenario."

"Why are you so emotionally intelligent, Jenn?"

"I don't know. But I know this much—every time you smile at me, all I feel is inspiration."

And that's the thing: it's all about perception, and the only ones that matter are the ones I love. My beauty, at its highest value, is worth only as much as I can value it. Whenever I attempt to hold My Body up to the standards of anything or anyone outside itself, I set myself up to have a bad day. This body of mine was never meant to be measured or graded on its aesthetic or societal currency.

The external validation I spent my entire life seeking can't hold a candle to what I give myself daily. I made a conscious decision that prosthetic teeth were not going to compromise my beauty or my worth, and I stand ten toes down in that decision every single day—including the bad ones. I celebrate my smile, wear clothes that make me feel like a babe, and am gentle with myself.

Like many, I navigate life in a body that has changed and will likely continue to change over time. This impacts my human experience, but in no way, shape, or form does it define it, let alone compromise its worth.

I want to tell you deeply that the body you embody in this moment is perfect, working for you, and giving you everything you need to be your best Self. But, if someone had told me that after one of my dentist appointments, I would have pulled one of the gauze balls out of my mouth and chucked it at them. So, I will not patronize you with wishy-washy affirmations or pretend that our struggles with our bodies are identical. Instead, I'm going to encourage you to live as loudly and proudly as possible with the body you have while you still have it. Because if you've made it this far in the book, you understand that we're only here until we're not, and we don't always have a say or get a warning of when our bodies change or stop working. No matter what stops working or needs to be replaced or removed, our bodies are whole and in need of our love and compassion.

Care & Intersectionality

■

*"My description cannot fit your tongue, for I have
a certain way of being in this world."*

—MAYA ANGELOU

A WORD ON CARE AND INTERSECTIONALITY . . .

In what ways is your life unique because of your intersection? Does your identity play a part in where you get to live? Work? When you make decisions about what's best for you, do you often have to factor in your race, gender, ethnicity, physical mobility, income, etc.? How compromised are your reproductive rights?

"Care & Intersectionality" is an examination of the ways in which our wellness, liberties, and opportunities are compromised due to our identities. No matter how often society suggests that pulling ourselves up "by the bootstraps" is the cure-all for facing adversity, it's a lot more complex for people who navigate marginalized intersections.

From finding a decent place to live to pursuing dream jobs and stability, overlapping oppression compromises every chance we have at pursuing an American dream. Rather than surrender to the realities of our oppression, the following testimonies examine the nuances, challenges, wins, and decision-making of those who are determined to live beyond the confines of oppression.

LAST MAMMY STANDING

◼

*"The myth of the strong black woman is the other side of the coin
of the myth of the beautiful dumb blonde. The white man
turned . . . the black woman into a strong self-reliant Amazon
and deposited her in his kitchen—that's the secret of
Aunt Jemima's bandanna."*

—ELDRIDGE CLEAVER

Lord, these corns are killing me!" As soon as I shoved the words
out of my mouth, I knew I was being laughed at and not with.

The year was 1997 and I was a freshman at Bay Shore High
School, auditioning for a role in *You Can't Take It with You*. The
production was based on the 1938 film of the same name. The
plot is centered on Alice Sycamore, a nice white girl from a well-
meaning yet eccentric family. The part I was instructed to audition for was Rheba, the family's maid.

At the time, I loved performing as much as I did write. I was in
tap class and the school chorus. Being on stage meant something
to me, and I always took note of teachers who complimented me
on my animated personality. I took that as a sign that I had that
special "it factor" that would get me noticed in life.

More than wanting to be on stage, I wanted to fit in; I needed
to fit in. I was fat, sheltered, and excluded from almost every inner
circle I tried to weasel my way into. A few weeks before the audition, Tamika Reynolds squirted ketchup packets on one of the free

sanitation pads handed out at the nurse's office and slapped it on my locker. A few classmates were actually more incensed than I was. I appreciated the support, but the damage to my self-worth was cemented. I figured that the dorks in drama club were the last peers on Earth who would take me in.

Finding out I'd won the role of Rheba was . . . bittersweet. My spot in the club was now solidified; all I had to do was show up. But, when I got the full script on the first day of rehearsal, I realized that showing up would not be easy. Every line Rheba spoke was in broken English. The way her appearance was described—handkerchief on the head, Southern drawl . . . I didn't have the verbiage for it then, but it was clear that this character was Mammy.

A BLACK WOMAN'S WORK

A photo of my maternal grandmother, Ma, sits on my altar alongside her four sisters, Christine, Ruth, Alice, and Lois. Each woman varies in height, hair texture, and complexion. The one thing they all have in common, aside from having the same mother, is that each woman was employed as a domestic. Ninety percent of Black women in the late nineteenth century were employed as domestic workers. That means damn near all of us. Domestic employment would be our dominant work well into the twentieth century.

"Domestic" is placed alongside many of my women-identified ancestors' names on various census records throughout the nineteenth and twentieth centuries. A simple term to disguise the unfair and commonly inhumane conditions under which Black women worked for white families, industries, and institutions. Domestic, such as washing the dishes and clothes, preparing meals, looking after children, wet-nursing white women's babies, etc. However, the term leaves out the nuances in the power dynamic between white matriarchs and Black servants, which brought many domestic workers back to their enslaved pasts. Black women employed as domestic workers spent more time commuting to and from their employers' homes than with their own families. The word "domestic" may paint a picture of fair employment, but the truth behind it is anything but just. For Black women, it would serve as a pigeonhole that reduced us to acts of servitude, sacrifice, and exploitation.

When Nancy Green, a Kentucky-based domestic worker who was formerly enslaved, was hired to portray Aunt Jemima in 1893, she was catapulted into American pop culture history, her image as well-known as Michael Jordan's one-armed dunk on a pair of Nikes. As the brand Aunt Jemima became successful, Nancy Green took off with it. She was booked and busy presenting as the syrup's namesake, appearing at stores, festivals, and fairs throughout the country. Her image would go on to further refine the physical embodiment of Mammy. Long after Nancy died in 1923, the image of Aunt Jemima continued to serve as the prototype for the Black domestic—wide hips, dark skin, a handkerchief-covered crown, and a beaming smile.

YOU CAN'T LEAVE IT BEHIND EITHER

"Don't you think it's racist to have only *one* character for a Black student to play?" We were a few days into rehearsing for *You Can't Take It with You*, and I was finally ready to confront Mr. Anthony about Rheba.

"Unfortunately, Black students don't seem too interested in theater." Mr. Anthony said it with a straight face and a condescending tone. It was the same response I would receive from supervisors, teachers, or coaches whenever I questioned why I was the only Black person in attendance. The suggestion that Black people are less *interested* in said experience, which is why they're excluded, is a racist code: *The opportunity for Black people to participate in this is so compromised that it's designed for them not to want to show up.*

"Maybe next year we'll get the rights to put on *The Lion King!*" he snickered.

I laughed along with everyone else but didn't find that funny. As the weeks rolled by, my anxiety over playing Rheba grew. I thought that perhaps I needed help from an adult to convince Mr. Anthony to change the script around and de-Mammify Rheba.

"It's racist and wrong!" I was in the office of my guidance counselor, Mrs. Pratt, explaining everything wrong with the play and me starring as Rheba—the broken English, the blatant racism, and only being offered that role.

"I'm so sorry to hear this, Tamela," she began. The tears fell as I processed her apology. I was just about to lean into the feeling of being understood when Mrs. Pratt pulled the carpet from beneath my feet. "It's been so hard for you to fit in this school year. I would think that you would want this to work out for you."

I was stunned. I knew that she was referring to Tamika and the ketchup period pad, but that wasn't my fault either. I was incredibly confused as to how the onus of fitting in and getting along was on me, even and especially when it was clear that very few people cared to get along with me.

"I do want this to work out!" I shrieked. "But I didn't choose this play or this role."

"That's how acting works, honey." She smiled as she said this, but her demeanor was far from pleasant. It was clear that she didn't understand or even care to.

"Mrs. Pratt, I'm *trying* to fit in, but not at the expense of humiliating myself and my race! That's not fair! Don't you think that's wrong?"

She sighed and slid back into her chair. Her unbrushed shoulder-length blonde hair obstructed the disconnect in her eyes.

"This isn't about race, Tamela," she lied. "This is about *perspective*. And you're choosing a perspective that . . . well, really . . . isn't good for anyone." She stood up, walked across the room, and opened the door. "I'm sorry you don't like your role, but we don't always get to choose in life. If you don't want to be in the play, don't be. But you won't have anyone to blame but yourself."

"Tamela, you need to walk a lot slower than that. You must walk like an old woman who's been on her feet morning, noon, and night. Remember, your corns are killing you!"

"You should be smiling more, Tamela. Rheba didn't like being a mam-maid—she loved being a maid!"

"I don't want you to walk with a limp, but throw in a bit of a . . . waddle in your walk. You know, like a penguin. Even better, George Jefferson!"

No matter how hard I tried to let it go, the nagging feeling that committing to this role would backfire taunted me. But each time I worried that the role I was playing would receive as much ridicule as I had welcomed it with, I would remind myself of the adults who assured me that this was the right thing to do. That a bit of discomfort could lead me toward acceptance. *Next year, Mr. Anthony will choose a play with more options for Black students. In a few years, someone will look back at me today and figure out I was right.* I allowed myself to get lost in a sea of what-ifs and maybes until I was sufficiently disassociated from the reality of everything.

"Why would you let them make you play a slave?" It was the Monday after opening night in Mr. Weinstein's English class. I had already been addressed by several classmates and even a few teachers, everyone wanting to know why. Why had I agreed to be in the play? Why didn't I speak up for myself and on behalf of the other Black students? Why didn't I question the integrity of the role? Each time, I would stammer over my words, trying to explain the same limp excuses handed over to me. *There aren't enough Black kids who tried out to have good roles. Rheba wasn't a slave; she was their maid and an integral part of the production.* By the time I got to Mr. Weinstein's class, I was fresh out of regurgitated responses. So, instead, I just sat there and stared at whoever asked a question. And oh, they asked:

"I'm just saying, like . . . didn't you feel bad? Didn't you feel stupid?"

"After everything we've been through in this country, why would you let them take us back like that?"

"Are you even proud to be Black?"

GOLDEN GIRLS

The original actor who played Rheba in the 1936 stage production of *You Can't Take It with You* was Lillian Yarborough, better known by the names Billie Yarbo on stage and Lillian Yarbo on screen.

Lillian was born in Washington, DC, on March 17, 1905. She would eventually go to New York, where her performing career would take off. She became a hit on Broadway and in Harlem, where she resided. Twentieth century Harlem was home of the Niggerati. It's not a stretch to imagine young, stunning Lillian smoking cigarettes lit by Langston Hughes and spilling industry tea with Zora Neale Hurston in the ladies' room. Yarborough would stand outside venues where she was set to perform and yell, "Come down and listen to me—the real Billie!" This was an egregious dig at Billie Holiday, a world-renowned performer at that time. Regardless of her personal comparison to Billie Holiday, Lillian was making a name for herself on Broadway. The *Pittsburg Chronicle* wrote of one of her performances, "Yarbo was never appreciated as an artist, and now she finds herself one of the most talked about performers in current successes."

Eventually, Lillian made her way to film. After several small parts, she landed the role of Rheba. The success of *You Can't Take It with You* helped to further Lillian's reach in Hollywood. She continued acting in film for nearly two decades until retiring and fading into obscurity. Lillian Yarbo died on June 12, 1996. By the end of her career, she had starred in at least a dozen stage performances and at least forty-nine films. Sadly, because Black actors were rarely credited for their roles, many of these performances fail to mention her.

I wanted to know more. Not just about Lillian but all the other Black women actors whose limitless talent was reduced to slapstick servitude, all because of their intersection of Blackness and womanhood. How were they able to make it out of their careers despite the stronghold that Mammy had over their images? How did the stereotype impact their lives offstage? What I learned was that, despite the racism of the entertainment industry and painful ridicule from both critics and Black people, Black women actors of the Mammy era helped pave the way for all Black actors that followed, both on stage and off.

Ask your average trivia fanatic about the first situation comedy to star a Black woman lead. They'll tell you it was Diahann Carroll in the 1968 television series *Julia*. Undoubtedly, the lead actor and television show were a first: a Black woman in a lead role that wasn't degrading in any way, shape, or form. However, *Julia* wasn't the first. More than a decade before the sitcom that starred Carroll, there was another show, another first, that centered on a Black woman. It wasn't inspirational or aspirational in any way.

The role would become so infamous that it would take three Black women actors to fill it.

Beulah was introduced to American entertainment in 1944 as a supporting character in the popular radio show *Fibber McGee and Molly*. The comedy was about a Black maid who worked for a white attorney and his family. Though the show boasted an ensemble cast, much of the plot focused on Beulah's attempt to fix problems. In the early twentieth century, it was customary for white performers to wear blackface and pretend to be Black instead of hiring Black performers, even on the radio. This was also true of *Beulah*.

The show would eventually hire a Black woman, and in 1950, it made the leap from radio to television. Despite an eager audience and impressive viewership, it would take three Black actresses who were willing to play the lead character: Hattie McDaniel, Ethel Waters, and Louise Beavers. On their own, these performers would create filmographies with movies that stand the test of time to this day. Yet, together, the three women would not only leave a progressive imprint on Hollywood, but they would also force Tinseltown to respect their Black performers, both on stage as well as in residential quarters.

Many may assume that the limited roles and cutthroat industry would create division among Black women actors in Hollywood. There did exist elements of competition and sometimes contempt; however, the three actors were more comrades than competitors.

By 1938, Hattie McDaniel, Louise Beavers, and Ethel Waters were among Hollywood's most gainfully employed Black actors. It made sense that the actors and other notable Black performers would want to live in the community that used them. At that time, the Los Angeles neighborhood was known as West Adams Heights.

Most California suburbs reflected the nation's upholding of white supremacy through its housing discrimination. In West

Adams Heights, that looked like restrictive housing covenants. These written guidelines spelled out clear discriminatory standards, like, "property shall not . . . at any time be leased, sold, devised, or conveyed to or inherited by . . . any person whose blood is not entirely that of the Caucasian race."

The covenants for West Adams Heights may have been overlooked when Hattie, Ethel, and Louise moved in, but by 1945, a collective of white West Adams Heights residents filed a lawsuit against thirty-one Black residents. Alongside legal counsel, Hattie led the charge to advocate for Black residents' right to live in West Adams Heights. She went as far as organizing Saturday workshops to strategize for the case and gathered as many as 250 supporters who attended the hearing in December of 1945. Ultimately, Judge Thurmond Clarke ruled to throw the case out the day after a personal visit to the neighborhood. "It is time that members of the Negro race are accorded, without reservations or evasions, the full rights guaranteed them under the 14th Amendment to the Federal Constitution."

The case set a precedent that would lead to the eventual disbandment of restrictive housing covenants throughout the country. And, for Hattie, Ethel, and Louise, it affirmed that, despite the characters they played on screen and stage, they were neither subservient nor complicit.

HATTIE MCDANIEL

Gone with the Wind was a 1939 antebellum film about the impact the Civil War had on affluent white Southerners. Scarlett O'Hara, played by Vivien Leigh, was a snobby, privileged daughter of the owner of Tara, a Georgia-based plantation. A deep South plot that made no apologies for sympathizing with Confederate soldiers while villainizing the Union and abolitionists, the film glorified chattel slavery. It bent backward to humanize the Lost Cause of the Confederacy.

Hattie starred as Mammy, the head domestic at Tara, who ruled the staff, children, and even Scarlett with an iron fist. While her existence was exclusive in her servitude, she was not docile. Some white moviegoers took offense to the bold character, fearful that her defiance of the social order of employer and servant would give other Black domestic workers bad ideas.

Just as there were white critics who opposed the Mammy character because of her abrasiveness, there were Black critics who detested the fact that Hattie McDaniel was in the film at all. The romanticized notion of "good old days" in the antebellum South was a narrative that Black folks refused to cosign. To Hattie's credit, her work behind the scenes was far less docile than the enslaved character she portrayed in the film. Like many Black actors of the Mammy era, she had to take diction courses to learn how to speak like a Mammy, seeing as how the Denver-born woman spoke "proper" English, not broken. However, she stopped short at playing in scenes that she felt were egregiously racist, changing lines and omitting the n-word.

Despite her best efforts, criticism of portraying Mammy roles overshadowed any notoriety she received for playing them well. Despite winning an Academy Award for Best Supporting Actress in *Gone with the Wind,* Hattie would spend the remainder of her career embroiled in a bitter feud with the NAACP over representation.

Refusing to apologize for the roles she portrayed, she clapped back at the stigma that preceded Mammy in radio, television, and film. She also acknowledged that she lived in a country that gave her very few choices of what to do with her life. In Carlton Jackson's *Hattie: The Life of Hattie McDaniel,* he documents a conversation Hattie had with a friend who challenged her decision to play "handkerchief heads." A handkerchief head is an outdated, offensive term that describes a subservient Black person, usually a woman, who has completely surrendered to white laws and hierarchies.

Hattie replied to her hating-ass friend, "Hell, I'd rather play a maid than be one."

Despite her Oscar win, nothing changed for Hattie in Hollywood regarding getting roles outside servitude.

Over a decade after her Oscar win, the Mammy trope would hit its theatrical peak when *Beulah* went from radio to television. Revamped into a thirty-minute situation comedy, viewers were excited to see the long-running radio show brought to the silver screen. However, they were surprised to turn on their televisions during that first season and not see Hattie McDaniel star as the lead character. Instead, the role was given to Ethel Waters.

ETHEL WATERS

"I never was a child" is Ethel's opening sentence in her 1950 memoir, *His Eye Is on the Sparrow*. Sis wasn't lying. Ethel Waters was born on Halloween, 1896. She was the product of rape, and her mother was barely thirteen when she gave birth to her. By three, her father would be poisoned and killed by a jealous lover. Her great-grandparents were enslaved, and she carried with her memories of not-so-post-abolished slavery. "Slavery had been abolished, but these white men were still making money by kidnaping little Negro children," she wrote.

Her young mother did the best she could. Still, the streets raised Ethel. Her only exposure to stable living would be when she accompanied her mother to work as a domestic. By age eighteen, she understood the drug game, running numbers, and the art of prostitution. Without a doubt, she would fully support the pro-hoe movement if she were still alive today. "I've always had great respect for whores," she wrote. "The many I've known were kind and generous." Of all the lessons she learned while growing up in the mean streets of Philadelphia, the art of entertainment would stay with her through the years.

Along with socioeconomic hardships beyond Ethel's control, the way her body was developing impacted her opportunities and how she was seen in the world, something that was not lost on her. "Sometimes I think this big size of mine has prevented me from becoming a human being. Nobody's protective instinct ever is aroused by a huge girl."

In EbonyJanice Moore's *All the Black Girls Are Activists*, she writes about the sexualization and adultification of Black women and girls based on the shape and development of our bodies. The issue is as old as Sarah Baartman, known as Hottentot. Sarah was an enslaved African woman who was caged and treated as a spectacle because of her curvy physique. White men have forever lusted over the shapeliness of Black marginalized genders, so much so that our humanity becomes secondary to their desires. So, when Ethel said, "This big size of mine has prevented me from becoming a human being," she was speaking on behalf of a collective lived experience that many of us Black girls and women can relate to but have yet to process fully.

Despite how she was perceived in her youth, Ethel would mature into a woman who understood how to use her divine feminine prowess. After years of traveling throughout the country, singing, and performing with greats like Bessie Smith, she would go to Broadway, where she became known for her singing voice. By the time she was cast as Beulah, she had already claimed a television first. In 1939, while Hattie was basking in the glow of the role which would crown her the first Black actor to win an Oscar, Ethel was becoming the first Black entertainer to star in a television program, *The Ethel Waters Show*. The variety show would be the first of many moments where the blues singer and actor would show off her range, including a performance based on South Carolina's Gullah community.

Ethel continued to work steadily throughout the 1940s. Though she was no stranger to portraying Mammy-like roles, she also embodied characters with range and dialogue that went beyond the traditional domestic. For example, Ethel costarred in the 1949 film *Pinky*, which critics so highly regarded that it earned her an Academy Award nomination. The plot is about racially ambiguous Pinky (played by Jeanne Crain, a white woman) who returns to her Southern town to visit her grandmother, Dicey, played by Ethel. The film centers on race, misogyny, and colorism.

Despite the promise the role offered her, Ethel walked away from the lead in *Beulah* after just one season. The official press release claimed it was due partly to scheduling conflicts. However, word on the street was that Ethel was tired of catching heat from Black folks and critics alike who were fed up with the inundation of Mammy. As soon as she exited, she was replaced with Hattie McDaniel. Sadly, Hattie would only star in one season of *Beulah* before a late-stage breast cancer diagnosis forced her to retire from acting. Her dying wish was to be buried at the famous Hollywood Memorial Park, where many other actors and notable celebrities were laid to rest. Sadly, her request was denied because Hollywood Memorial Park didn't permit the burials of Black Americans. Instead, she was the first Black person to be buried at Rosedale Cemetery in Los Angeles.

In a final twist of fate, Louise Beavers would be cast as the final actor to play Beulah, connecting her with Hattie and Ethel one last time.

Of the three actors to be cast in the role of Beulah, it's fair to say that Louise was given the shortest stick in Hollywood. Though her career as an actor spanned the course of five decades, from the 1920s until 1961, it was her portrayal of Delilah Johnson in 1934's *Imitation of Life* that made Louise Beavers a household name. Like *Pinky*, the film's plot was about a racially ambiguous Black girl and her complicated relationship with the Black elder in her life. However, unlike *Pinky*, the protagonist, Peola, played by Fredi Washington, disavowed her race. The film interrogated the nuances of colorism, the act of white passing, and self-hatred. Despite high praise from Hollywood and an Academy Award nomination, the role did Louise's career little favor. By the time she took on the lead role in *Beulah*, she had played in more than fifty films as a domestic servant.

By 1953, *Beulah* had run its course, and the show was canceled. Louise would act in ten more films, appearing in all of them in the Mammy form. After a series of illnesses, including diabetes, she died in 1966 at sixty.

In 2009, actor and comedian Mo'Nique became the fourth Black American woman to win an Academy Award for Best Supporting Actress for her role in *Precious*. She donned a beautiful flower pin in her hair in an ode to the one Hattie McDaniel wore the night she won an Oscar. Mo'Nique proceeded to thank Hattie for her contribution to television and film.

Ethel Waters would be the only one to experience the blessing of time and creative liberty. She would continue acting in a series of stage, screen, and television productions and write not one but two autobiographies.

The backlash I received from playing Rheba in *You Can't Take It with You* was insufferable. Convinced that I needed a fresh start, I badgered my parents to let me live with Sissy in Queens until they relented. While there, I auditioned and was accepted into the performance art program at Hillcrest High School. A moment of redemption allowed me to continue exploring my creative side, but wherever I went, there I was. I began experimenting with re-making myself, going through various styles and personas, each further removed from anything resembling Mammy. I wanted to be sexy, I wanted to be cool, and I wanted to be the main character.

It's easy to say that we become the people we choose to be — that who we are, our behaviors, characteristics, and other traits are based solely on our innermost selves. If only that were true. For those who navigate marginalized intersections, especially Black marginalized genders, much of our existence is spent bobbing and weaving among the racial tropes that assault our identity. The act of attempting to show up as our whole authentic selves is much like trying to walk straight in a crooked room, a brilliant metaphor Melissa Harris-Perry uses to describe what it's like for Black women to show up in a society that expects us to present in the ways they are willing to accept us. Do we play the part and appease the misogynistic audience, or do we rebel and tilt which-ever way the room sways us? I chose to rebel. Sadly, I did so in ways more seeped in being someone else than in honoring myself. In my effort to abandon Mammy, I abandoned Tamela.

THE STAKES IS HIGH

■

"This dream, and we'll get to the dream in a moment, is at the expense of the American negro. You watch this in the deep south in great relief. But, not only in the deep south."

—JAMES BALDWIN

CONTENT WARNING: MOLESTATION

In one way or another, I have been violated in every hood I've ever lived.

Where in America will my Black body be safe? I've been searching for the answer to that question my entire life. So far, I've lived in one major city—New York—one small town—Bay Shore—and two that stay on the struggle bus—New Orleans and Miami. Each has its respective perks, but none passed my safety smell test. I've visited big cities like Atlanta and Los Angeles on several occasions. Fun? Sure. Landscapes and backdrops that will make your Instagram profile drool? Absolutely. But a community that offers physical, psychological, financial, and legal safety? At this point, fly me to the moon because there ain't no safety on this land for my Black body.

That good old American dream makes us believe we'll be all right if we can just get inside this utopia known as the suburbs. My parents bought into the same hope that all Black families who moved to Long Island were sold: Everything will be better. Better schools, better living conditions, and better quality of living. For Black New Yorkers in the 1980s, *better* was anywhere else but the concrete jungle. We didn't know then that the American dream that white supremacy was luring us into was just as dangerous as the hurdles we jumped in the inner city.

NEW YORK STATE OF MIND

In the winter of 1984, just a few days before Christmas, Darrell Cabey and three friends were riding a Bronx-bound 2 train. A few stops into their ride, a white man, Bernard Goetz, also boarded. One of Darrell's friends, Troy Canty, who was nineteen years old, approached Goetz and asked, "Can I have five dollars?" Goetz contends that he said, "Give me five dollars." *Can I have* versus *give me* shouldn't make much difference, but it ultimately changed all five men's lives.

"I've got five dollars for each of you," Goetz responded, then went in his pocket, whipped out a gun, and shot Darrell and all three of his friends.

Various versions are told about what happened on that number 2 train; some say the group was creating trouble, while others claimed they were rowdy but far from violent. The one fact to be proven was that Goetz shot four Black kids.

By the next day, Goetz had gone into hiding, three kids were recovering, and Darrell was fighting for his life. It sounded like an open-and-shut case. However, there was a mixed reaction from New Yorkers, many of whom commended Goetz for acting when the city was riddled with crime.

The gunman was revered as a hero and quickly dubbed The Subway Vigilante. In the *New York Daily News*, Bob Kappstatter reported, "By Monday, a police telephone hotline had received just a handful of tips but more than 500 calls from New Yorkers who desired to congratulate The Subway Vigilante. Several of them offered to pay his legal expenses when he was arrested. A World War II veteran named Fred Pollizi called the *Daily News* to offer the gunman his Bronze Star." In reality, he was neither a vigilante nor a hero. He was a trigger-happy white man who had been rightfully denied gun ownership in New York, so he took off to Florida and got one there.

Three victims recovered from their wounds, but Darrell's fate was touch and go. He would ultimately survive but suffer from severe brain damage and paralysis from the waist down.

The narrative that the young victims were the antagonists only grew. As more footage of his police confessional was released, it became clear that Goetz wasn't simply defending himself.

"You look like you're doing okay," he confessed remarking to Darrell before shooting him again. As time passed, Goetz went from New York's darling to another perp. Twelve years later, in a civil case that Darrell's family had filed on his behalf, Goetz admitted to saying that New York would be a much better place if "they got rid of the niggers and spics." He also admitted, under oath, that he believed Darrell's mother, Shirley Cabey, would have been better off having an abortion.

Those who stood beside him quickly wrote him off as another New York City "wacko." Despite their pivot, the damage had already been done. People of all races were okay with violence against Black children. For my mother and father, both from Queens, who were the parents of two young Black sons, the fear of white supremacist murder was all they needed to stay the hell out of New York City.

NOT FROM THE PJS, BUT . . .

Only months after the Bernard Goetz shooting, my family moved to a small hamlet on Long Island called Bay Shore, a little over one hour east of New York City. We had lived in a neighboring town, Brentwood, for several years. But, after missing too many mortgage payments, the house foreclosed, and we were sent packing.

During this time, my parents were going through a rather . . . troubling chapter in their union.

"You are *never* getting in my bed again, you raggedy-ass nigga!" Mom told Daddy after he spent another night out with his mistress. The word *never* seemed to crawl out of the bowels of Mom's guts, a tone of finality so sharp that Sissy, seventeen at the time, would pick her head up from the picnic table in our backyard and mutter, "Damn."

The year was 1986, and I was four years old. The six of us were having our first family cookout in our new backyard. Sissy, the eldest, was there, along with my two elder brothers, Terrell and Tyrone.

Daddy's mistress, Dianne, was a poorly kept secret in our family. At his lowest, he took Sissy and Tyrone to the zoo with Dianne while Mom was in the hospital recovering from the birth to Broner.

"You getting too emotional, Bren!" Daddy responded, his Cuban accent dripping off his slurred speech. He sat there with his US Navy cap on, even though he was never in the service, attempting to squirt mustard on his hot dog, though most of it landed on his french fries. Daddy, a functional alcoholic, had mastered the art of getting plastered from Friday evening until Monday morning, sobering up with black coffee and dry bread on his way to work.

My siblings and I sat at the picnic table in our backyard, sandwiched between our parents and their resentment for each other, wondering what Mom would say next.

"I hope you both get AIDS and get hit by a fucking bus!" she yelled at Daddy. I watched her long, mascara-drenched lashes bat furiously, her cheeks flushed pink from the emotions Daddy alleged. Her complexion identical to the color of sand, thick relaxed hair bobbing back and forth in her ponytail while she yelled.

"You so dumb, Bren!" Daddy snapped. "We gonna get . . . AIDS? Do we know we got the AIDS when we got hit by the bus? Man, you dumb!" He laughed.

The boys sat there shaking their heads while Sissy stared at Daddy in disgust. I began to laugh, my usual reaction whenever Daddy laughed, which I believed wasn't often enough.

"You think that's funny?" Mom asked me. Fearful to be on the other side of her fury like my father, I stopped giggling and stared at my burnt hot dog, waiting for someone to dress it with mustard and ketchup. "You heard me, Tamela?" Only then did I pick up my head. She looked me directly in the eye. Her expression was serious, like the one she would give before smacking me behind the neck for talking back or running around the grocery store. "I'ma show you something funny." She took the aluminum pan filled with barbecued meats—hamburgers, hot dogs, chicken wings, and sausages—and pulled out a hot dog. Instead of placing it in a bun, she snapped it into three pieces with her hands.

"Use a knife, Mommy!" Tyrone ordered.

"I don't need no knife," Mom calmly replied. "Listen!" she yelled at Daddy. She took one of the end pieces of the hot dog and flung it directly in his face, smacking him in the nose. My father reacted like an invisible ghost had pinched him. He rapidly stared around us all, confused as to what happened.

"Oh snap, Mommy!" Broner yelled, his oversized glasses bobbing up and down the bridge of his nose as he laughed. His birth name is Terrell but Broner is the nickname I gave him. Ever since he broke his glasses playing basketball and had to duct tape the legs back to the frames, they never quite fit the same.

"That's what you get, Daddy!" Sissy laughed.

"Nigga, if there's anybody dumb at this table, it's *your* dumb ass." WHACK! went another piece of hot dog, this time hitting Daddy's chin. "Cheatin'-ass, nasty-ass self!" She threw the last bit at him as we all watched the tip smack into his forehead, making a loud clap before flopping into the baked beans on his plate. My siblings and I erupted into an uncontrollable state of laughter, the kind that's lasted for years.

Daddy may have been raggedy in Mom's eyes, but that never stopped him from being my favorite person. At a very young age, I understood that alcohol changed my father's behavior, but I felt like his intoxicated presence was more enjoyable. There were often illogical behavior and outbursts, but there were also times when he took me to the park or toy store.

"Whatever you want!" he would tell me, then unleash me into the store while I filled our arms with toys and gadgets that would only occupy me for a few hours.

Despite their personal challenges, my parents tried hard to give us a well-rounded upbringing. Mom worked full-time as a data operator twenty minutes away from home, and Daddy still worked at the phone company in Manhattan. We were the family with domestic disputes, but we were also the family that loaded up the caravan with snacks on the weekend and watched movies at the local drive-in. Every Easter, after attending our first and only service of the year, we'd all go to Bob's Big Boy Buffet in the same parking lot as the mall. And we spent the Fourth of July at Lake Ronkonkoma running around and watching fireworks.

Bay Shore, known for being a pass-through town to get to Fire Island, prided itself on its "diverse" community for decades, among the highest number of Black residents on Long Island. It's not uncommon for people to use the term "melting pot" when describing the community's demography. Words like "diverse" and "melting pot" are code for Black people and people of color. While there was no disputing the presence of Black and Brown people, that "melting pot" was more like a slow burn of racial tension. What my parents didn't know about this little hamlet we called home was that it reflected Long Island's deeply rooted white supremacist culture.

In 1947, William Levitt of Levitt and Sons, one of the nation's most prominent real estate firms, began construction on a massive community called Levittown in Nassau County, Long Island. With 17,000 units, it provided homes for as many as 84,000 residents. These homes were catered to the working class, charging as little as $7,900 per unit to own. The units were modern with new appliances, lush green lawns, and white picket fences. It was not long after World War II, and Levitt and Sons targeted consumer veterans who were ready to settle down with their families. The requirements were flexible and the amenities abundant. There was only one catch: homes in Levittown couldn't "be used or occupied by any person other than members of the Caucasian race." Levitt and Sons would be neither the first nor the last to draw white supremacist lines in the residential sands of Long Island.

At his peak, New York architect Robert Moses had as much political power as any senator or governor. Responsible for New York landmarks, including Riverside Park, the United Nations headquarters, and Lincoln Center, he used his power to design the parkways and state parks to make Long Island an upper-class destination stop—and keep Black people out.

Several long bridges throughout Long Island connect to the powder-and-shell beaches that line the Atlantic Ocean. These bridges are off-limits to public transportation and private buses, keeping out many local Black and working-class people. The man behind the innovative infrastructure, Robert Moses, was behind the construction of Jones Beach, Meadowbrook Parkway, and a host of other Long Island roads and landmarks. At the height of his career, Moses would have more political capital than any city or state politician in New York. How much of his designs were motivated by segregation is up for debate. But what's known is that rarely, if ever, did he intend on making his properties accessible to Black and/or poor people.

I'll forever wonder what life would have looked like for Brenda and Walter if they knew they were moving to land that was intentionally designed to exist without their presence. Because it was their understanding that money was the name of the game, and seeing as how you had to pay to play, we were good to go. Now that the ugly truth of white supremacy and red lining is spread out before us, it's clear as day that the game was rigged the whole time.

Mom bought the biggest turkey she could find for our first Thanksgiving in our big three-story house. Daddy stayed up late the night before to make sure the Christmas tree was up for us all to awe and take pictures. Mom's parents, Ma and Papa, drove in from Queens.

Before we ate, we held hands, beginning a tradition that would remain with us on the last Thursday in November and for the rest of our lives: telling one another why we are grateful. We didn't know it then, but this would become a tradition that defined us — one that kept us rooted in our personal and collective missions to stay spiritually and emotionally grounded and remind us how blessed we are. Years after that first roundtable of thanks, the six of us can still be found in the family chat asking on an early morning, "What are y'all grateful for? I'll go first . . ."

I was last up and excited to call out my list. I continued filling the room with every fiber of gratitude my four-year-old body had to give. Everyone sat back and smiled, allowing me to suck up the air in the room. And then, *"BAM!"* The sound of an explosion interrupted my speech. Every head at the table turned to the front door. Mom raced to the living room window.

We all gathered outside, walking down the long driveway that led to our narrow street. There, we found the remains of what was once a nice, ordinary mailbox left by the homeowners before us. Shards of wood and smoke were scattered everywhere. Across the street, I spotted the red flag you flip up when you've got mail to ship. I crossed the road and retrieved the flag.

"Get out of the street, Tamela!" Mom yelled. All our neighbors were outside, everyone standing over the remains of our mailbox, pointing at each side of the street, attempting to guess which way the culprits went. It didn't feel like Thanksgiving anymore.

Daddy told me to return inside, but I didn't want to. I wanted to stay and ask a thousand questions. *Who did it? Why? Are they coming back? Can we eat now?*

As I returned to the house, Ma stood at the doorway watching. She still had both legs, but diabetes had compromised her ability to walk without pain, so she avoided stairs as often as possible. Within five years, she would have both her legs amputated and pass away when I was only ten. "Somebody blew up our mailbox, Ma!"

"I know." She nodded, plopping down on the living room sofa. "That's why I would *never* live near these people."

Eventually, we were all back inside our home. Nobody was in the mood to celebrate or go down a list of reasons to be grateful.

We were hyperaware that someone didn't want us there; someone hated us enough to destroy our property on one of the biggest holidays in America. It could have been one person or perhaps even a gang of people. Despite following up with the police report, my parents were never contacted by the police with information on the case—if there was one.

The second time our mailbox was blown up was the following Thanksgiving, in 1987. This time, Ma and Papa stayed in Queens, waiting for us to visit them for our big meal. After the explosion, our next-door neighbor, a cute white guy named Billy, ran up and down the street with clenched fists. "I've had it with these bastards!" he snarled. He and Daddy cleaned up the remains quietly. When we sat back at the table, Mom was mad and silent. Daddy was pissed because he did not want to spend another Friday off once again reinstalling a new and expensive mailbox. We didn't call the police that time.

"They didn't do shit the first time, so what's the point?" Mom shrugged.

With a new home comes new schools, neighbors, and cultures, all new to me. Because I was born after our city days, I had nothing to compare Long Island to. However, transitioning from city life to the burbs was brutal for my siblings.

"I'm telling you, Mommy, he touched me funny!" That's how my eldest brother, Tyrone, described a disturbing interaction with our new pediatrician, Dr. Cohen. During what was supposed to be a routine physical, Tyrone detailed weird questions Dr. Cohen asked him about masturbation and sex. Only fourteen years old, my brother mostly laughed it off and assumed Dr. Cohen was teasing him. But when he began rubbing and tugging on Tyrone's genitals, he knew something was wrong.

"Doctors are supposed to touch you down there, Tyrone," Mom assured him. "It's normal."

That would be the last time Tyrone brought it up. However, three years later it was reported that Dr. Cohen was being charged with molestation and endangering the welfare of a child. A total of six boys between the ages of ten and fourteen confessed to being sexually assaulted by the doctor. In 1991, a jury found Henry Cohen guilty of sodomy, sexual abuse, and endangering the welfare of a child. He was sentenced to twenty-five years behind bars.

What should have been a moment of justification for my brother was instead a sad reminder that of all the voices that were heard, his was silenced.

"I wish somebody would have taken me seriously," he admitted years later.

Broner blossomed into "the popular one." Though he was born in New York City, he only attended Long Island schools like me. Taking after Mom when it came to looks, he was the lightest in complexion of the four of us, with deep natural waves that never called for grease, gel, or a durag. He had a lean shape until he hit fifteen and grew into a very tall, broad version of himself.

On the morning of my sixteenth birthday, I awoke to the news that Broner had been violently attacked by a bar bouncer just a few miles away from home. A verbal dispute with a bartender resulted in the bouncer and owner of the bar attacking him, stomping him repeatedly. The beating left my brother with serious injuries to the right side of his face, primarily his eye and cheekbone. He would endure several reconstructive surgeries.

Neither the bouncer nor the owner of the bar faced criminal charges for the attack.

Broner's physical injuries would eventually heal, but the impact of that night would have a lasting effect. Not long after the attack, he studied with The Five-Percent Nation, a Black nationalist movement influenced by Islam. During this time, my brother would develop rather radical opinions about white people and Black women.

"She knows her shirt is too revealing; that's why she keeps tugging on it." That's what he had said while we watched Lauryn Hill accept an award. She was wearing a white tank top, her brown skin illuminated under the glossy lights. She was on the heels of *The Miseducation of Lauryn Hill,* a culture shifting album that advocated for a more virtuous Black woman, unlike Lil' Kim and Foxy Brown, popular rappers who owned their sexuality and bravado.

"What?" I shrugged. "She's wearing a tank top."

"A *revealing* tank top. A woman should never wear clothing so revealing that she has to adjust herself publicly."

"Seriously, bro?" I giggled. "Then what's the rule about guys who let their ass cracks hang out of their baggy jeans?"

Fast forward to 2003, when I was twenty-one years old, a sheltered virgin still living at home, sleeping in the same bed as I did when I was a child. On a sunny Monday, around noon, our house was again attacked. Two gunmen barged into our home and held Daddy and me at gunpoint while they rummaged through the house. Minutes later, our home was filled with apathetic detectives treating us like the assailants rather than the victims. They paraded through our home, touching stuff without asking, looking behind our furniture, and entering rooms with closed doors.

Eventually, they left us with only a ransacked home and a few business cards from the lead detectives. My parents would call these numbers regularly for weeks to see if they found any information and were close to catching the men who threatened our lives. Just like the mailboxes, we never got answers.

STRONG ISLAND

In 1992, William Ford was like many other young Black Long Islanders. At twenty-four, he loved sports, working out, and cruising around town with his friends. He was a tall, beautiful man. Dark, creamy skin, high cheekbones, and a killer smile. Despite being tall and built big, he was described by his loved ones as beautiful, soft, and kind.

"Do you know how beautiful you are?" his younger sister, Laura, recalled him once asking her. "You're beautiful. Beautiful. Don't forget that." He was the oldest of three, big brother to his siblings, Laura and Yance.

Like Brenda and Walter, the Ford parents had been high school sweethearts. Also like the Gordons, the Fords relocated to Long Island from New York City. They settled in Central Islip, about five minutes east of Bay Shore.

Central Islip was and is still known as one of the "pockets" on the island to which Black folks are designated. My family would quickly realize that our neighborhood in Bay Shore was just outside several Black pockets. One of William's surviving friends would explain, "In that one neighborhood, it was a haven. When you go *out* . . . you know, you might be running back for your life."

After a dispute with a local mechanic about a fender bender that had taken place weeks before, William and his friend went to the auto shop where it was said to be repaired. William went unarmed to the chop shop one evening, demanding to get his car back. Instead of leaving with his car, he was shot and killed by Mark P. Reilly, a then nineteen-year-old mechanic.

"Wait until we get to court" was the only comforting attitude Barbara had as she looked at the body of her dead son in his casket. Naturally, it was believed that the case would be open and shut. Sadly, the day in court Barbara yearned for would not bring the justice the Fords deserved. An all-white grand jury in Suffolk County acquitted Reilly of all charges, stating that his decision to murder William was rooted in self-defense.

William was no stranger to crime and justice. His mother, Barbara, ran a school program for women at Rikers Island. This inspired William to become a probation officer. Sadly, his acceptance into a rigorous training program came through only six weeks after his murder.

"We weren't received as parents of a victim," Barbara said in the 2019 documentary *Strong Island*, produced by William's sibling, Yance Ford. "I was foolish enough to think that, well, you know, it's going to be okay." William's friend, who was there with him the night he was murdered, confirmed the apathetic approach he received from the assistant district attorney and detectives. They asked him how big William was and how often he went to the gym. They were more invested in portraying William as a threat than an innocent, unarmed man who was murdered.

The disrespect William's family experienced is similar to my family's experience after every instance of injustice. When our mailbox was bombed, the police officers scribbled down details in their notepads and left with a shrug. "Try to enjoy the rest of your dinner," one said while strapping his seatbelt. There were no arrests of the men who violently attacked Broner and no follow-ups after the home invasion.

The American Dream is racist bullshit, yet we continue striving toward it. New York is known as the best city in the best state in the entire world. Yet, for Black people, the struggle to remain equitably housed and safe was as challenging on Long Island as in the city.

I'd love to say that my childhood home will always be on the list of places where I feel safe; however, the memories of explosions and invasions still haunt me. I aimlessly traveled to different big cities hoping to feel even a suggestion of home. Ultimately, when I paired my income with my preferences, I was always led to the unsavory, often dangerous parts of an otherwise promising city.

To this day, my parents still live in my childhood home in Bay Shore. "Trust the devil you know over the one you don't" is the motto Mom often recites when considering relocation. It's her way of acknowledging that, while life is less than ideal in Bay Shore, there's a good chance that it only gets worse when we leave our segregated pocket of society. Sissy would eventually split her time between New York City and Miami, and Tyrone settled in Atlanta with his wife and two sons around 2010. For Broner and me, our attachment to our friends and the life we knew on the south shore would trump the experiences that shook our youths. But my concept of home would become an ongoing riddle—one that would lead me to various cities and states in search of some-where relatively safer.

PAN(IC)DEMIC

■

"I am often struck by the dangerous narcissism fostered by spiritual rhetoric that pays so much attention to individual self-improvement and so little to the practice of love within the context of community."

—BELL HOOKS

Where were you in March 2020 when the COVID-19 pandemic swept through the globe, demanding strict quarantines and social distancing? Who helped you prepare for the worst and navigate the complexities of a pandemic society? How did COVID-19 impact your health—both physical and mental? Your social life?

I spent the better part of COVID-19 lockdowns by myself in my small studio in Little Havana. With a compromised income and no in-person support system, the mandated isolation had a major impact on my mental health, income, and quality of life.

Up until that point, my framework on wellness was solidified off the idea that with the right combination of self-care practices, any person could greatly enhance their quality of life. However, left alone to my own devices for months on end, I learned the hard way that trying to get by on self-care without strong communal ties and an in-person support system was like trying to drive cross-country with a half-empty tank of gas. I can't make it.

MARCH 11, 2020

"Make sure you have enough toilet paper and albuterol," Simone said over the phone.

"I'm pretty sure I'm good." I snickered. I had about four rolls under the sink in my bathroom and figured I'd just buy another six-pack the next time I remembered.

"Have you been watching the news, sis?"

I spent the first six months in Little Havana allowing myself to get lost in my own world of self-discovery and healing. I watched very little news, rarely read the paper, and deactivated all the no-tifications from my phone. I had seen more than my fair share of Black people murdered to know that the American media was not to be trusted with my mental health. I did watch PBS NewsHour a few times a week, but besides that, my feet were in the sand, and my hands were in my journal. I felt that I had been exposed to enough horrors of the world and didn't need reminders of how shitty everything had gotten. But Simone's alarm level made me wonder exactly how much I missed.

Later that night, while cooking enchilada de camarones con blanco arroz, I blasted CNN from my television in the TV room, which was only five feet away from the kitchen. Within ninety seconds, news anchors not only talked about COVID-19 in detail, but also how many people had died, how many more would die, and how many institutions and nonessential establishments would be indefinitely shut down.

Umm . . . are we going to fucking die? I texted Simone.

No, girl, but you need to get prepared.

Disaster preparation was something I had only kind of consid-ered when moving to Miami. I knew to have a flashlight, nonper-ishable foods, and plenty of water. Outside that, I was clueless. I had always lived with another person who was either more responsible or more prepared than me. The idea of having to take care of me on my own was new territory.

Because COVID-19 was airborne, staying away from public spaces was essential. Order groceries online, but make sure to check the no-contact option. Get plenty of masks to protect me from germs when I go outside. Take vitamins.

I did well for the first two weeks. It helped that I foolishly believed this was a very temporary situation. I treated it like a major blackout, only global. And mad people were dying.

Like many, I attempted to use this newfound "downtime" productively. My social media newsfeeds were inundated with, "If you're not learning a new trade during these lockdowns . . ." I felt I had no choice but to pick up a new hobby or hone an old one. The only issue was the constant fear of death, my own or someone I love, which affected my productivity.

A kind soul from the internet gifted me a tarot card deck—the first I'd ever owned. It was Courtney Alexander's Dust II Onyx, which was very popular. Huge, dark, celestial-like cards with images of fantastical Black people. Getting a feel of the cards became my hobby, and a lot of my free time went to intuitively getting a feel of each card, as well as watching YouTube videos about tarot. *This whole lockdown thing may actually work out in my favor.*

APRIL 9, 2020

Quarantines and lockdowns were enforced indefinitely. They said it was only going to last two weeks, but I found that hard to believe. Miami had a series of curfews because tourists were still arriving for spring break. It was pretty disturbing. The entire world was instructed to stay inside, but on any given block in South Beach, the party was alive, well, and unmasked.

I would have loved to celebrate the traditional fancy birthday dinner with Sissy, where we ordered a seafood tower and drank too many martinis. Instead, I had to settle for a goofy Facebook Live "party" with a handful of online friends. It was just me talking into my phone and thanking people for their little hearts and laughing emojis that popped up while I tried to make light of a pitiful situation.

I desperately wanted to be one of the people who came out on the other side of this pandemic thinner, more successful, more together. I wanted to learn something new, bake bread, and teach English as a second language. But the fear that I would die from this weird disease only increased with the national death toll.

Death, which used to be a personal topic, the thing you only bring up to the closest loved ones, the ones in your will, was now as fluid as a boldfaced number on the right screen of CNN—all day. The death toll was monitored hourly, and the most trending news was knowing exactly how many people had died and where they were dying the most. There was also a good head count on how many ventilators were in use and how many would be needed as more people got closer to death.

I almost felt guilty for being sullen about my cyber party. Every day, thousands of people across the globe were dying, and thousands more were fighting for their lives, hoping that there was a ventilator with their name on it to keep them alive. But I also knew my disappointment had less to do with the desire to celebrate and everything to do with missing being in the same room with people I knew. I had sat through a host of Zooms and video chats with friends and clients, their children and pets crawling over them, partners calling their names in the background. It was such a cruel reminder that my greatest struggle in solo quarantining, even greater than the fear of death, was the reality of being alone, indoors, twenty-four seven, indefinitely.

MAY 20, 2020

My beloved neighbor from Bay Shore, Mrs. Perez, died of COVID-19. She was seventy-two years old, only two years older than my mother. I couldn't believe it. Mrs. Perez was a vibrant woman, always kind and chatty. Mom used to love bumping into her at ShopRite, the two exchanging good news about their children and the latest news about our hood.

"I think you should come home for a few weeks, sis." I was on a late-night call with Simone, where we were both too tired and vulnerable to play off the impact of our trials and tribulations on our spirits. Simone was one of the very few people with whom I kept in contact.

Even though, before the pandemic, I struggled with maintaining connections with family and friends, I had never experienced this level of aloneness. Before it was self-imposed with quarantine lockdowns, spending long bouts alone was a treat. I allowed myself to get submersed in solitude and got used to going days, sometimes an entire week, without talking with friends or family. I didn't mind it one bit. But, after a month of lockdown, I was regretting my flippant attitude toward maintaining the relationships I left behind in New York. And, having gone so long without returning phone calls and texts, guilt prevented me from reaching out.

The effort it took to function throughout a single day required every fiber of energy I had. I often wanted to return phone calls and text messages but could not respond. The impact of isolation paired with my pre-pandemic neurosis completely altered my ability to engage and maintain relationships, some of which I highly valued. When I left New York, I was so deeply invested in starting fresh that I was okay with letting many of my old relationships fall by the wayside. It helped that my decision to divest from social justice resulted in being unwelcome in many of the communal spaces where I had friends.

My distance was mistaken as a slight from some folks I was in community with, especially those who had fundraised and helped me get from New York to Miami. Some expressed contempt toward my isolation, which was rarely said directly rather through condescending comments and passive shade. Like the post from a former friend, one who had actually helped the fundraising efforts that covered the cost of moving to Miami and furnishing my apartment:

It must be nice to say fuck it all and eat mangos all day. But some of us, who are real and serious about liberation, must do this work.

I wasn't tagged or named in the post, but it wasn't necessary. A few days before, I'd made a short video about a mango I ordered through Instacart, which rivaled with the size of a football. It was huge and juicy and only cost ninety-nine cents. It was only a month into the pandemic, and I had very little to look forward to. I didn't post it to be cheeky or suggest that I had no worries in the world. As I rebranded my page to center more of my life and divest from anti-racism content, I allowed myself to share the things that actually excited me. On that day, it was a mango.

My pivot in content didn't garner nearly as much traction as I experienced during the 2016 election, but I was okay with that. At least I knew that the people who subscribed to my work and engaged in my comment section were genuinely interested in me and what I had to say. I was free from educating and being referred to as a "teacher" or "resource." I was beginning to understand how wrong it was that, to provide for myself, I had to become some relevancy tool for white people who only wanted to appear as though they were dedicated to dismantling systems of oppression.

I may have been at peace with my decision, but people like my former friend were not. It disappointed me, but I also understood the nuance of it all. Don't we all want to be free? Don't we all want to have time for ourselves to figure shit out? Grow through our traumas instead of stew in them? I wasn't ignorant of the ills of the world and the dangers that taunt my intersection on a daily basis. But I wasn't willing to sacrifice my entire life for the struggle.

Just as I looked at others, jealous of their filtered families and lives filled with other humans, some looked at me with jealousy, wishing they had the time, support, and guts to take off and start over.

JUNE 16

Aside from the whole everyone's-dying crisis was the inevitable racial uprising, which really . . . bothered me.

To be Black in America is to have such an intimate understanding of white violence that we don't have to actually see a Black person murdered or dead to know that it was brutal, intolerable, and outrageous. We understand that while the murders of Breonna Taylor and Sandra Bland were not recorded and broadcast worldwide, they were indeed murdered and deserve justice. Still, the recorded murder of George Floyd was, sadly, what inspired white people throughout the country to take to the streets.

At least seven hundred Black Americans were murdered by the police between 2017–2019. Many of these murders were not captured on video, but some were. Why would we be so incensed, so outraged by the one murder that we saw televised when there have been thousands of murders just like that one? The answer "because we saw it live" gives little excuse or explanation. Worse, it only affirms that we are not believed as Black people until we can trace the bloodshed back to live footage.

I feel bad for George Floyd and everyone who ever loved him, knew him, or was impacted by his brutal murder. And I also feel bad for every other Black human whose life was taken by police violence. Our rage should go deeper than the pop-off during the 2020 uprising. And it should have more range.

JULY 2

With the exception of a brief visit from Sissy and my siblings, I had no in-person contact with a human being outside of two visits at Presidente Supermarket.

Shit was starting to get weird.

I gave up on trying to learn how to bake banana bread. I couldn't care less about learning a second language, and I stopped making my bed every day. I began blocking pages that dared to inspire survival in style, learn a new skill, or buy an LLC.

Long gone were the shopping sessions at Whole Foods, where I would walk with my cart very slowly so as many people as possible pay attention to the fact that, yes, I am the Black woman who spends seventy-five dollars on her produce, even though I intend to steal the better part of it. Now, I order my groceries from Instacart or sometimes Amazon Fresh, which, while it feels dirty, also delivers alcohol. While deprived of pushing a grocery cart, I now have the added benefit of ordering all the processed, boxed food that I would never be caught with in person. And so, I began ordering unnecessary cakes, pies, and ice cream. A diet that once consisted of fresh fruits, vegetables, and the occasional pescatarian dish was now replaced with boxes of Tyson's fried chicken, Mrs. Field's frozen peach cobbler, and Talenti ice cream.

I woke up one morning, surprised not to have gone into sugar shock during my sleep but feeling sluggish from a dinner that consisted of half a Publix key lime pie and a box of SeaPak coconut shrimp.

I felt like a loser.

AUGUST 22

I prolonged the day by staying in bed and scrolling through Facebook and Instagram, judging anyone who seemed to be doing anything productive. A word that used to inspire me into a state of movement now moved me to nauseousness. I once associated productivity with writing, working out, and washing my dishes daily—all activities that I was now detached from.

After hate scrolling for about an hour, I concluded my daily morning routine by logging on to Pornhub.

A simple two-minute clip of "MILFS TRIBBING" or "SENSUAL EBONY LESBIAN" was enough to tickle my kink pickle. But, with the boredom I'd hit in the past two months, it took more than two women rubbing thighs to get my rocks off. I was tempted to go down the rabbit hole of taboo I'd recently deviated into. However, reminders of that filthy feeling that washed over me immediately after climaxing pumped my brakes. Even though the smutty category guarantees a quick orgasm, I would hate myself for three days: lesbian squirt orgy.

Lesbian squirt orgies are just . . . fascinating. A group of women in one room, fresh from the pool, oiled down like WWF stars. There are three kinds of lesbian squirt orgy scenes that I'm familiar with: The one where one woman is expected to drink as much squirt from as many squirters as she can swallow. Then there's the kind when the porn stars are scattered about in groups of two or three, more like a workgroup session. And, finally, my favorite is when they perform as an ensemble cast. Each porn star masturbates in a circle, squirting one by one. What I appreciate most is the level of teamwork involved. They're not all fighting to be lead squirter. Instead, they encourage whoever looks closest to erupting. Regardless of the choreography, they rub their kitty cats vigorously, ravenously. When one is near climax, the others surround her, egging her on. They all begin moaning like alley cats as though an orgasm by one is an orgasm by all. And then, when the woman finally climaxes, liquid gushing out of her kitty, the other women crowd around her, opening their mouths in an attempt to drink her juice. They continue moaning in satisfaction, making it easy for a naive viewer to consider that the elixir must be in the pussy juice. And then, they crowd around the next woman, wash and repeat.

The energy often turns me on, but I'm also mystified at how they can do something with their body, on command, that I've never come close to. I've had many an orgasm, but never via penetration. In lesbian squirt orgy videos, these pros use everything from dildos, vibrators, fists, and palms pressed against their clitorises.

I want to do that; I want to learn how to make my kitty cat squirt. Instead of scrolling through videos, I Googled "How to make my pussy squirt." Much to my delight, a stream of articles, videos, and how-tos popped up, and I dug in.

Within minutes, I learned the basics: not every person with a vagina can squirt, learning takes time and patience, and the best way to accomplish it is by playing with the G-spot. I roll my eyes at the mention of this hidden pocket inside my vagina, somewhere toward my tummy, that's supposed to send me into euphoria when I play with it right. For years, I have attempted to find my G-spot, both on my own and with partners, to no avail. Typically discouraged, finding out that the mystery pleasure spot was the conduit between my bed and soggy sheets changed my perspective.

I went into my closet and whipped out the big guns: my pink rabbit, of which I'd just changed the batteries, my skinny dildo with the curved tip designed to penetrate the G-spot, and CBD lubricant that I'd gotten from a friend. After cleaning each toy, I lay towels on my bed, convinced that by the time I was done, I'd need a raft to wade through my own juices.

I did what one of the articles said and rubbed one out as a precursor to getting warmed up and relaxed. When I was done, I got started with the pink rabbit. I played with that for a few minutes, but it didn't move me. I switched over to the curved dildo but found myself equally underwhelmed. After half an hour, I was exhausted.

I need to learn how to squirt! It was odd how I'd never given squirting much thought, but in that moment, it was my deepest desire. Having access to that level of alone time made me feel like I should push the limits with what I did with it. I was over baking bread and trying to learn a new language. I also liked how it would sound whenever someone asked, "So, did you teach yourself anything cool during the lockdown?" And I'd be like, "Yes, actually, two things. Tarot cards and squirting."

Despite my yearning, after nearly an hour of playing with myself, there was no flood. Apparently, this wasn't going to be an overnight job. It was going to require practice and patience. Instead of getting discouraged, I decided to get prepared. I planned on treating this occasion like a date. I needed to get really nice and sexy, treat myself well, eat something fresh, and take my time.

AUGUST 28

I diligently prepare to squirt for the remainder of that week. And I ate extra healthy the day of. I drank lots of water and walked across the street to Presidente for produce. Instead of trash frozen food, I broiled some salmon and air fried a fresh veggie medley. I ate dinner with a glass of red wine and some Anita Baker. Then, I took a long bath with goat milk and Himalayan sea salt. After I dried off and lotioned down, I slid into my lingerie.

By the time I got into bed, I was feeling so sexy I didn't even need Pornhub. I took my time and got started with my curvy dildo.

I was enjoying myself; it felt good. But after a while, the pleasure wasn't elevating. Legs up, legs down, on my stomach, on my back. Nada. I decided to take a break and put the dildo on the nightstand. I sat up, looked at my kitty, and attempted to have a heart-to-heart. "This is good for you," I whispered. "You haven't gotten laid in five years! Don't you want to have a good time?" She didn't say a word. And so, I lay there, surrounded by dildos and lube, feeling like a failure. This disappointment was overwhelming. I rolled into my pile of pillows and wept.

"I am such a lonely fucking loser!" I sobbed.

The sulking would last for a few days before I got over the fact that I was not a part of the 60 percent of people with vaginas that can squirt. That didn't bum me out so much as the fact that the long bout of solitude was driving me back to places where I sought validation and pleasure from something I could get neither from. As usual, I was in a state of high anxiety, and, as a form of disassociation, I took it out on My Body. Only, instead of trying to put something in it like cocaine or alcohol, I was trying to get it to release something it likely doesn't have the capacity to do. The pressure to perform and squirt hit the same peak anxiety as trying on a pair of too-tight jeans in a department store; the disappointment was brutal.

What's really going on with me?

SEPTEMBER 14

At first, it seemed like people were finally beginning to acknowledge the impact of white supremacy on Black people. It was a conversation, front and center. Everywhere. In commercials, on your favorite sitcom, on that obscure history podcast that normally only covered the twentieth century. The dominance of anti-racism discussions throughout pop culture made it easy for anyone to be hopeful that the conversation would evolve into actual liberation. Unfortunately, that was far from the result.

Sadly, the racial uprising of 2020 was quickly whitewashed and commodified, reduced to Black Lives Matter bumper stickers and lawn signs, with hollow promises that We Support Black Lives on the walls of yoga studios. The performative allyships were empty, as they could never hold a candle to the tsunami of hate that the pro-Trump crowd brought with them.

Cubans are a proud people. Proud of their legacy of rebellion and uncompromised culture. Sadly, a substantial number of Cubans in America were also thrilled to be Trump supporters. They rode down Calle Ocho in droves for hours, honking their horns, waving their goofy flags and racist, xenophobic paraphernalia.

"Unreal!" I said to one of the cashiers at Presidente while the bigots paraded down the street.

"Why?" she asked, slowly sipping her cafecito.

Of course. I sighed. *She's one of them.*

"Because," I began, "as a Black woman, Trump and his supporters are against my rights, my existence!"

She gave me this quizzical glance as if I posed a riddle. "*Mami,* you no Black. You Cuban!"

So much of what was happening in life confused me, but I knew one thing for certain: I had to get the fuck out of Florida.

CASA DE TAMI: KIT

Kit Fenrir Amreik

■

BLACK NONBINARY TRANS WOMAN – SHE/THEY
– AGE: 27 – FROM: BOSTON, MA

Today is amazing!" Kit sighed. We sat on the balcony of Wet Willie's, a major tourist spot on Ocean Drive known for its tropical daiquiris, fried seafood, and amazing view of the Atlantic Ocean. It was only day two of Kit's stay, and already we managed to get pedis, waxing, and frolic on the beach. *I love it when a plan comes together*, I thought to myself. Of the four guests scheduled to stay at Casa de Tami that month, Kit was one of two whose trip was 100 percent crowdfunded, from her flight, ground transportation, and dining expenses, to spending money for souvenirs and other expenses.

Kit is the kind of trans woman who doesn't adhere to gender norms like shaving her beard or chest hair. Her time in Miami was intentionally centered on leaning into her divine feminine without being cheesy or performative about it.

At twenty-seven, Kit was at that age where she was just as vulnerable to surrender to the world of activism as she was on the streets. I was thirsty for her not just to survive but to live a life she enjoyed that stretched beyond the margins of activism, organizing, and servitude.

"Picture time!" I squealed. Kit stood up straight and leaned against the railing, two teal-painted metal bars. Her chest and chin protruded, the thick curly hair that coated her breasts springing out of her bathing suit top. I noticed the springy coils in her mane gathering themselves together as curly fros do.

"I can't wait to wash this sand out of my hair." I sighed, rubbing my hands through my scalp and watching the grains fall down my shoulders. "What are you going to do with your hair?"

"Nothing." She shrugged. "I don't usually do anything to it."

"Want me to give you a wash and go?" I offered.

"I would love that!" She beamed. I had planned an itinerary that was filled with sexy nights out on Ocean Drive and gay bar hopping. But, realizing that my good Black sis had yet to have the full-fledged get-your-hair-done-by-grandma-on-Sunday-afternoon experience, I made an executive decision. Instead of taking a disco nap and getting ready to go out all night, we picked up some snacks at a local CVS and then returned to my apartment. I put out my favorite shampoo and conditioner for Kit to use in the shower. When she was done, I had the TV room prepped with Xtreme Wetline gel, four hair clips, and a detangling comb.

Who teaches a young Black trans girl about basic haircare? How does she learn the art of slicking down her edges and maintaining a hairstyle for a week with nothing more than a silk bonnet?

And how does a young trans man learn about a proper lineup when he's never stepped foot in a barber shop?

Unlike many Black girls, Kit didn't grow up spending Saturday mornings in the salon with her mother or hours in a beauty supply store trying to get the right lace front and still have money to spend through the weekend. She never got to spend her lunch period in the bathroom with seven girls, one tub of Eco Style hair gel, and three toothbrushes, each girl expertly explaining their magic trick on how they get their edges to curl and blend to perfection. Those moments meant everything to me as a child, and I value them even more as I look back. Sadly, for Kit and so many Black trans girls, these experiences were sworn off.

By adhering to heteronormative standards and expectations, trans children are forced to play the part of the gender they were assigned rather than live out the gender they identify with. This deprives them of crucial identity, hygiene, and passage rites allotted to children identifying with their assigned gender.

Kit's family was conditioned to believe that because she was assigned a boy at birth, she had to behave as such. What's cruelest about this imposed gender identity is that when trans people are brave enough to identify as who they really are, they're often met with the argument, "It's not the same for a trans girl because they were born a boy and got the benefit of being a man, even if it was at a young age." In the reality of Kit and so many trans girls, being a boy was never a "benefit." It was no privilege for her or other trans kids forced to perform as a gender outside their identity.

I sat on the sofa and placed a pillow cushion on the floor between my legs. Kit sat down on the cushion. I gently clutched her shoulders with the grip of my thighs, just like Mom or Sissy would do when I was young. As I parted her hair into four sections, I massaged her scalp with a light peppermint oil, saturating her prewashed hair, by section, with the water spray bottle, then working the gel into every strand. I took my time to explain each step and why it was so important. Keeping the hair wet helped detangle and catch the curl in its most springy state. Just enough gel for each section—too much, and you look like you got a Jheri curl; too little, and the curls won't hold. While doing this, we watched YouTube videos of what the influencers put in their hair, laughing at some concoctions that looked much more like smoothies than deep conditioners.

We discussed everything from boys, money, stealing, and where we envisioned ourselves in five years. It was clear that Kit was full of goals, full of love, and full of life. But the hustle that comes with surviving aged her in ways that made it impossible to enjoy the reckless youth that comes with being twenty-seven. As a way of encouraging her to make even more mistakes, I told her about all the times I had fucked up when I was her age.

After putting her under a hooded dryer for about twenty minutes, I finally let her get up and look at her new 'do in the mirror. She didn't have to say a word; her smile said everything. For the remainder of the evening, Kit and I got stoned and laughed in our bonnets and lingerie. The next day, after brunch, shopping, and another day on the beach, I redid Kit's hair, this time giving her a twist-out.

"Okay, long hair!" She giggled in the mirror, swaying her head from side to side as her long, now twisted locs bounced back and forth. Afterward, we each slid into our lingerie and bonnets, me wearing my usual indoor beat-up black bonnet. Kit wore a new big, bright pink one I gifted her for the occasion. We smoked a joint and giggled and went to sleep like schoolgirls.

GIRLS JUST WANT TO HAVE FUN (AND CODE)

by Kit Fenrir Amreik

■

During the time in my life when I stayed at Casa de Tami, my life was heading in a stressful direction. I was working with a nonprofit, Rebel Cause Incorporated, and facilitating reparations transactions for Black folks from white people. My mission was—and still is—helping people use transformative and restorative justice to further communal safety and collective liberation. Most people don't even understand the difference between transformative and restorative justice, and that's a major problem.

Transformative justice has two main tenets: to stop violence and harm and to transform the conditions that lead to the harm so it never happens again.

Restorative justice is solving problems interpersonally and within the community and using community voices that create dynamics that allow people to be seen, heard, and restored.

Facilitating this work is important and often fulfilling, but it also requires much energy and puts me in vulnerable situations.

Attempting to be a conduit for resolution in sometimes highly intense conflicts exposes me to all kinds of anger and negativity.

And, while I was working hard to keep the peace and integrity strong within my greater community, things were far from healthy at home. I was dealing with a toxic roommate who was sometimes volatile. She would disrespect my belongings and even throw and break them. After asserting various boundaries to create safety, it became clear that these were short-term solutions, and I needed a way out of this living arrangement.

When I arrived at Casa de Tami, I felt a deep shift within myself. The energy of Miami is so vibrant and fun! I felt like I was on a tropical island instead of Southern Florida.

I got to choose which kinds of self-care I was interested in before I arrived, and one of the areas that intrigued me was spiritual self-care. So, each morning, we would spend five minutes breathing with intention, followed by ten minutes of meditation and then journaling. I learned a lot about ancestral veneration, setting up my altar, and incorporating it into my manifestations. What I love about spiritual self-care is that I was familiar with many of these practices even if I hadn't fully incorporated them into my lifestyle. It felt as though these practices were innate and had always belonged to me.

We also got to check out the metaphysical store, House of Intuition, and go crystal shopping. I'd been to metaphysical stores before, but this one was pretty impressive! It was ethical and very high-vibing. There were rows of crystals with detailed descriptions, every kind of incense you could imagine, and a cool collection of books and tarot cards. I've always known that I'm a magical being, and I've dabbled with different spells and rituals, but after practicing magical mindfulness with Tami, I realized that I hadn't been applying my magic to its highest potential. My current relationship with my spirituality is a lot more connected these days. I can hear their comforting presence, like a hand on my shoulder to provide me with that solace whenever I need that reassurance. I have been able to follow my intuition and dream again. Much of my spiritual self-care involves tarot and altar work.

A personal highlight was having brunch in Midtown Miami with Tami and her sister. The three of us just camped out at this pretty fancy spot, indulging in our food and cocktails, laughing, and having a good time. Being in the presence of other Black women really filled me up. And, at that moment, I wasn't a community organizer, I wasn't an activist, and I definitely wasn't there to serve. I was just one of the girls, my hair hanging down and my spirit light. I remember thinking about how much more of those times I wanted to experience.

I went home, realizing I was craving more joy and ease, but it was necessary for my survival. I was tired of being so serious!

Having someone invest in my wellness inspired me to do it for myself regularly. I know that Tami had her challenges, but through it all, she was incredibly happy, fun, and had so much love and care to give. I know that came from taking care of herself. I made a personal vow to have that same diligence with my own care to pay forward the magical experience I'd been blessed with.

A few weeks after I returned home from Casa de Tami, the dynamic with my roommate got so abusive that she tried to harm me physically, and I was arrested. Ultimately, I wasn't physically harmed; however, the stress of being under arrest, along with knowing that I had to sleep with one eye open, made it clear that I had to move, and fast. I was a part of many queer and trans-friendly communities, but because they catered to teens and young adults, eventually I could no longer fit in there. I'm grateful there are resources for young trans, nonbinary, and queer folks, but it can get challenging once you enter adulthood. Not having the safe spaces I once had access to also affected my decision to leave Boston.

I had some connections in Denver, where I was teaching transformative justice classes at a kink convention. I already had friends who'd relocated there, and they encouraged me to have a better life. I was apprehensive about the idea initially, but the more I thought about it, the more I could envision a full life there. I needed a home and a community where I could be safe, experience new things, and come out of my comfort shell. I wanted the same support and protection I offered others but wasn't getting.

My love life in Denver is moving more slowly than in Boston, and that's partially because my work has been steadier in terms of getting reacquainted with My Body and new avenues of exploring kink, pleasure, and what is affirming for me. I have met more BIPOC people out here in Colorado, who are especially supportive and understanding about my transness, which is a nurturing presence to me that I haven't felt too much back home in Boston. I think people are courageous and considerate out here as well. There have been more honest talks about sexual health, consent, and friendship overall. I would say that I practice open dialogue, communication, and polyamorous dynamics with my two comet partners back home in Boston.

My time in Denver hasn't been perfect; it's been fulfilling. I'm safe here. I'm free to embody my whole Self—the quirky Kit and the divinely feminine Kit. Just like when I was frolicking in a two-piece on South Beach, I can gallivant in Downtown Denver without feeling like I will be harmed because my existence is threatening someone's bigotry. Of course, safety is relative, but it's related to my connection with the community, and I have that here in ways that I'd been previously yearning for. I can say, unapologetically, I love my hood!

I think there's been a lot of growth in becoming the woman I am today. Being able to go outside, dress up, and feel comfortable in my skin. To have people smile at me and wave and be receptive to that. People see me as a full human. For some, those are just small exchanges in a normal day, but for me, it affirms that I'm loveable and worthy of being seen. I'm feeling a semblance of peace and happiness and joy.

My fashion style keeps expanding as I gain confidence in my skin. I'm definitely wearing more dresses and crop tops, showing off this cosmically delicious melanin. I'm also enjoying lingerie more and getting more comfortable with pampering myself. My sister, Yesinia, has been amazing in getting me new shoes, such as flats and small-inch heels, for those extravagant brunches and club nights. She's a vital part of my community and always challenges me to feel safe and secure in connecting fashion with my womanhood.

I always get compliments when I wear makeup. I'm starting to feel nude without it! The compliments do not inspire me, even though I appreciate them. It's the being seen part that affirms me.

There was a time when I didn't have the money or freedom to wear makeup. My entire transfeminine teenage years were ruined because I had to present as a boy. In school, I was in JROTC, where there was no room to suggest queerness, let alone show up to target practice wearing lipstick and faux lashes. And my mom was not playing that with me. There were actually times as I got older that she'd catch me wearing makeup around the house and not comment on it. But that was strictly forbidden outside the house.

Digging into my relationship with fashion has really allowed me to bond with the parts of myself that needed to feel their beauty. Even if others attempt to invalidate me, I need to know that my existence as a nonbinary trans woman is as important as it is beautiful. I deserve to feel pretty.

As of late, exploration has also included body piercings and tattoos; I have a bridge across my nose and a septum piercing. Yesenia and I have matching Virgo tattoos because our birthdays are one day apart.

A lot has changed, but I'm still a passionate advocate. I'm also a bomb-ass teacher. I recently got a certificate in coding, which required hundreds of hours of studying and research. As daunting as it seems, I'm determined to make a way for myself in this industry, even if it is congested with white men. Working as a software developer has been a dream of mine since I was a child. In many ways, my sheer existence in finding success in coding is a form of activism. I understand now that liberation must start with me; it must start from within. As I break down the limitations within myself, I further that liberation through my career, which only makes room for other Black marginalized genders who want to follow my path. What I know about myself today, which I didn't give myself credit for previously, is that I never lose when I bet on myself.

I'm currently manifesting a future that's centered on financial freedom. I want to nourish myself based on my preference, not my bank account. I want to own items that will enhance my ability to live, whether it's toiletries or a Peloton. And I want that for the people who are precious to me. I want to buy a home and have a place to lay down roots. I want to look out into a skyline of mountains and sit on a porch with a dog and my partner. I'm manifesting fulfillment.

I would love to travel with ease and explore different countries and experiences that I felt got reignited when I had the Casa de Tami trip; it would be a blessing to teach classes abroad in person as well.

Kit is continuing life and community organizing in the Denver area.

THE SOUTH'S GOT
SOMETHIN' TO SAY

■

*"For too many years, the American South
has been evoked as a shorthand for African American
misery and oppression."*

—TAYARI JONES

By the late summer of 2020, I had an idea to write a book proposal for nonfiction about inclusive self-care. The issue was
that I could barely string together a grocery list, let alone a book
outline, overview, and other parts of a proposal.

I had hit my creative peak in Little Havana. I decided to take
off to New Orleans for a creative breath. I'd been there once before and found the city as stimulating as it was fun. And, after
seven months of solo quarantining, I needed to be in a community
with something to offer besides good produce and the beach.

The two-month excursion in the Crescent City cost a pretty
penny, requiring me to hustle harder than I ever had and fundraise for the remainder. I was able to come up with enough money
to cover my rent and utilities in Miami for the two months I was
away, but fundraising for the cost of the Airbnb, food, and travel
expenses didn't come easy. I wasn't surprised. People quickly do-
nated funds to extreme, destitute situations, like money for rent or
baby milk. But, when the cause was a single Black woman trying

to sow her creative oats and further her career, people—white people especially—felt a lot less generous. Fortunately, a $1,500 donation from The Black Feminist Project covered whatever I couldn't come up with. The money was deposited into my PayPal account with a simple message: *Black women deserve to create. Good luck, my nigga.*

I found a one-bedroom loft on the corner of Canal and Magazine St., a central location between the famed French Quarter and New Orleans's upper-class residential Uptown neighborhoods. The loft was basic but much bigger than what I was used to in Miami. A long hallway with a modest, windowless bedroom off to the right, a cute, modern kitchen, and a living room with wall-to-ceiling windows. The floors were hardwood, there was exposed brick in the living room, and it was on the seventh floor, blocking out any would-be noise coming from the crowded streets below.

I want this, I found myself thinking. I preferred more natural light and a balcony, but the space and architecture inspired me to dig deeper into what I wanted from a home. After getting so used to living in small spaces, rented bedrooms, and rough neighborhoods, I was tired of settling for what I could afford. That Airbnb made me crave space and light. And a washer and dryer. My desires only increased the day I met Knight at their house.

Knight was a friend I had made on social media, a fellow Black marginalized gender—pronouns, she/they. We vibed off Black literature and pop culture but often discussed everything else under the sun. They were also a writer and a two-time winner of one of those game shows where only geniuses need apply.

"What you doin' today, baby?" my Uber driver asked. He was a Black man, straight from New Orleans. His gold teeth glistened in the driver's mirror as he smiled, speaking with the New Orleanian accent I instantly fell in love with. Separate from every other

city in the South, locals spoke as though they were singing, even
when they yelled.

"I'm going to visit a friend," I responded. Under normal circumstances, I would never engage with a man who called me
"baby" without my consent, but in New Orleans, the word "baby"
was no different than the New York variation of "shorty" or "ma."
I quickly learned that the city's lingo was unmatched by any other,
and exposure to it was a gift to appreciate, not shun.

"Well, your friend must have a whole lot of money living
around here!"

I snickered at the driver's comment, but as we got closer to
Knight's residence, I understood what he meant. Beautiful three-
story houses with huge porches poked between oak tree-lined
sidewalks. This was no barrio.

When we pulled up to Knight's house, they were standing on
their porch, perfectly decorated with rocking chairs, colossal ele-
phant ear plants, and money trees. Looking just like their profile
photo, a full, multicolor-dyed Afro, wearing a knitted romper like
one I'd stolen from Target. They were sans makeup, bra, and
shoes. They were effortlessly beautiful.

"Welcome!" they said as I climbed the massive stairs that led to
the porch. Forgoing hugs as we were social distancing, we gave
each other a warm smile and bumped our elbows together. As we
did, I noticed two things: a thick patch of hair under their arms,
and the distinct whiff of undeodorized pits. The freshly waxed
Miamian in me was fascinated.

As we sat on the porch, my intrigue of them only intensified.
They explained that they were in the late stages of editing their
manuscript, which was under contract with a reputable publishing house. They lived with their partner, a white guy who owned
the house, which I would later nickname a McMansion. They
spent most of their days writing on their back porch, which

overlooked their inground pool and trees that dripped limes and avocados.

"So . . . what's next after this?" they asked as our legs dangled on the shallow end of the pool. I told them my plans to relocate to Los Angeles, and they snickered, a reaction that left me surprised and pissed off by equal measure.

"You know your preferences better than I do, but I feel like you'd have the same struggles in Los Angeles as in New York. Maybe even more." They went on to list the myriad challenges for a poor Black woman like me to make a way on the West Coast, aside from needing a car—a big nonnegotiable for me—culture, or lack thereof. After seven months of solo quarantining, I was hungry for people, interaction, and engagement, and Los Angeles, for the most part, isn't a very "walkable" city. People stay in their cars and their homes. And, of course, the rent is astronomical, which would have meant that I'd likely have to go back into the food service industry—another nonnegotiable.

"Too bad I can't afford to live in a place like this." I sighed.

"Who said you can't?" they asked. Then they started pointing at the houses surrounding their backyard, listing off the rent in various units ranging from $675 to $1,200. I was shocked.

We hung out for the remainder of the day, well into the evening, drinking daiquiris and talking. I returned to the loft late that night, reconsidering everything I wanted.

As I spent more time in New Orleans, it became easier to envision myself as more of a resident than a tourist. My comfort in the city made me reflect on why I had chosen Little Havana and how much my needs and desires had changed since I lived in New York. I enjoyed the water therapy from living so close to the beach, and my homemade black beans rivaled my abuelita's. My Body gained a new sense of attraction and favor from hot days without makeup in sundresses. And above all, I had proven that I could do it—I could survive on my own and do hard things. It wasn't always pretty, and God knows I took advantage of all the help I could get my hands on, but either way, I did that! For all the years I struggled in New York questioning my capabilities and doubting my talents, I had proven without a shadow of a doubt that I had the capacity to live a life of my design.

What halted my sunny-forever-after in the 305 was the unbearable reality that Florida was one of the country's most oppressive states, fully committed to attacking queers, Black and trans people, and even/especially the autoimmune compromised. Then newly appointed governor, Ron DeSantis, had enforced rules that required children to return to school while many across the country were still operating under lockdown-imposed Zoom classes, mocked mask-wearing, and challenged the rights of trans children. To paraphrase a famous quote from the late great Audre Lorde, if my people weren't free there, then neither was I.

I'd never considered living anywhere in the South, let alone the *Deep* South. Like many who lived in Miami, I considered it separate from most of the Southern region. Because of its predominantly Latino and Caribbean population, it felt more tropical than American. Thinking about the distinction reminded me of a joke once told to me by a white Uber driver who picked me up from Miami International Airport.

"You know what I love about Miami?" he asked me after flinging my suitcase into the trunk.

"What?"

"It reminds me of America!"

Of course, the politics and quality of life for the most marginalized Louisiana residents weren't much more impressive than in Florida. For starters, it was known for being among the worst school districts in the country. New Orleans, like many other big cities, was high in crime and poverty, and the numbers reflected the state's deep-seated racial disparity. I wasn't impressed by the statistics, but I was also childfree and had only lived in cities that were rough around their lower-class edges.

But there was a challenge I had to overcome in making peace with my newfound desire that had a greater impact on my resistance than the statistics or politics—my own anti-Blackness toward the South.

Slow. Both in speech and movement. Poorly educated. Subservient to white supremacist culture and norms. Uncouth. Behind the times. Those are just a few stereotypes I had about the South growing up, as do many coastal and Midwest Black Americans. If the Black court of popular opinion ruled on a location of Black American liberation, New York would be at the top of the food chain, and the Deep South would be at the bottom.

The chokehold big city Black Americans' have on the culture isn't as tight as they think it is. Fifty-six percent of all Black Americans live in the South. That means that if you combined all the Black folks from the East, West Coast, and Midwest, it still wouldn't equal the amount of us that hold a stake below the Mason-Dixon. In the spirit of power in numbers, the South brings much more to the table than a Southern drawl and sweet tea.

These were the things I considered as I prepared to relocate from Little Havana. I can't say that I was sold everything would "work out" for me if I made a sudden Southern pivot, but by the time I returned to Miami in January 2021, I was ten toes down in my decision; what I yearned for most was waiting for me in the Deep South.

I took the same steps in New York when I desperately wanted to relocate to Florida: I sought guidance at my altar, prayed, and meditated on it heavily. I was still waiting for internal approval about this shift for a while, but instead, I heard nothing. It wasn't until I spread myself out on my bedroom floor with a stack of magazines, a long piece of cardboard from an Amazon box, some scissors, and a glue stick that I heard something. Unlike other times, the message wasn't in fragments, it wasn't unclear, and I didn't have to piece it together. It was almost as if my Internal Self was discussing with my Highest Self:

Highest Self: Last time, you manifested an apartment out of desperation. That's how you wound up broke and lonely in the barrio. This time, you're going to dream bigger, and you're going to manifest opulence. You're going to live in a McMansion, you're going to have your own washer and dryer, and you're going to have friends.

Internal Self: But that doesn't make sense because—

Highest Self: Shut up. We don't make sense anymore. We make moves, we make art, we make a way. The way is in a fabulous apartment in New Orleans. You want hardwood floors, exposed brick, a spacious balcony, and neighbors who care if you're breathing. Let's go!

I was so intimidated by the tone of Highest Self that I didn't question it; I simply cut and pasted. The more I thought about the conversation, the more I realized how true it was. I had, in fact, manifested Casa de Tami out of desperation. Sure, the greater parts of my list of needs had been checked off, but there was so much that I had forgotten to aspire toward. Like comfort, stability, and in-person community. I decided that this go-round, I was going to aim higher, a lot higher, and ask for what I needed and what I yearned for. I wanted the kind of apartment I loved, not just one with a roof.

For months, I kept my plans and details of my relocation to myself. I had no money or prospects to even suggest that I had a shot of living this "opulent" life that I dreamed up, but I held on to the dream anyway. Every morning and evening, I looked at that vision board and repeated, "I want that for me, and I know I deserve it. I'm really excited about that life!" I began watching *New Orleans Foot Tour* videos on YouTube to familiarize myself with the city. By the spring of 2021, I knew the difference between Uptown and the Lower Garden District and how to make red beans and rice from scratch.

Three days later, after an especially grueling round of extractions at the dentist, I got a call from Knight.

"So, I know this is pretty random," they began, "but the married couple that lives in one of the two units I told you about? Well, they're getting a divorce and . . . they're moving!"

"No way!" I responded. My surprise was sincere, but I was a bit thrown off as to why they'd felt the need to reach out and tell me this.

"Yeah, so, if you're still looking for a place to stay, we can totally hold that unit for you." I replayed their words in my head over and over, still struggling to process them. That house, the McMansion, the beautiful porches with an inground pool. That place. Held. For me.

"I don't know if I got that kind of bread though," I confessed. From what I recalled, the two units in Knight's house were both above $1,400. Even though I was barely paying my one grand a month by the skin of my teeth, I still felt like I could afford an extra two hundred if necessary. But anything more than that was too sweet for my blood.

"I know," Knight replied. "I asked Max, and he said he could go down to $1,200." Knight went on to explain that, if I could come up with the first month's rent and $1,200 security, the apartment was all mine.

"Yes!" I exclaimed.

With a solid four months to save and get my shit in order, I facilitated yet another fundraiser, this time vowing that it would be my last.

I know I'm not the only person in these streets struggling, I began on a Facebook post, *but I also know what I'm able to do with resources when I get ahold of them, and y'all do too. I'm grateful to have a roof over my head, but I'll be forty next year, and I deserve more than a roof. I found an opportunity to live a life of my design, in a community that can hold me. I just need help securing that security and covering my moving expenses.*

I set a goal of $5,000, set up a GoFundMe, and even sold tarot card readings. With help from friends, my online community, and Sissy, I got that money up. One month post-extraction, less than a week shy of my lease expiring, I was on a one-way flight to New Orleans.

My dream apartment was so perfect that I feared it. There were two faux fireplaces lined with exposed brick. The ceilings were thirty feet high. There was a balcony that overlooked Magazine Street. It was so long and wide I was pretty sure it was the size of my old studio. There was a washer and dryer, a huge bedroom, and a tub.

I spent the first several months tiptoeing between rooms, from one end of the apartment to the other. When I sat on my balcony to drink tea or smoke a joint, people stopped and waved. At first, the constant acknowledgement felt intrusive, but eventually I got used to it. Eventually I began waving back if they're Black.

Across the hall from my apartment was another unit where my neighbor, Candace, lived. Candace was a cool white chick who, like me, worked from home and smoked too much pot. She was in her late forties and single with two adorable pugs that she walked twice a day. Within the first three months, she gifted me a

lightly used white love seat and two four-shelf bookcases I so desperately needed.

At Knight's insistence, I joined their Mardi Gras krewe, which
came with an instant community of friends. We met monthly to
plan events, supported one another's endeavors, and spent time
together just because. Catt, a white girl originally from Arkansas,
became a friend in whom I openly confided about my struggles
with dating and meeting romantic partners. Ashley, a Black
woman who bartends in the Quarter, expressed her appreciation
for sharing my dental woes and often encouraged me to come out
more. And then Michelle, the resident "mom" of the group, who
happened to be, by far, the coolest of us all. A dark-haired white
woman a few years older than me who randomly decided to get a
T-Boz haircut one spring. "Only Black women compliment me
on it, but it's because they get it." She's an unapologetic spirit who
never tired of hearing me rant about my writing challenges or
home decor decisions.

I did my best to show up for events, but the urge to leave early
often drove me to hop in an Uber when the party was just getting
started. The need to be alone would get the best of me, leaving
me to fake a migraine. Knight once mentioned my pattern of awk-
wardly early exits, but I brushed it off. However, on the day of
Mardi Gras, the jig was up.

At the last minute, I decided I wasn't going to go. I'd spent
weeks preparing my costume, covering my pink tutu with rain-
bow rhinestones and all kinds of glitter. I just really didn't feel
like being around a bunch of strangers—drunk strangers at that.
Even though I'd never attended Mardi Gras before, I was convinced that the day was going to demand every inch of my energy, and I just didn't want to give it. I was turning forty in two
months and felt like I was too old, lonely, and weird to prance

around the city. When Knight knocked on my door, I attempted to go back to sleep, but then they kept knocking. And knocking. A touch of aggression grew with each. They weren't leaving anytime soon.

"Are you trying to get a hold of Tam?" I heard Candace ask Knight.

"Yeah, she's coming with us!" Knight responded without a hint of condescension or fear that I was backing out. This made me feel guilty—so guilty that I felt dirty. I quickly popped in my teeth, threw on some clothes, and dragged myself to the door.

"What time is it?" I asked after sliding open my door. I rubbed my eyes and did my best to give off a disoriented vibe as if I'd only been sleeping, not lying alert in bed waiting for them to leave.

"It's Mardi Gras time, darlin'!"

Within twenty minutes, I packed my costume, untwisted my hair, puffed it out, and slid out the door with Knight and company. We spent the next few hours getting ready at Catt's apartment in the Tremé.

As we got settled at Catt's and started slipping into our costumes and slapping on glitter, Knight asked if I had received the note from Candace. She was planning on wearing a too-tight dress that she knew she'd need help getting out of and wanted to make sure I'd be around the next day.

"I got the note," I confirmed, remembering plucking it off my door the night before when I returned from throwing out the trash. "She never came by, though."

"She did, Tam. She left that note on your door seven days ago," Knight confessed.

My dirty secret was out; despite having a career and money, I was still going days, sometimes *weeks*, without leaving my apartment or engaging with humans outside of Knight. This problem would soon get much-needed attention from my new therapist.

But, on the morning of Mardi Gras 2022, the dirty little secret got nothing more than a *Girl, I know your life* glance from my concerned friend.

Knight and Catt were prepared to go all out for my fortieth birthday. They kept asking my thoughts about themes, venues, and settings. What was my color theme? Was I thinking funky and poppy, or did I want to get elegant, à la black and white? I told them I wanted a simple pool party. Michelle came with Paradise Park beer, and Ashley brought chicken wings and daiquiris from Melbas. Just before sunset, Knight appeared with a batch of cupcakes they made, and everyone sang happy birthday to me. It's hard to explain even now, but this was one of the best moments of my life.

By the time my birthday rolled around in April, I'd already had a series of discussions with my therapist about my challenges with socializing and going outside. I agree that my issues went deeper than simply not liking people or not wanting to go out. My natural introverted ways combined with the impact of two years of quarantining solo engulfed into a serious case of social deprivation. I was familiar with the term after learning about it in *Restart*, my friend Doreen Dodgen-Magee's book. Rather than simply "will my way" through it, I would have to methodically, consistently, and patiently create practices that reintegrated me into the world without feeling like I was buck-ass naked.

Because I never actually contracted coronavirus and I didn't lose a job or a business, I never considered that I had lived through any kind of COVID-related trauma. But the more I unpacked my feelings in therapy and waded through *Restart*, it was clear that the pandemic unearthed a host of fears I'd been keeping below the surface. The fear of dying, the overwhelming loneliness, the isolation from the rest of the world may have been experiences I felt in Miami, but they followed me to New Orleans.

I assumed at first that by leaving the house more often I would naturally break the cycle of self-imposed isolation. It wasn't that simple. Leaving the house proved to be the easy part, and staying at an event became the challenge. Eventually, friends stopped inviting me out as often because they assumed I didn't want to go long enough to stay. Realizing that the impact of social deprivation was leading to the destruction of newly developed relationships broke my heart. Friends and community were things I yearned for, yet it seemed that I didn't have the capacity to foster the very relationships I desired.

"It's not a failure; it's a process," Doreen said to me during one of our Zoom sessions. She never acted as my personal therapist; however, after confiding in her my challenges with "post" pandemic isolation, she was willing to listen and help me unpack it all.

"I know," I agreed. "I just hate that this process back to normal-ish is taking so long." Doreen reminded me that during my time of isolation I was taking care of myself all on my own, running a growing brand, which now incorporated spiritual self-care content into my platform, all while surviving a global pandemic, a racial uprising, and even learning how to chew and talk again after getting all my teeth removed. Shit was heavy.

"I think you should be open with your loved ones and let them know the hard time you've been having," she suggested. A strategy so honest and forthright I hadn't even considered it. I'd spent so much time playing off my neuroses, blaming them on being "super introverted," I never considered admitting, "I want to let you know, I had a really hard experience back in Miami, and I'm still working through that. So, sometimes I show up a little weird—or don't show up at all." But that's exactly what I started doing.

"I had a feeling it was deeper than just digging into solitude," Knight responded when we talked. "Totally understandable."

From that point forward, we planned different strategies for when I would attend an event. No hard and fast rules, more like friendly guidelines that ensured I could continue fostering meaningful in-person relationships while honoring my own comfort. Sometimes we'd come up with hourly check-ins, and whenever I was ready to peace out, there would be no objection because I did my best. Other times, I would simply let my friends know, "I'm going to do my best to show up, but please don't hate me if I have to leave a little early."

I also submersed myself in the New Orleans writing scene, which was far more robust than I could have imagined. I made friends with Dr. Megan Holt, who runs One Book One New Orleans, an amazing program that brings free books to New Orleans residents as well as inmates at Louisiana State Penitentiary. They also host various book discussions and events throughout the city, which I eagerly attended. I got to experience firsthand what it feels like to be a Black writer in a community with other Black writers. Well-known, established journalists and authors like Jarvis DeBerry and Maurice Carlos Ruffin went from names on my bookshelf to writers I engaged with. I no longer felt too far removed from having "what it takes" to be taken seriously as a writer. I was on the inside now, brushing arms with some of my favorite literary giants, picking their brains, and asking for advice about writing and business.

I spent hours writing at Baldwin & Co. bookstore and attending writer meet-ups held by Third Lantern Lit, a local organization that promoted inclusive writing workshops. I participated in timed writing contests, and I always won. Afterward, we would sit around drinking craft beer and commiserating over our creative woes. I made friends with Erin, a white chick from Texas who used to work heavily in the documentary industry. We hung out in our downtime and exchanged battle wounds from online dating fails.

The lifestyle I sought didn't come easy, but eventually, it came. With time, I was able to build a substantial social circle, pay my bills, and solidify myself as not only a writer but a sensitive reader and developmental editor. Living in my dream apartment allowed me to pursue desires I didn't realize I had, like creating a beautiful balcony garden, as well as a meditation room where I relax, read, and give tarot card readings.

New Orleans operates at a slower pace than New York and other coastal cities, but it's an intentional pace deeply rooted in pleasure and ease. They take their time not because they are slow, but because there's an understanding of what's missing when life is rushed. I may have gotten my grills and my sexy in Miami, but without question, I got my life in New Orleans. And it would have lasted longer if it weren't for the abortion bans.

THE SWEETEST SUNDAY EVER KNOWN: SELF-CARE SUNDAY & CHATTEL SLAVERY

"This sense of not belonging and of being an extraneous element is at the heart of slavery."

—SAIDIYA HARTMAN, *Lose Your Mother: A Journey Along the Atlantic Slave Route*

CONTENT WARNING: ABUSE

One of the greatest myths about people within the Black diaspora is that we're monolithic. Because many of us are born with a strong command of our cultural and racial language, there are things we will forever gravitate and celebrate together, i.e., ingesting ginger ale for medicinal purposes, acronyms (IKYFL, IYKYK, ATEOTD, etc.), washing our ass on the daily (above *and* below the knee), etc. However, outside of some common quirks, we are far from monolithic. Like any other race and/or ethnicity, our ideologies are formed not just by our race but our upbringing, personal experiences, the nuances of our intersections, etc. One of the best examples of the contrast in our opinions can be found in our views regarding film and television programs that center on chattel slavery.

"I'm not watching any more slave movies!"

"Enough with the slave shows and films."

I disagree with the reasoning, but I get the sentiment. We are, after all, a people with a rich history that goes back to the start of civilization. Every era in human existence includes a collective of Black people doing something magical, revolutionary, and worthy of a four-part miniseries on PBS. It's understandable to question why film and television are fixated on the era when we were ripped from our freedom, held captive, and forced to produce labor that would subsequently build entire nations. There's an emotional and psychological pull we experience whenever faced with dramatizations of the inhumane true tales of our past. And, when the retelling is in the hands of bigwig white Hollywood producers, "What's the *real* reason?" is a valid question.

White people have been the most dominant oppressors in the history of humanity, yet nobody craves to be oppressed as they do. It's why they develop weird fetishes with our cultural norms that they try to pass off as appreciation. For example, Black Americans nationwide still fight for our right to wear cornrows and locs in the workplace without punishment or ridicule. As of June 2023, only twenty-three of America's fifty-one states passed the CROWN Act, CROWN standing for Creating a Respectful and Open World for Natural Hair. The act protects Black people who wear their hair in natural styles, braids, or locs. Meanwhile, white people proudly sport theirs and claim that its origins are from the fucking Vikings. Or, like the way most of the white boys I went to school with memorized all the lyrics to Wu-Tang Clan and 50 Cent albums, yet today they're now proud Republicans who believe that cops murder Black people because we're "noncompliant."

White people have repeatedly proven that their intrigue in Black and Indigenous culture has more to do with colonizing than celebrating. As Sissy often says, "They want our rhythm, but they get off on our blues." For that reason alone, suspicion is valid whenever the latest wave of chattel slavery and Jim Crow–era content emerges on the big screen and primetime television.

Still, an unfortunate impact of America's fetishization of Black people in bondage is our own disownment of our lineage. In recent years, statements like "I am not my ancestors" and "You may have got them, but we built different" have popped up everywhere, from T-shirts to Instagram memes. The verbiage often varies, but the objective is the same: I am unlike those you violated the first time. This attitude suggests that our enslaved ancestors were docile and, in many ways, responsible for their entrapment. No one captured this sentiment better than the artist once known as Kanye West when he said, "Four hundred years? That sounds like a decision to me."

Because of the deep misrepresentation and lack of education regarding our ancestors, too many people perpetuate binary ideas about The Enslaved. Examples: those who were assigned to labor in the house were all light-skinned and experienced more favorable treatment, and there were few attempts at running away and fighting for liberation; many were so complacent in their entrapment that they favored living under the ruling of their owners instead of fighting for liberation, etc.

It's one thing when we distance ourselves from the history of our ancestors and chattel slavery because of the pain and rage that overcome us. However, when we do so because of ideologies suggesting that enslaved Black people were in some way docile or complacent, we do a great disservice to our lineage and ourselves. And, worst of all, we deprive ourselves of the magical connection of who we were, what we've become, and the liberation that awaits us in this very moment.

Whether we're comfortable with it or not, the legacy of chattel slavery is deeply embedded in every fiber of the entire universe's fabric—even the wellness industry.

As Patricia Hershey continues revolutionizing our relationship with rest, labor, and ease, the American wellness industry has quickly followed suit. It's not uncommon for the regular-degular white influencer to interject messages of "take a nap" and "lean into your soft season" into their otherwise vanilla, capitalist-fueled platforms. While to many it's nothing more than a trend, for The Nap Ministry and Black folks as a collective, the rest revolution is a path of liberation, with bricks laid by our enslaved ancestors. It's from them that the roots of self-care Sunday were born. I learned this firsthand during one of several visits to the Whitney Plantation Museum in Louisiana.

A bus picked up tourists at the French Quarter, taking us to the plantation, about ninety minutes outside New Orleans. During the ride, a sweet white woman named Rose greeted us with a smile and a slice of king cake provided by her husband, who worked at the local factory where it was produced. She was about five foot four with shoulder-length blonde hair that had streaks of gray flowing through the front. She was likely in her fifties and seemed very sweet.

The group of tourists was a mixture of Black and white people, though predominantly white. I was immediately on guard, wondering exactly what kind of experience these people were looking for.

"I hope everyone understands that you are about to visit a very sacred land that tells a true story about the lives of Black people here in Louisiana. A story that's not told enough." As we licked glittery frosting off our fingers, Rose explained that the Whitney Plantation Museum is unlike any other. Its sole purpose is to pay homage to the enslaved Africans who were forced into the brutal culture of chattel slavery. As she continued to inform us of the land we were about to explore, my tension dissipated. I realized that her compassion for the Black people who lived and died at the plantation. Of course, she was a paid host, but also, she was a human. And she spoke about The Enslaved with the same reverence as I would expect anyone would speak about their ancestors, a rarity in white people.

The owner of the plantation was a farmer turned slave captor who emigrated from Germany in the 1720s. At the height of his operations, he had purchased and enslaved twenty Africans. As the plantation was passed down through generations, that number would swell to almost one hundred enslaved Africans and their descendants. Forced labor of The Enslaved produced lucrative crops which varied from indigo, rice, and then, primarily, sugarcane.

By the time Rose was done giving us basic information about the plantation, the mood on the bus had shifted from giddy to unsettling. That pleased me. Unlike other museums like the Guggenheim or a museum of modern art, the Whitney Plantation is centered on human lives. It's not meant to be a backdrop for an Instagram reel.

When the bus arrived at the plantation and we took our first steps on the land, the dirt was muddy from rain the day before but caked before my eyes under the heat of the relentless Louisiana sun.

"For those who are hot, imagine what it felt like working in this heat," our tour guide, Michael, explained. He was a white kid, a college student with a shaggy haircut. Like Rose, the consistency with which he centered the lives of The Enslaved allowed me to receive him with a different, more receptive lens. His intention was on-brand with the museum.

As we walked through the plantation, carefully, Michael explained in painful detail the importance of each structure.

He took us to the slave cabins, smaller than my studio in Little Havana.

"Each cabin was built to fit one family," he explained. With nothing but a brick wall dividing the already compromised space, it was hard to imagine life as a woman, a rambunctious child, or an elderly person. Privacy was beyond their reach for them—a reality that broke my heart.

Next, we got to "the big house," the residence of the enslavers and their families. A sprawling, wide, two-story home, clearly built with pompous privilege.

"The enslavers would use a young enslaved child to act as a fan to cool them down while they slept," Michael explained when we entered one of the bedrooms on the second floor.

"I don't understand," a white woman whispered.

"They used babies to fan them at night," a Black tourist reiterated. His tone was stern and disturbed.

The big house, often romanticized as a less harsh forced work environment for The Enslaved, offered no salvation for Black people. Stephanie E. Jones-Rogers, author of *They Were Her Property: White Women as Slave Owners in the American South*, delivered gobsmacking details of the lived experiences of The Enslaved, not only in the field but in the homes of their captors. Of all the heart-wrenching stories, that of young Henrietta King stayed with me. Henrietta was only nine or ten when her mistress, the unassuming term for "woman captor," accused her of stealing candy. As punishment, the woman captor wedged Henrietta's head under a rocking chair and rocked for about one hour while her daughter beat the helpless girl. This act of torture resulted in Henrietta being permanently disfigured and unable to digest solid foods.

Being relegated to forced labor in or around the big house was little solace for Black people, women and girls especially, who were forced to dwell in the belly of their captors' domain. That proximity only meant they were vulnerable to rape and torture by their captors.

We made our way to the part of the plantation where sugarcane was milled and processed.

"It's important to understand the conditions under which these people were forced to work," Michael explained. "With temperatures that could reach as high as one hundred ten degrees, not including the heat from the boiling sugar."

In Angela Davis's *Women, Race & Class*, the activist and author detailed the horrendous conditions enslaved Black women were subjected to in the field. Those who had just given birth were still expected to work only one day postpartum. They were forced to leave their newborns unattended in the wilds of the unsanitary field, vulnerable to infection and mother nature.

The picking of cotton and tobacco has been widely referenced and documented. So much so that the tips of my fingertips tingle with discomfort when I think of my ancestors' pain as they sifted through hundreds of tiny, sharp seeds imbedded in raw cotton. For all that I knew and understood about picking cotton, rice, and tobacco, I was unaware of the dangers and backbreaking labor required to harvest and process sugarcane in the Deep South.

Colonizers used two systems to enforce labor: the task system and the gang system. The task system was based on an expected quota: hoe x amount of field, pick x amount of cotton, sow x amount of crops. When the quota was met, The Enslaved were permitted to retreat from their place of forced labor back to their living quarters. This system was more customary. The gang system, practiced more in the Deep South, was known for its harsher, higher expectations and was not led by a quota. Instead, work was expected from sunup to sundown, Monday through Saturday. There were three stages of labor required to turn sugarcane into sugar and rum: field maintenance and cropping, extracting its juice, and boiling the liquid down until all that was left was sugar in its purest form.

The first gang was responsible for cutting the sugarcane down in the field and transporting it to the mill area. Sharp machetes and billies were used to whack down the thick stalks, then they had to carry them from the field to the actual mill location. And, because raw sugarcane has such a short shelf life once cut from its root, getting it to the mill for conversion had to be done quickly so the juice didn't ferment. This work was deemed less dangerous than what gang two was tasked with: the actual milling and boiling sugarcane juice. However, with heavy sugarcane stalks taller than people, in that Deep South heat, there was little safety in cutting sugarcane.

The second gang was responsible for converting the sugarcane and boiling it, by far the most dangerous part. From crushing the cane though mills, then boiling it down, it was common for enslaved laborers to lose fingers and arms in the milling process and face severe burns during boiling.

"With the combined heat from the boiled sugar, along with Louisiana's oppressive heat, this work was known to kill the men who labored in around seven years. They were, literally, worked to death." I, along with other Black tourists, openly wept.

And lastly, there was the third gang, also known as the grass gang. They were in charge of gathering grass to feed animals and weeding crops. Applying the gang system to a sugar plantation like the Whitney ensured that captors of The Enslaved had optimal free labor around the clock.

In 2017, Mom and I began tracing our ancestors back through census records on ancestry.com. We learned that Papa, Mom's father, was born and raised in Bacon Level, Alabama, on the same plantation land where his paternal grandparents were enslaved. I walked through the plantation, my heart seething with anger as I wondered what proximity my ancestors were to boiling sugarcane. *How the fuck did they survive this?*

In another area of the plantation was a church. It was a small one-story building the size of a large shed. When we walked inside, there were life-size bronze statues of enslaved children. Some were smaller than others, but none of them looked older than five or six years old.

"Each statue represents a real child that lived on the plantation," Michael softly explained. His tone told on his feelings of sorrow.

Many children were born and died on the Whitney plantation. So many that the museum created a special memorial for them. It was a concrete and marble square with four walls lined with plaques. Each one was engraved with the children's names, alongside their ages. Many of them were three, four, and five years old. Some died of poor conditions, others from disease. None lived long enough to know, understand, or experience freedom.

"So, slaves were allowed to go to church?" a white tourist asked.

"The Enslaved," others and I corrected. Normally I wouldn't correct people on their grammar, but this was different. Slavery was a lifestyle that Black people were forced into; however, that was not their identity. They were Africans who had been kidnapped and forced to build nations while the roots of their lineage, autonomy, and native tongue were stripped from them. Reducing the lives of the most violated humans who ever lived to "slaves" was nonnegotiable.

"From the eighteenth century until the end of chattel slavery, Sundays off was a law in the state of Louisiana as well as other French colonies within the Caribbean and Gulf of Mexico."

The law was one of several decrees known as The Louisiana Black Code. A variation of France's Code Noir, The Black Code was a collection of laws that ultimately defined the culture of chattel slavery in the Deep South up until the Emancipation Proclamation. The Louisiana Black Code had two major objectives:

enforcing Catholicism as the primary religion and protecting the rights and profit of the chattel slavery industry.

The first article called for the expulsion of all Jews, regarding them as sworn "enemies of the Christian faith." The rules that followed further cemented Catholicism as the only religion of the land, one that slave captors were instructed to enforce on The Enslaved. The fifth decree in particular is one that offered only slight reprieve for Black people:

> V. Sundays and holidays are to be strictly observed. All negroes found at work on these days are to be confiscated.

Because slave captors provided the barest of minimum, the onus was on The Enslaved to produce anything deemed as "extra," such as meat and fish, shoes and clothing, linen, and cabin repairs, etc. The concept of spare time was not allotted within a gang system labor structure, so all hygiene and domestic duties such as haircare and domestic tasks were also handled on Sundays. With all that needed to be taken care of, Black folks still found a way to practice care, both personally and collectively, on Sundays. The best example of this can be found in the history of Congo Square.

Located in the Tremé/Lafitte section of New Orleans, Congo Square was a lively market on Sundays, exclusively for Black people to gather, play music, and exchange goods. Loved ones and spouses who were enslaved on different plantations blissfully, albeit briefly, reunited. Black children ran around and laughed without the threat of punishment or death looming over them. Africans maintained their culture by playing native instruments like banzas and bamboulas. Couples got married. Hustlers sold goods. Heads of households bartered fruits and vegetables from their gardens, and women sold fabrics they strung together from unwanted scraps. Sundays were magical for The Enslaved in ways the whites couldn't or can't ever understand.

You could hear a pin drop on that bus ride back to New Orleans. We all stood in the face of the ugly horrors behind chattel slavery, not the theatrical images from *Django Unchained* and *12 Years a Slave.*

I stared out the window, fixated on those majestical Sundays. It says so much about a race of people who, even when stripped of every rightful dignity deserved to them, found a way to not just survive but to thrive. To celebrate, to show out, to prosper, to give. To dance!

Long after the end of chattel slavery, the legacy of self and communal care on Sundays continues. For many, it still includes the act of worship, but for most, rest, ease, and gratitude are a given. The connection that Black people have with Sunday is unmatched by any American norm; it's deeper than just laundry and sleeping in late. It's a big dinner with a table set for twelve. It's the gratitude from within for the week we survived and the faith in knowing we will conquer the one that's ahead.

In my family, Sunday was the day Mom didn't remove her head scarf and tried her best not to leave the house. The aroma of yams and baked chicken filled our household by the early afternoon. While the deep cleaning was done on Saturdays, Sundays were reserved for making everything nice; with fresh flowers and water on our altars, The Clark Sisters and Yolanda Adams blasted from the stereo while we all delicately floated around one another.

Of course, Black people aren't the only ones who have connected rest and domestic upkeep with Sundays. The concept of "self-care Sunday" is a capitalist goldmine. The truth is that what the industry promotes isn't even self-care; they're expensive, consumer-driven forms of self-soothing. The difference? The soothing of Self, while it does help to alleviate stress, is a short-term fix for the average person who's spent an entire week filled with labor, stress, and responsibility. Whereas caring for Self aids in long-term betterment and addresses our needs and desires. Self-care is the upkeep of Self but also the service of Self. Practice it with consistency, and life improves. Of course, we all depend on being pampered and self-soothed, but why should it cost money? Moreso, why only on Sundays?

I recently saw an Instagram story from the author of the 2023 memoir *A Renaissance of Our Own*, Rachel Elizabeth Cargle. She was curled up on her sofa, eating cereal and watching Saturday morning cartoons. At first glance, it looked like a cute, personal ritual. But, on a deeper level, it was a sheer act of revolution—the kind that The Nap Ministry has taught us only comes when we prioritize rest and ease.

Personally, I don't do shit on Sundays. I'm not cleaning nothing for nobody, I'm trying not to go anywhere, and the only ones I'm cooking for are me and my ancestors. When I think about the people I come from, and how they had to go through six days of invasive torture just for a precious Sunday, I remember that I am my ancestors, and I must rest for them. America can suck my eggplant; it's self-care Monday–Saturday in this bitch. Sundays are for being still, for being mindful. Sunday is for *being*.

There will always be more heartbreak than revelation regarding my diaspora's brutal history with chattel slavery. It's not meant to be romanticized or reimagined. But it shouldn't be forgotten either. Through its darkest of truths are revelations about who we were, how we survived, and why we should be proud. We turned Sundays into magic, and there's nothing docile about that. Truths that can't be taught in Hollywood but, rather, our very own bloodlines. I'm forever grateful to be a descendant of my ancestors, but most especially on Sundays.

BUSTIN' NUTS IN AN ANTIABORTION STATE

◼

"Witnessing an embodied yes in the body of a historically oppressed person is irresistible to me."

—ADRIENNE MAREE BROWN, *Pleasure Activism: The Politics of Feeling Good*

The last time I had sex, I was so high on cocaine that I had to stop midway to check my pulse.

"Is it good to you, baby?" he asked.

"I DON'T KNOW, I THINK I'M HAVING A FUCKING HEART ATTACK!" It was Cinco de Mayo, 2015. Obama was president, I was giving friendship bracelets to people whom I wouldn't be able to pick out of a lineup today, and I got most of my haircare tips from Black vloggers on YouTube. He was some white guy I'd picked up on the D train after bartending a double at work. A different time indeed.

That version of me needed a break from the fast life, which, at that time, included promiscuous sex. It wasn't based on morals but rather impulsive decision-making fueled by self-sabotaging and sometimes dangerous behavior. My immediate desires haunted me until I fulfilled them. I had to learn to honor my best interests more than my reckless cravings. So, I spent time working through my impulses in therapy, rebuilding my self-esteem, and finding the validation that I once sought from bed partners within my actual Self. In the meantime, I explored my level of arousal with toys and porn (shout-out to the Rose) before I was brave enough to get back in the saddle with another human.

By the time I moved to New Orleans in late 2021, I felt like a new woman. It had been seven years since I'd kicked (most of) my addictive habits and developed a healthier, more intuitive relationship with My Body. I had been creeping up on the first anniversary of living in the Deep South, and most of my pleasure boxes were checked: social life, interpersonal relationships, and career. The one challenge I had yet to unpack was my almost eight-year celibacy.

To be clear, I'm actively divesting from all fetishization and romanticization of any and all purity tropes. A good kitty is a good kitty because it's a good kitty. It doesn't matter who makes it purr, how many make it purr, or how often it purrs. Okay? Personally, my kitty is magnificent because she knows herself like the back of her hand.

Besides cold feet, there was another reason why I was hesitant to start dating and having sex again. Much like the rest of the Deep South, the politics around reproductive rights in Louisiana was pitiful.

In June 2022, Louisiana had become one of several states— most in the South—that adopted antiabortion laws. I had never had an abortion, but I was never opposed to having one if needed. The idea of a forced pregnancy mortified me. And that was just the half of it.

The maternal death rate among Black Americans is a national crisis, with Black birthing people three times more likely to die from birth-related causes than white women. With statistics that pair better with poorly resourced third-world countries, Black birthing people are at constant risk of complications and death to both their lives and that of their unborn children.

As I write this, Louisiana has the highest rate of maternal mortality in the nation. Not only could an abortion mean the difference between my life and death, but should I keep a pregnancy, there was a disturbingly high chance that I wouldn't survive. Maternal mortality is a nationwide crisis, but as usual, when it comes to intersectionality, no one is more impacted by this than Black birthing people.

> "About a third of our population is African American; African Americans have a higher incidence of maternal mortality. So, if you correct our population for race, we're not as much of an outlier as it'd otherwise appear."

That's a quote from Louisiana state Senator Bill Cassidy, attempting to suggest that the maternal mortality crisis only *seems* high because Black American birthing parents are included. Senator Cassidy is proof of why there's yet to be tangible assistance to combat a crisis that claims Black birthing people three times more than whites or Latinos. And, for those thinking that one would have to be an actual physician to understand the gravity and nuance of the maternal mortality crisis, Senator Cassidy is indeed a licensed physician. That is not the kind of leadership I want to have final say over what I do with my kitty.

Almost fifty years ago, research proved Black women face severely high medical risks, not because of genetics but misogynoir. The perpetual exposure to racism and sexism causes irreversible weathering of bodily organs and arteries. Dr. Arline Geronimus discovered the weathering hypothesis while working for a maternity program in Trenton, New Jersey, in the 1970s. Since then, medical research has expanded the weathering hypothesis and found a direct link to maternal mortality. Yet, lawmakers continue to dismiss the facts despite the plethora of information.

When the rights of marginalized genders and reproductive agencies are on the line, many have failed to take on both issues with an intersectional approach. With the current bans on abortion further compromising Black birthing people at high risk of pregnancy complications, no one will feel the consequences more than Black marginalized genders.

For Senator Cassidy, it's a Black people problem. To others, it's a socialist problem that a Healthcare for All bill could solve. But ultimately, the maternal mortality crisis is a white supremacy problem that not even classism can counter.

As much as I loved my ginormous apartment in my fancy neighborhood in cool-ass New Orleans, I hated having sex in an anti-abortion state. Living in New Orleans meant that I was at least three states away from the nearest clinic that performed abortions—two, but only if I were willing to travel through Texas, and ain't nobody got time for that. After months of internal deliberation, I finally caved and created an online dating app. I posted my cutest pictures and put up several full-body selfies, so suitors knew I was fat.

Black people were my preference, and I stated as much in my profile, yet white men were tripping over themselves in my DMs to get my attention. At first, I overlooked them, but after a while, I thought, *Well . . . why not?*

One guy, in particular, caught my eye. Not because he was cute but because he said his favorite musical artist was John Coltrane. I figured anyone with such good taste couldn't be that bad. I figured it wrong.

His name was Steve, and we met up on Frenchman Street. I could have sworn we discussed going to a jazz lounge to catch some live music, but when we got together, Steve had other plans. He also had a completely different aesthetic and body type than what he posted on his profile. For starters, his beard was a lot longer, and he was shorter than the five foot nine he claimed to be online. And then, there was the issue of lips—or lack thereof. I can't say he didn't have lips; I couldn't find them. *The nerve of you*, I chastised myself. I mean, there I was, hoping that my Fixodent would keep my dentures in place all night. Meanwhile, I was judging this short, hairy, lipless man for his appearance. I quickly got over myself and remembered the mission: to get laid, not married.

"So . . . which way is the jazz spot?" I asked. He grinned sheepishly and then looked down at the concrete. It was then that I realized he was nervous, and I thought that was kind of cute. I didn't bother to dress up, knowing that the New Orleans aesthetic is casual, but I still looked really hot in my too-tight black jeans and green Peaches Records tight tee. That morning, I gave myself a good wash and go, so my curls spiraled out of control around my face. I topped it all off with red lipstick. I was *giving*.

"Yeah . . . I was thinking we could just walk around and talk," he suggested. "I mean, it's a really nice night out."

"Sure." I shrugged. *This motherfucka's broke*, I thought. Still, who was I to judge? I'd been broke a lot longer than I had money. So, off we went, two people and one pair of lips, walking around hand in hand. Steve did most of the talking. He was a rather verbose talker. I'd try to get a word in, and sometimes he would listen, but only so he could relate it back to himself. We were only fifteen minutes into our walk when I admitted to myself that I was beyond bored, but getting out of the house was nice.

Eventually, Steve asked if I wanted to sit at a table across the street in front of a bar. We made our way over and sat down. I waited for him to ask me if I wanted a drink.

"Are you going to get anything to drink?" I asked.

"Nah," he casually responded. He sat there with one hand in his rusty jeans and another clinging to his phone. While he wasn't using it, he kept tapping the screen to ensure it was on.

"Waiting to hear from someone?" I asked. Part of me was joking, but another part was genuinely hoping that some kind of emergency would give us a reason to call it an early night.

"Nah." He shrugged. "I'm just waiting on my dealer."

"I'm sorry?"

"My weed guy," he explained. "You toke up, right?"

"Um . . . yeah. Yes, yeah, I do." I was stunned, but it was all beginning to make sense. Walking around, not-so-aimlessly, sitting on the corner in front of a seedy bar. That was it for me. While Steve started telling some boring story about some great show he and his band put on a few weeks prior, I pretended to care by nodding while ordering a Lyft. When he got to the part about their alleged encore performance, my car had pulled up.

"All right, I'm out of here!" I exclaimed. I was so proud of myself for making a smooth exit that I barely noticed Steve's look of disappointment.

"Wow, just like that? Can I call you?"

"I don't know." I shrugged. "I mean, this was fun. But maybe we should cut our losses." Steve stood up to me and walked closer. I extended my right hand, ready to give him a shake, but he took his pudgy hands and used them to grab my waist. *Not him wanting a hug,* I thought. But it was worse than that. He took his lipless mouth and pressed it onto my face. The next thing I knew, a tongue and a beard pressed against my lower lip, thrashing against my chin. I quickly pulled away, my eyes bulging out of my head.

"Whyyyy did you do that, bro?" I asked, wiping off the saliva from my chin.

"Because you're hot!" He smirked. I stood there and gave him a look like I smelled a fart and ran into my Lyft.

"Yuck!" I shrieked once I sat in the backseat. The driver, a cute older Black guy, started laughing.

"Looks like you caught a bad catfish, huh, baby?" he snickered as we pulled off.

"Yeah, and it was poisonous with no lips." We both started laughing. For the rest of the ride, we talked about how strange the men downtown were and how I'd likely have better luck looking for a man from the Seventh or Ninth Ward. "You need a good man from the East." He was saying, *You need you a Black man.*

After sifting through the sludge of mediocrity of hetero males that dating apps had to offer, I finally found someone who seemed suitable. Marvin. Twenty-nine years old from New Orleans East. I would typically never date someone my junior. Still, after consulting with my therapist, I decided it was okay to make an exception because what I was looking for was . . . seasonal.

We met at Lily's, my favorite Vietnamese spot a few blocks from my apartment. He thought we were just on a date, but really, my kitty was just putting him through a minor preliminary check. She wanted to make sure he was hygiene-conscious, wouldn't fuck up my perfect pH balance, and that he wasn't a killer.

He was a lot cuter in person than his profile picture, which pleasantly surprised me. He was taller than me but not quite six feet. He had light brown skin with full, beautiful lips. His eyes were deep brown, and he had huge cheekbones. He wore his hair in cornrows that fell down to the nape of his neck.

I could tell by the way he looked at me that we were going to fuck. The pho hadn't even hit the table, and his goo-goo-eyed gaze was stuck on me. Obviously, he had good taste. I had my titties shoved up to my throat, and I was giving sex. But also, fat Black women are the bad bitch prototype in New Orleans.

It was my second date in almost eight years, and I felt so alive. We talked about our childhoods and giggled at how we held our chopsticks. I told him about the book I was working on and how much fun I had in New Orleans. He told me about his work as an Uber driver and his love for playing the trombone, an inherited talent that his father had taught him, and his father's father had taught him. He also told me about an eight-year relationship he had just gotten out of. As he talked, his tone got softer, and he stared into his pho more than my eyes, which I could tell was a sign of emotion he was keeping to himself.

"We had been engaged for a while, but, in the end . . . just couldn't make it work." He shrugged. As much as I was attracted to him, in that moment I was grateful that I wasn't actually falling for Marvin. His heart was with his ex, and, given the chance, that's where he'd prefer to be. I was just fine being his rebound. Ultimately, I was using him to get over someone too—I was getting over an outdated version of myself instead of someone else.

"So, what's next?" he asked, picking up the thirty-five-dollar check and slipping forty-five dollars into the checkbook. "Keep the change," he told the waiter when he came to pick up the bill.

"I mean . . ." I began, fake coy and shit. "We could go to a local bar. Or . . . we could get a bottle and go to my place. I live right up the street." My own forwardness took me aback. Back when I was a partier, this would have been pretty on-brand, but it felt like new territory for a girl who hadn't been back in the saddle in years. I had to remind myself that I wasn't a girl but a woman. One with her own place, career, and right to be as suggestive and forward as I pleased.

"I'ma tell you what I want to do when we get outside," he said with a smile. We stood up, and he rushed to the door to open it for me. Social Justice Tamela knew I should point out that her feminist ideology didn't welcome chivalrous behaviors like "ladies first" and door opening. But, soft, delicate Tamela hadn't had anyone do anything for her in such a long time, so a little chivalry was welcome.

We crossed the street, and I walked to the passenger side of his car, watching his shadow swallow mine whole against an oak tree. I turned to him, and he slowly leaned his body against mine until my back was pressed against the passenger door of his Jeep. His hands pressed against my waist, and not a single part of me flinched. He pulled my face toward his and slowly pressed his lips against mine. His lips, full and in control, sucked on my bottom lip. He gave me soft pecks on my cheek and then whispered, "Where do you think I want to take you?"

Once Marvin started the engine, Bootsy Collins filled the car with "I'd Rather Be with You." He had no idea that I love the old shit, that I'd moved to New Orleans because they worship all things old shit, all the things my daddy listened to while drinking. "I hope you don't mind the oldies," he said.

"I love it," I assured him. We headed to a liquor store on St. Charles and picked up a bottle of Casamigos and a pack of Dutches.

"Anything else?" the cashier asked.

"Do you have condoms?" I whispered.

"LET ME GET A BOX OF MAGNUMS!" This nigga was so loud, I couldn't tell if he was talking to Siri or trying to order from the store across the street. Still, I respected his excitement, as did Kitty.

We returned to my place, snuggled on the sofa, and turned on Netflix. Not even five minutes into finding something to watch, he started nibbling on my ear. My right hand found its way to his dick, and his lips moved from my ear, lips, neck, and tits.

"Let's take this to the bedroom." I giggled. When we got there, I made the first two of four announcements: 1. No street clothes on my bed, and 2. Hands must be washed before playing with my kitty.

While he headed to the bathroom, I pondered how necessary announcements three and four were. Announcement 3. I haven't had sex since niggas was dancing to "Hotel Bling," and announcement 4. These aren't my natural teeth.

He came back naked and clean, and I decided to wing it. We kissed and touched, letting our bodies take their time to know each other. Eventually, he pulled me to the edge of the bed, got on his knees, and buried his face between my legs. His tongue swiveled around my clit while I giggled nervously, then cooed with pleasure. Those full lips latched on to my clit and sucked the life out of me until I came.

"Are you okay with giving head?" he whispered. Such an unfair time to ask, seeing as how he just spent the past ten minutes buried between my legs. It felt like the prime moment for announcement number four, but I didn't want to ruin the mood. Horror stories from my denture support group crept into my mind, along with the taboo kink of a "gummy," euphoric head from a person with no teeth. Naturally, I was intrigued at the idea of something usually seen as a handicap enhancing my unicorn appeal. But . . . it felt too soon. So, I decided to test the waters and give faux tooth head.

Much to my surprise, it wasn't different at all. I did notice that I had to open my mouth wider than I used to back in the day, but seeing as how prosthetic teeth take up a substantial amount of space in the mouth, it's to be expected. Marvin moaned loudly and pulled My Body closer to him by wrapping his legs around me.

His dick was something beautiful. It was about seven inches long and thick, but not overwhelming. A few shades darker than his light-brown complexion with a slight curve to it. Once I got over my nerves, I began enjoying it. My confidence got the best of me at one point, and I attempted to deep-throat. At first, everything was fine, but as the tip of his circumcised penis pressed against my tonsils, it pulled back against the back of my upper denture. I felt it and am convinced he did too. As I looked up, I could see that his eyes, which were once closed, were now open and he was alert. I tried to play it off by licking his dick ravenously, yanking it, and moaning nonsensically.

The embarrassment I felt was akin to when I once farted in the supermarket, convinced that it would be a silent killer, and instead, it was a loud, boisterous gust of stinky wind with bass and baritone. I turned to see a young mother looking disgusted while her toddler son stood beside her, near tears. "Mommy, why she did that?"

When I finished, I hopped back on the bed. Marvin stood up, rock hard, and put on a Magnum. He wrapped his arms around my thick-ass thighs. He was about to slide it in, which, for some reason, felt like the perfect time for announcement three.

"I just want you to know that I haven't had sex in seven years and five months!"

"You lyin'." He gasped. His grip on my thighs loosened, but he didn't let go.

"No." I giggled nervously. "It's not a big deal. Just be . . . easy."

"That's why you get so wet?" he asked, biting his lower lip.

"Yes," I lied. The truth is that I just naturally get very wet. But I learned early that it does more for their ego to let them think it has something to do with their personal prowess.

Marvin pressed against me and slowly slid himself inside. It felt good . . . mostly. That curve, though. Just when I would get into the groove, the sharp poking of his tip would make me squeal, both of us unsure if it felt good or irritating. Still, he seemed to know how to move it.

We fucked for around fifteen minutes. I lay on my back on the edge of the bed with my legs wrapped around his shoulders while he fucked me standing up. Then I got on my stomach while he lay against my back. And, finally, it was him on his back, and I pressed against his body. The sex was exciting but tender.

Afterward, we curled under the covers and lay in each other's arms. I drifted to sleep, and he woke me up around midnight and said goodbye. He texted when he got home, as well as to say good morning the next day.

Not hearing from him for the remainder of the week, I sent a friendly check-in. I was surprised when my phone rang a few moments later.

"Hello?"

"THE FUCK YOU WANT WITH MARVIN, YOU OLD BITCH?!"

"Um . . . who is this?" I asked, though it was clear. Marvin had mentioned that he was just getting out of an eight-year relationship. It was clear that by "getting out," Marvin meant that the mothafucka was still in an eight-year relationship.

"BITCH, LEAVE MARVIN ALONE!"

"Girl! Relax." I was as calm as a cucumber but disappointed. I had a really good time with Marvin. He was tender, sweet, and attentive to my kitty. But my attachment to him was purely physical, thank goodness.

"HE DON'T EVEN WANT YOU, YOU DUSTY BITCH!"

"Baby, he wanted something. Also, are you the one who taught him how to nibble on the clit? Because he did it just so and—"

"BITCH, WHERE YOU LIVE AT?"

"You want to know where I live? Why? You want to fight me?"

"I WILL *DRAAAGGGGG* YOU, BITCH!" She said this with such deep intention that I found my hands on my neck, clutching my imaginary pearls.

"Let me tell you how to get to my place. Take Marvin's dick, hold it close to your ear, AND FOLLOW THE YELLOW BRICK ROAD, BITCH!"

Click.

The following Monday, I made an appointment with a local Black gynecologist.

FOR BLACK GIRLS
UNSHIFTING . . .
(Originally published in 2018 via Medium)

■

Hey, sis. Are you tired of policing your thoughts, behavior, and image? Are you starting to feel like you're not keeping it all the way . . . real? You may be suffering from a bad case of code shifting . . .

When I had something to say in white-centered spaces, I made sure there wasn't a single wrinkle in my name-brand blouse or stray hair popping out of my kitchen. I spoke with an English literature professor's diction and carried myself with Michelle Obama's poise. My neck didn't dare rotate, and I never spoke higher than my indoor voice. I filtered my opinion, sedated my conviction, and weeded out everything that nodded to a stereotype before parting my lips to speak. Code shifting is a lot of work.

Not to be mistaken with speaking properly or having manners, code shifting is a fluid behavior we take on to survive. It requires intentional distance from the race, ethnicity, and culture we were born into. Ultimately, it's a universal experience faced by many Black and Brown people, especially those forced to navigate white environments. However, no group of humans is more pressured to fall into the white-passing formation than Black women and other Black marginalized genders. Code shifting is a way of escaping the many racial tropes that follow us. It only takes one misinterpreted action to assume that a Black woman has an attitude, is sexually reckless, poorly mannered, offensive, uneducated, etc.

To be fair, code-shifting—also referred to as cultural assimilation, has its benefits. For Black folks, it works best during job interviews and office hours, interactions with the police, on campus, applying for residency in apartment complexes and gated communities, and situations where staying alive and blending is a priority.

There comes a time when a Black person consciously detaches themselves from their *other* Self; that's usually when the process of unshifting begins. As liberating as unshifting is, it can be pretty scary. It requires intense emotional labor. There's no road map to direct you to your most organic Self. It requires a consistent dedication to listening to who you are beyond the white gaze and chains of respectability.

To help others who are emotionally prepared to begin their unshifting journey but don't know where to begin, here are some tips and tools to ease the process of unshifting.

STAY WELL READ

Audre Lorde. Melissa Harris-Perry. Brittney Cooper. Tamara Winfrey-Harris. Angela Y. Davis. Isabel Wilkerson. Assata Shakur. Terry McMillan. Zora Neale Hurston. These intellectual Olympians will take you by your literary hand and guide you through the path that leads to your most authentic, Blackest Self. Reading about Black women who understand the duality in our identity is a balm for the unshifting soul. Here's a few books written by Black women who will help you reroute back to yourself:

- *Shifting: The Double Lives of Black Women in America* by Charisse Jones and Kumea Shorter-Gooden, PhD.
- *Sister Outsider: Essays and Speeches* by Audre Lorde
- *Sister Citizen: Shame, Stereotypes, and Black Women in America* by Melissa Harris-Perry
- *The Sisters Are Alright: Changing the Broken Narrative of Black Women in America* by Tamara Winfrey-Harris
- *More Than Enough: Claiming Space for Who You Are (No Matter What They Say)* by Elaine Welteroth

SPEAK LESS AND PAY ATTENTION TO EVERYTHING

Rather than force yourself back to the *other* version of yourself in white-centered spaces, decide not to speak if you won't sound, act, or behave like You. This doesn't mean you should be rude, but you should show the utmost restraint around non-Black people during these crucial stages of unshifting. We don't owe anyone small talk, and we are by no means obligated to make them feel comfortable in our presence. Silence is a virtue, and when it comes to unshifting, it's a necessity.

GO ON A WHITE CLEANSE

Some may think that the idea of a white cleanse is radical, but some allow goats to sniff their butts while they appropriate yoga, so . . .

The objective of a white cleanse isn't necessarily to rid oneself of white people—entirely. For many of us, our interaction with them is unavoidable. That's why a white cleanse aims to center, amplify, and focus on uplifting and exploring Blackness as much as humanly possible. From the music you listen to, the people you hang out with, the food you eat, the stores where you shop, and the shows you watch. All. Black. Everything. Stay away from

Friends binge-watching or scrolling through those weird "Vote Blue No Matter Who!" Facebook groups.

When I did my first white cleanse, I went on a strict cultural diet, only allowing myself to indulge in music, art, and entertainment centered on Black women. I started my first one-week white cleanse in January 2017, and I'll be done . . . any day now.

GET INTO YOUR SCALP

There's no woman whose body is more political than that of one with unapologetic 4C coils. Whether you're team natural or about that bundle life, embrace your hair. It's literally the Blackest thing about us, and they're all going to die mad about it. Do you wear your hair in the style it's in because you love it or because it's . . . presentable?

Maybe you've been aching to do the big chop or had your eyes on a twenty-two-inch Brazilian lace front. Create a sacred ritual of massaging your scalp (mine looks like red wine, *Queen Sugar*, and my handheld scalp massager). Or sit your ass down for enough hours to get those Janet Jackson braids you've always wanted. Whatever look you go for, get into it. And not because people are less likely to get on your nerves, but because it's the hair you want to rock.

LEAN INTO US

During the embryonic stage of my unshifting, I had no Black girlfriends, which made my unshifting process even more challenging. To forge meaningful relationships with Black marginalized genders that reflected the person I was, instead of the old, assimilated version, I had to lead with intention and patience. I also had to divest from many ideas and judgments I had previously held toward Black women. I struggled to get along with Black women for the longest time and assumed it was because I was so "different." However, as I unshifted, I realized that I was giving them the outdated, white-approved version of myself, and most of them were simply uninterested and not having it. The more I discovered my authentic tone and Self, the easier it became to bond with other Black women.

For those who live and dwell in predominantly white spaces, do your best to seek the environments where we are. And until you find them, join as many offline meetups and online groups that are facilitated and cater to Black marginalized genders. Unshifting requires community, and there's no better support than your own kind.

FORGIVE YOURSELF, SIS

Every time you've allowed white paws to poke at your coils without smacking their hands will surely haunt you during the unshifting process. Long-lost memories of misogynoir, bias, and racial disparities will run laps in your brain. This is rough but also necessary.

I wasn't proud to admit how much I enjoyed playing up to the "exceptional token" trope, but I wouldn't be keeping it real if I didn't admit that I did. And rule number one about unshifting: always keep it real (or at least when it won't get you fired or incarcerated).

Be gentle with yourself as you revisit the times you chose to blend instead of resist. Remember that you would never have shifted if you didn't feel like you had to. Instead of beating yourself up about the past that you can't change, be grateful that you love yourself too much to pretend to be anyone else today.

CANCEL ANYONE WHO DOESN'T "GET" IT

When I first started unshifting, I wanted the world to know that there was a whole other me I had been suppressing—a me I hadn't even met yet. Sadly, a few "friends" couldn't understand the depth of the challenges I was experiencing. I found myself in a weird headspace anytime I was around these "friends" who refused to believe that code shifting was an actual thing that was eating me alive. I don't mess with those people anymore.

The process of unshifting is complex, isolating, and at times, incredibly emotional. The only friends you need during this process are those willing to hold space for you as you walk through this journey of self-discovery. You've been exposed to more than enough ridicule and gaslighting; you don't need any more during this delicate transitional period.

LET GO OF RESPECTABILITY

Those unspoken rules and codes that stifle our liberation and restrict our growth are cancer to our unshifting souls.

One of the most complex challenges with unshifting is recognizing how we have adopted and accepted respectability and acknowledging that it's bullshit. Respectability politics police Black women, restricting us from exploring cultural, intellectual, and artistic images of ourselves that would be deemed stereotypical. It also causes damage to our relationships and views of other Black women. When we adhere to respectability, we enforce it on others, making us feel entitled to label other Black girls and women with the same racial tropes we run from.

Unshifting allows Black women and femmes to embrace the reality that we are non-monolithic unicorns, unbeholden to tropes, stereotypes, or respectability. So, stop making fun of the Black woman who doesn't code shift and realize she is free.

TRUST THE PROCESS

There will be times when you want to return to the way you were. Maybe you'll miss your old friends or the habitual routine centered on being that "other" you. The closer you get to your organic Self, the more you realize that you didn't like things you thought you had and enjoy things that would have seemed foreign to the "other" you. You may find that the person you are, unshifted and organic, is too unfamiliar to your liking. Don't stop now, sis. There's a breakthrough that's bound to bloom from this breakdown.

Unshifting is scary, and it's supposed to be. Most people live and die trying to fit in and blend. It's worth the moments of confusion and second-guessing during this process. There's something at the end of unshifting that every Black woman deserves: her fullest Self.

Care, Community & Activism

∎

*E*ven though we're only two decades into the twenty-first century, we've already encountered two major social justice movements that have shifted our cultural landscape: The Black Lives Matter movement, which led the way for the 2020 racial uprising, and the Me Too movement. Both movements, which eventually went global, were founded and led by Black marginalized genders. While the world benefitted and, in many ways, was entertained by these separate fights for equality, those who had their boots planted on the ground faced levels of violence, vitriol, and even death.

What becomes of the community who has no one to depend on but themselves when it comes to their safety and rights? And what about the activist whose personal stand leads to collective liberation? How can we effectively move forward in our fight for equality if we still struggle to see one another as equals?

Care, Community & Activism is about the lives, movements, and communities who have, despite the grimmest of odds, found ways to not only advocate but also, in turn, make the world a better place for them as well as us.

CASA DE TAMI: SHEVONE

Shevone Torres

■

BLACK AMERICAN AND INDIGENOUS WOMAN – SHE/THEY – AGE: 42 –
LOCATION: NEW JERSEY

'm telling you right now, Tamela! Make me take another step,
and I'ma punch you in your fuckin' gut!"

Shevone Torres and I were on her second day at Casa de Tami.
It had been going great—at first. But the moment we hit the sand,
she started getting weird.

"I'm not gettin' in that water," she kept repeating as we searched
for the ideal spot to spread out our blankets and beach bags. Her
hair, jet black and super curly, was pushed back with a headband,
and she was rocking a really cute blue-and-pink bathing suit.

"Relax. You're going to love it," I assured her. Looking back, I
probably should have taken her declaration more seriously. However, she checked the *yes, I'd like to add beach and swimming to
my wellness itinerary* box on her assessment form. She was also
from Jersey, so I assumed she'd spent a weekend or two at the
Jersey Shore. I couldn't have been more wrong. It took fifteen
minutes just to convince her to get knee-deep in the water.

"Let's just take a breath and a step at a time," I kept encouraging. I lightly held on to her fingertips, slowly taking baby steps so tiny I was sure she wouldn't notice. She noticed.

"Nigga, you can *breathe* all you want! I, Shevone, am not gettin' deeper in this water! Hoe."

It would have been hard to tell at this moment, but Shevone and I were, and still are, very good friends. Like Holly, we met on social media, but our friendship evolved into an in-person dynamic soon after. If I wasn't going to Jersey to check in with her, she was coming to New York to see me. She even helped moderate several online spaces I facilitated, helping me navigate the nuances of holding equitable and safe spaces for people.

Through her, I learned the importance of being self-aware of the privileges and energy I bring into a room. Despite being a person who navigates a marginalized intersection, I embody a unique combination of privileges, such as two supportive parents who have always provided shelter and resources when I lacked, as well as the societal perk of assimilating, moving through mainstream and white spaces that are more abundant with access to valuable resources. Understanding these privileges doesn't invalidate my life experience or make me less.

For as long as I'd known her, Shevone's life was centered around two things: her two sons and activism. The real frontline shit—the dangerous part of the movement that leads to direct interaction with the pigs, getting doxxed, and incarceration. When she wasn't flying around the country for random protests or injustices that any given Black person faced, she was collaborating with a local Black organization that regularly held protests against their county's police force as well as state officials. She'd been arrested several times in the four years that I'd known her.

I have been a staunch believer that Black people should stay as far away from anybody's "frontlines" as humanly possible—most especially Black marginalized genders. I believe that the dangers we face on a regular basis, the perpetual fear of murder and incarceration, has put too much strain on our already compromised well-beings. This couldn't be truer for Shevone, who lives with sickle cell anemia and idiopathic chronic pancreatitis. When she wasn't fighting for justice in the streets, she was fighting for her life in the emergency room.

In February 2019, after a series of complications and medical neglect, Shevone was hospitalized and in need of expensive medication along with financial assistance to help cover her bills, as she was immobile to hustle as she normally did. I, along with a collective of other Black marginalized genders, fundraised the money through social media. It was a small action as far as we were concerned, but it was also the kind that helped people like Shevone get the medical treatment and resources she needed, as well as people like me maintain housing.

I've never been the kind of person who references the acts of kindness I've done for someone else. However, when scrolling through my Facebook feed and seeing a video of Shevone screaming through a bullhorn while marching down the street less than one week after getting discharged from the hospital, I felt some kind of way.

"Was that a throwback video of you protesting in the street?" I intentionally FaceTimed instead of our normal text message mode, knowing it would throw her off.

"Yeah." She sighed. She went on to explain the situation that led to the protest.

"Do you feel like being there for those people, for that situation that's going to exist whether you're dead or alive was more important than your health?" As I look back, a small flash of guilt comes over me for being so harsh with my friend. But, also, the memories of praying for her life at my altar touch me too.

Years later, the two of us stood in the water, face-to-face with a fear Shevone didn't even know she had.

"We could just . . . stand here and let the water splash on our legs!" I suggested. When somebody forewarns that they'll resort to bodily harm, I believe them. I was still determined for Shevone to experience a proper dip in the Atlantic, but I knew not to push too hard.

We stood there in silence. I figured Shevone was still contemplating if she was going to punch me. But then, her vibe shifted. Her chin quivered, and the puddles in her eyes grew. The gentle splashes of warm water against her bare skin sent her over the edge.

"You know what? Let's not even focus on the step part!" I encouraged. "Let's just breathe, girl!"

A gasp of air passed through her mouth, and her shoulders collapsed. I considered walking her back to our beach blanket and calling it a day. Water therapy does wonders for a stressed body, but nothing is therapeutic about being scared to death. I was still debating, and Shevone was still quivering, when two small brown children splashed their way between us. They couldn't have been older than six or seven. The same waves that splashed against our knees delighted the kids as it practically swallowed them.

"See." I grinned, pointing at the children. "Fun! Swimming is fun. I promise!" It would take another ten minutes of "*a breath and a step,*" but eventually, Shevone was waist-deep in the water. And then, breast-deep. Each time she got a little deeper, it was as if she had amazed herself.

"I feel like I could float if I wanted to," she said, bobbing up and down, taking huge gasps of breath before plunging her body to the ocean floor. Soon enough, she was wading around, her head barely poking above the water. For hours, we jumped.

Swayed. Floated. Splashed. Exhaled. We laughed at nothing at all. We surrendered to the current, allowing us to do the one thing that was too dangerous to do on dry land: let go.

Hours later, over mojitos and Cuban food, we reflected on how necessary it was to exist in moments not reliant on our sacrifice. We didn't have to campaign to have a good time; we could go and have one. Like me, Shevone had been programmed to believe that joy, rest, and adventure had to be "earned." Societal and cultural standards expect us to appear as Mammies, mules, and fixers. These tropes have such a significant impact on the lives we live, we inhabit their characteristics without even realizing it. By enjoying nature, air, and life, we're resisting in the most radical way possible.

As the mojitos kicked in and our coils bounced back, Shevone opened up about the stress she'd been carrying from intense community organizing. The never-ending conflicts from a male-led organization constantly challenged her boundaries, skills, and needs.

I told her there was more than one way to pursue liberation and that it should never involve us showing up as a sacrifice. I also reminded her about how many Black marginalized genders have died giving to movements that have yet to protect or even respect them. Marsha Johnson. Erica Garner. Venida Browder. Sandra Bland. Korryn Gaines. Oluwatoyin Salau. To their last breath, each one of them sacrificed all they had for a movement that cost them their life. I didn't want that for Shevone or anyone. I don't need bloodshed to be free.

"The thing is that I don't have a lot of time left," Shevone responded. "It's important that I do as much work toward my mission as possible to continue to create change, even when I'm not here."

"What is your mission?" I asked.

"I want to open up a space called Imperfect Village that provides resources and aids in building community by collecting its fractured parts." She started perking up, and her eyes widened as she spoke. She had so many ideas for Imperfect Village, so many resources she was ready to organize and provide for her community.

For the remainder of Shevone's stay we had a really good time. I showed her around Miami, specifically Little Havana. We did some light shopping and sightseeing, but most of our time was spent at the one place where she wanted to be: the beach.

I MADE A WAY

■

by Shevone Torres

■

I'm not one who got into activism because it was cool. I fight for my rights. Literally, it's something I've had to do my entire life as a Black woman, so there's nothing new or strange about doing it now regularly.

Activism is essential to me because there are so many racist, ableist, queer-hating systems of oppression that need to be dismantled, and we don't all have the capacity to stand up against them. I'm one of the people with the capacity, so I rarely stay seated.

Before I got to Casa de Tami, I knew the problems I had with leadership at the organization I was a member of were severe, but I didn't want to admit how bad it was. A lot of infighting, patriarchal bullshit, and toxic dynamics made it hard to focus on the work and center liberation. How can we get liberated if we're constantly coming at each other?

I know how serious Tami is about self-care and mindfulness, so I was ready for meditation and hydration. I needed it, so it was welcome. But I wasn't expecting to have my comfort level pushed the way it was at the beach. I said I was interested in the ocean but didn't realize how uninterested I thought I was until the plane started flying over Florida and I saw all that blue water. *No, thank you,* was my first thought. It looked pretty, but that's because you can't see the sharks and undercurrent.

Looking at that body of water reminded me of when I was a kid and went swimming with friends and family. At one point, I almost drowned. Thankfully, there was someone around who could swim, and they saved me. I must have buried that memory deep in the back of my mind because I didn't remember it until I was on that plane.

By the time we reached the beach, I was in full PTSD mode from that near-drowning. I love Tam to death, but I was serious when I said I wasn't taking another step. It wasn't until those kids started splashing around and Tam said, "Come on, let's live" that I realized something. I get emotional admitting this, but I'd been so consumed with death that living was just happening before death for most of my life. When you've got a severe and life-threatening illness, you are not thinking about where you're going to be when you're eighty; you get to work on what you want from life right now. When I finally let go and went into the deep part of the ocean, I let go of all those fears and thoughts of death. I was alive, and I was well. The high I got from being in that water was unlike anything I had ever hit off a blunt. My Body felt healthy too!

I've always had someone push me into leading something, taking over something. I never really had anyone push me to do something fun for me. It was such a thrill.

When I returned to Jersey, I could only think about the beach. I started Googling all these different cities and countries with amazing beaches—the Caribbean, Mexico, Central America. I wanted more of that experience. The thought of going somewhere exotic and tropical excited me for a while, but life got in the way. I went back to protesting and organizing and the same old routine. But then, about three months after I returned home, something changed. There was a conflict in the organization I was a part of. It wasn't even a big deal, but it was something that proved to me that their objective and mine had become totally different. So when somebody asked me to do something, I said, "Nah, I'm out." Just like that! I didn't even feel sorry about it. I felt like, seeing as I don't know how much time I have left, I can't be playing around in spaces that take up time but don't offer any real change.

I need to be a part of communities serious about caring for one another. I realize now that my time and my spirit are best served in spaces where I am offering direct care and support to my people. I will always be Shevone, an activist. But, I will also be Shevone, the human. I understand now that my activism can change and expand over the years and shouldn't come at the expense of my happiness or livelihood.

That's what inspired me to get Imperfect Village Org started. I finally did it—I am the proud founder and president of a nonprofit that provides for the community everything from holiday meals to book bags and school supplies.

I also work as a drug outreach volunteer helping people who struggle with substance abuse. It's not easy, and even when I can help someone off the brink of death, I still worry about them and hope they'll be okay. But, at least in that moment, I'm there for them, and it's help that I know they need, whether they want to take it or not.

Since I've taken a big step back from frontline activism, my health has stabilized. I haven't been in the hospital in almost a year, and for the most part, I feel healthy. Of course, my illnesses aren't curable, but at least, at this point, they're managed, which is the most I can ask.

The most shocking thing about my life that's changed since my stay at Casa de Tami is my love life. At the time, I was in a dead-end relationship with someone more of a comfort than an actual companion. Someone who was around because we were used to being around each other. But, as I started changing my life, I cut off much of my access to that person. And then, one day, I decided to check out one of those dating sites. I don't know what I thought I was looking for, but I was looking for something. What I found was Matthew.

On the one hand, we had a lot of things in common in every day—little things like food and music. But for the most part, we are really different. For starters, he's Asian. Never in my life did I see myself dating outside my race, but here I am! Plus, Matthew lives all the way in California. When we started talking, I was like, "Oh, so we never going to meet, huh?" And then he told me he would fly me out and take care of my lodging. I thought he was playing at first, but he kept pressin' it. So, after a while, I was like, "Book that flight, and I'll show up." He booked it, and I showed up.

I've made several trips to California, and I love it there. It's beautiful, it's spacious, it's clean. And, of course, I love spending time with Matthew. He's not my first partner, but he's definitely the first man who's been attentive to my needs, listened to my opinions, and taken care of me. It's not easy to trust people, especially men. But I definitely trust him. He has my best intention at heart, and I love him for that.

I knew it was real the day he took me to the beach. I had only been back to the beach a few times since I'd come home from Casa de Tami. I heard about West Coast beaches being different, but I was blown away. I mean, I thought it was beautiful. And being able to enjoy it with my partner felt really special.

I take everything a day at a time, but in most moments, I'm doing really well. Life still isn't easy, but at least I'm not afraid to live anymore.

ME TOO . . .
BUT WHO ALL GONE BE THERE?

■

"Nobody's free until everybody's free."

—FANNIE LOU HAMER

We like our activists to be sanitized, perfect, and, above all, palatable to the white gaze. Mainstream activists must balance advocating for the disenfranchised while winning the graces of the disassociated. It's messed up, but that's how it's always been.

There's a level of pageantry an activist must navigate to gain the respect of both their communities and the powers that be; the categories include respectability, adherence, able-bodied, desirability—bonus points for racial ambiguity.

What happens to the people of the movement who, despite existing outside the margins of respectable-approved intersections, have something to give? For two significant movements, The Alabama Bus Boycott and #MeToo, the answer was simple: replace them.

Claudette Colvin and Tarana Burke gave everything they had to a movement they knew would uplift the collective they were part of. For Claudette Colvin, it was remaining seated on that segregated Montgomery, Alabama, bus in 1955—nine months before Rosa Parks would also be arrested. And Tarana Burke is responsible for #MeToo—from the hashtag to the framework. Yet, when a second-wave Me Too movement emerged a decade later, this time fronted by two-thirds of the cast of *Charmed*, it was as if someone took a perfect potato salad and ruined it with raisins.

Is it ever okay to adjust the goalpost to meet white-gaze-approved standards? How far can a movement go if those in positions of power prioritize respectability politics over people? Can a movement even move if it isn't intersectional? Let's get into it.

PART I:
SHOUT-OUT TO
CLAUDETTE COLVIN

"To me, it doesn't bother me not being named. As long as we have someone out there so we can tell our story."

—*Claudette Colvin*

Just as Detroit was the home of Motown, and Oakland was the breeding ground of radical Black activists, Alabama was the flagship state of the Civil Rights Movement. Even though Black Christian males traditionally led activism efforts, the state's youth were rising in representation. As the NAACP expanded, they created a student council, giving Black teenagers education, resources, and communal support to help them push back against the Jim Crow laws that stagnated the generation of Black Americans before them. Children shouldn't have to be educated on protecting themselves from police and white supremacists, but America had proven that not even Black children were safe from white terrorists. An example of the injustices Black children faced was the case of Jeremiah Reeves.

· · ·

SOMEBODY'S SON

In one of two well-known photos of young Jeremiah, he's sitting in a chair with his long, lean legs crossed. He appeared to be wearing a conk hairstyle, popular for Black folks in the 1950s. He's looking away from the camera with a cigarette dangling from his left hand. Dark skin, thick lips, and curious chestnut eyes. His young face, drawn in by a so-serious, almost melancholy expression, screams beauty and youth.

Jeremiah was a senior at Booker T. Washington High School, one of two segregated schools for Black students in Montgomery. He was also a drummer in a jazz band. He was known for his style and warm, charismatic personality and also for balancing his studies, his passion for music, and his work.

Employed as a delivery boy for a local grocery store, the young teen made stops for several white customers in Montgomery. One of them was Mabel Ann Crowder. During a delivery in the summer of 1951, neighbors would catch an image of Mabel and Jeremiah undressing together in her home.

There's little information available about Mabel regarding her age and marital status at that time, but what is clear is that she was an adult. Many Black people in the community had already suspected the two had a consensual ongoing affair. However, at just sixteen, on the weaker end of the power dynamic between adult and child and white woman and Black boy, it's fair to assume that Jeremiah was more victim to the entanglement than he was the pursuer. Of course, the politics of white supremacy held no space for Jeremiah's humanity, let alone his youth. So, upon realizing that their intimacy was no longer secret, Mabel cried rape.

The young teen was immediately arrested, taken to Kilby Prison, and detained overnight. During this time, police officers put the teenager through a cruel interrogation, forcing him to sit in Yellow Mama, the prison's nickname for their faulty electrocution chair. Under the extreme fear of meeting his fate with electrocution, Jeremiah was forced to say that he had not only raped Mabel but several other women as well. Under great duress, he provided the false confession. He would recant it almost immediately, but the damage had been done. Jeremiah Reeves was convicted and sentenced to death after a trial that lasted only two days, followed by a jury deliberation of under half an hour.

Claudette Colvin watched sixteen-year-old Jeremiah get carried away by Montgomery police, never to see the free light of day again. She was crushed by the injustice Jeremiah was facing, whom she considered a friend. "When I was in the ninth grade, all the police cars came to get Jeremiah," she recalled in a 2020 interview with *The Guardian*.

PARTY OF ONE

As an NAACP Youth Council member, she deeply understood the inhumanity of Jim Crow laws and the urgency of standing against them. And as a Black girl growing up in Montgomery, she knew the power white people had due to Jim Crow had to end. Nearly four years after Jeremiah's conviction, he still sat in jail facing the death penalty, while the NAACP and local activists raised funds for Jeremiah's legal fees and campaigned for his freedom. Among his advocates was a newly appointed minister of Montgomery's Dexter Avenue Baptist church, Dr. Martin Luther King Jr.

By the time Claudette was fifteen, she wasn't just hyperaware of the injustices of her and her people—she was fed up. At their best, Jim Crow laws were a nuisance. Restricting Black Americans from establishments and resources and using the threat of violence to enforce said restrictions made even the simplest of tasks challenging for Black people.

"You had to take a paper bag, draw an outline of your foot, and take that to a shoe store to get shoes," Claudette explained in an NPR interview. By the time she was fifteen, Jim Crow laws were regulating every Black liberty it could get its hands on, creating ridiculous decrees that upheld stereotypes about Black people that maintained our second-class status.

After wrapping up a month-long celebration of Negro history at her high school, Claudette stared out the window of the bus on her way home from school, marinating on stories learned about Sojourner Truth and Harriet Tubman. When the bus driver demanded that Claudette sit in the back of the bus and give her seat to a white woman, the teenager remained seated. "My head was too full of Black history, the oppression that we went through," she said. "It was as if Harriet Tubman's hand was pushing me down on the one shoulder, and Sojourner Truth's was pushing me down on the other." As she sat unmoved, white passengers berated her, attempting to convince her that, by law, she had to give up her seat. "You gotta move! You gotta move!" they yelled at her. This only fueled the teen more. "I felt like, this was my time to take a stand for justice," she said.

Claudette may have only been a teenager, but her righteous indignation toward Jim Crow laws could match any radical activist in her era. "It's my constitutional right!" she repeated, as two officers handcuffed her, dragged her off the bus, and placed her in jail. Claudette was charged and convicted of violating segregation laws, disturbing the peace, and assaulting a police officer.

Later that evening, she was bailed out of jail by her pastor. When she returned home, her father sat at the kitchen table with a shotgun. "The KKK is not going to take you out tonight," he told his daughter.

Claudette was not the first Black woman to refuse to get in the back of the bus—and, of course, she was not the last either. But her solo protest was unique because she walked away with more than a fine. Her case was ideal for dismantling the Jim Crow law that dictated where and how many Black people were allowed on a city bus. One would think that the young teenager's actions would have been met with support and gratitude. Unfortunately, that would not be the case for Claudette.

"They [local civil rights leaders] wanted someone, I believe, who would be impressive to white people, and be a drawing. You know what I mean? Like the main star. And they didn't think that a dark-skinned teenager, low income without a degree, could contribute," she said. The Black leadership Colvin referred to was Montgomery's NAACP chapter.

There was a pattern of preference among the civil rights movement leaders—male-led, Christian, and light-skinned. The idea was that to capture white America's attention and respect, we had to present ourselves in a perfect image of Black dignity. By centering irrelevant traits like skin tone and ambiguity, those who didn't fit the aesthetic or pedigree were deemed less valuable to the movement. This proved true when Black leadership passed on the opportunity to continue supporting Claudette and using her as the face of the bus boycott. Gwen Patton, a Montgomery activist who volunteered during the bus boycott, said, "It was partly because of her color and because she was from the working poor."

Claudette may have been a revolutionary, but she was also a dark-skinned girl from the hood. In her teenage years, her family lived in King Hill, one of the rougher, segregated areas of Montgomery. "Middle-class Blacks look down on King Hill," she said of her hometown. "We have unpaved streets and outside toilets."

Not long after her arrest, Claudette became pregnant. A poor, dark-skinned, fifteen-year-old soon-to-be mother was short of the perfect victim they sought. Instead of continuing to amplify Claudette's case, they decided to wait nine months for another woman, one who was more mature, lighter, and primetime ready.

THE LOOK

Nine months after Claudette refused to sit in the back of the bus, Rosa Parks would do the same. Only this time, the NAACP and Montgomery civil rights leaders would back Rosa and make her case the catalyst for the Montgomery Bus Boycott, which began shortly after Rosa's arrest. At the time, Rosa Parks had spent years deeply invested in activism and education within the NAACP, and at one point was somewhat of a mentor for Claudette. She was married, light-skinned, mature, and college-educated. Dr. King said of Rosa Parks, "Her character was impeccable and her dedication deep-rooted." In other words, Rosa was the perfect victim.

The concept of the perfect victim is to use the injustice against an individual with an impeccable background who could not be proven wrong or deserving of their mistreatment in any way, shape, or form. The hope is that, in an effort of proving the victim in question, in this case, Rosa Parks, is upstanding, culturally assimilated, and therefore worthy of equity, the wrong doers have no choice but to take accountability for their actions. The issue with the perfect victim strategy is that it still places people who navigate marginalized intersections in positions that force us to "prove" that we were undeserving of whatever wrong happened to us. It's also why innocent victims of heinous crimes are portrayed as assailants instead of victims. Even Trayvon Martin's youthful misgivings were used to manipulate his character and distort the innocent teenager into a thug.

By playing into the ideology that one must live an exemplary life in order to be deemed a victim, society leaves the door open for countless people who are excluded from all forms of justice and retribution simply because their lives are not in formation of respectability politics and assimilation. For Claudette, that meant, despite being a revolutionary, that she was not valued by the very people she advocated with and for. The result was a series of hardships and isolation.

Rosa Parks's arrest would jump-start the Montgomery Bus Boycott. Like Neil Armstrong, Jackie Robinson, and all the other firsts highlighted in the history books, Rosa would become the poster activist for not only the civil rights movement but the feminist movement as well. She would reach an iconic level of fame and reverence—all of which was deserved. When it came to liberation, Rosa was loyal to the soil. Still, it was Claudette's case that would legally dismantle bus segregation in the state of Alabama.

One year after her arrest, Claudette would serve as a plaintiff in the Supreme Court's groundbreaking *Browder v. Gayle* case, along with three other plaintiffs, all Black women from Montgomery who refused to move to the back of the bus. The women were Aurelia S. Browder, Susie McDonald, and Mary Louise Smith (Ware). When Claudette was cross-examined, under oath, as to why she stopped riding buses the first day of the national bus boycott, her tone and frankness were just as unwavering as her mission to dismantle a racist law: "Because we were treated wrong, dirty, and nasty." Many have said that Claudette's testimony was the most succinct and effective at calling out the insidiousness of white supremacy and Jim Crow laws.

The case resulted in a ruling that the Fourteenth Amendment classified bus segregation as unconstitutional. The moment marked the beginning of the end of segregation and Jim Crow laws. At only sixteen, Claudette had taken on the city of Montgomery, the state of Alabama, the American judicial system, and Jim Crow itself.

Claudette's contribution to the Civil Rights Movement should have been met with unwavering gratitude and support. Sadly, because she fell short of being the perfect victim, she was ostracized from her community and under the constant fear of retaliation. In the fall of 2021, Claudette Covin returned to Montgomery, Alabama, to file for her 1955 charge of resisting arrest being sealed, expunged, and destroyed. After more than six decades, Claudette was still on probation. In her affidavit, she wrote the full story of her experience on that day she got arrested, the impact, as well as her opinions on where we are today regarding racial justice.

FROM THE BOYCOTT TO THE BRONX

After getting kicked out of high school, Claudette eventually got a GED, which did little in helping her gain employment. The teen's reputation preceded her. The most accessible hustle, domestic work, scared her the most. "You never know who's in the Klan," she said. The thought of being in the belly of the beast, only for them to learn that she was a radical activist against white supremacy, prevented her from even considering that kind of work. Claudette lived in a state of fear that rape and/or murder would find her, and that it would most likely come from the Ku Klux Klan. "I didn't want to be in those people's homes."

To avoid them as much as possible, she decided to work in the food service industry. However, after finding out that she was "that nigger," she was quickly fired. "I was notorious, and hiring me was a liability."

After five years of toughing it out in Montgomery, she took off to New York, in the Bronx. Now the mother of two sons, she left for the North in hopes of providing her family with a better life and more opportunities. She fell into community with the local Jamaican women and worked as a domestic there. "But we unionized with 1199," she noted proudly.

It was in those early days in New York that Claudette made the decision to reimagine herself without the binding limitations of her old Southern identity. The reality was, outside the Deep South's control of Black people's lives, New York was a place where the cloud of white supremacy didn't hover so low. "The American South was like South Africa apartheid back then," she said. "My Jamaican friends were used to riding the subways with all different races, and there were no segregation laws. They simply would not have understood giving up your seat and that white people could be so evil."

Though she moved away, she would continue to visit Alabama during the summer to see her family. And, while the reunions were welcomed, the fear of retaliation shook Claudette's parents. "I know they were terrified every time I came home because I was on probation from the court, and they were afraid of the consequences for having me there."

When leaders of the civil rights movement played Claudette by not giving her the flowers she so deserved, they played themselves and compromised the integrity of the movement. It's nearly seventy years after the Montgomery Bus Boycott, and American activism is still steeped in the performance of respectability. The same NAACP that ridiculed Hattie McDaniel instead of advocating for her is the same organization that left Claudette Colvin in the wind. The eras, locations, and circumstances are different, but the objective is identical: center those who are aesthetically appealing and socially favorable and put the rest of *them* in the back.

The impact from upholding respectability will always deliver the highest consequences to the most vulnerable within respective communities. When it comes to activism, Black women and other marginalized genders will always be a target.

Time can't undo the missed opportunities to uplift and center Claudette Colvin for her tremendous contribution to the greatest social justice movement of the twentieth century. However, we can do our part by not only remembering her place in history but also amplifying it every chance we get. Shout-out to Claudette Colvin.

PART II: ME WHO?

■

*"The glare of Hollywood and social media won't provide a
pathway for that to happen; only we, in our community, can forge
that path, and so I stay and keep on trying."*

—TARANA BURKE, *Unbound: My Story of Liberation and
the Birth of the Me Too Movement*

About thirty-seven years after Claudette Colvin's winning lawsuit against the state of Alabama for their discrimination, another young revolutionary would rise in the deep South. She, too,
would be motivated by injustices to Black Americans and spear-
head a movement that would change the landscape of American
activism and civil rights. Her name is Tarana Burke.

Just as the unlawful arrest and death sentence of Jeremiah
Reeves motivated Claudette Colvin to take a stand, Tarana would
also be moved into action because of the unjust treatment of
Black people. Only this time, they lived on the other side of the
country.

It was the spring of 1991 when Rodney, along with two passengers,
was pulled over by five officers from the Los Angeles Police Department. What followed was a brutal beating, with Rodney experiencing the worst of it. Police brutality has never been a secret
within the Black community; however, it was caught on videotape

this time. The footage circulated throughout the globe for all to see. An unarmed Black man was mercilessly attacked by police officers with batons, tasers, and guns.

Just two weeks after the Rodney King beating, fifteen-year-old Latasha Harlins would walk into one of her local grocery stores and never walk out again. Latasha wanted to purchase some juice. When the store owner, forty-nine-year-old Korean American Soon Ja Du, accused Latasha of trying to steal, they had a heated exchange. Despite the young teen holding the money she intended to pay in her hand, Du grabbed Latasha by her sweater and snatched her backpack. After Latasha broke away and attempted to leave, Du reached under the counter, pulled out a revolver, and shot Harlins in the back of the head, killing her instantly.

One year after the beating of Rodney King, a jury acquitted all four officers charged with assault and excessive force.

Two Black people violently attacked, both caught on tape, and one resulted in the murder of a fifteen-year-old Black girl. Tarana wasn't havin' it. A college student at Alabama State University, the verdict snapped her into action, and she immediately began planning a protest.

After searching around campus for students who were as incensed as she was, the young college student grew underwhelmed by her peers' indifference at the unfolding of racial injustices. The Bronx-born teen had already been involved in protesting and organizing back home in New York City, from the murder of Yusuf Hawkins to understanding the nuances behind the Central Park Jogger case. Los Angeles was a long way from the Bronx, and other students may not have been as viscerally affected as she was, but for Tarana, seeing the footage of each assault "made it feel like our backyard."

Tarana created handwritten fliers that said, *IF YOU ARE ANGRY ABOUT RODNEY KING AND LATASHA HARLINS,*

MEET ME IN FRONT OF THE MAIN DINING HALL TO-MORROW AT 12 P.M. Then, she cut her long black jersey cotton headwrap into strips. She headed to the main dining hall with a crew, her fliers, and the black strips of cotton. She encouraged everyone to attend the impromptu rally she was facilitating—one she'd yet to organize. Tarana also encouraged her peers to wear the black cloth around their right arms to show solidarity for Rodney King and Latasha Harlins.

Ultimately, Tarana cofacilitated a successful rally. School officials were involved, as were several school organizations, and even the press showed up. This wasn't necessarily new for Tarana, who had been engaged in activism before relocating to Alabama. Still, she proved to herself and others that she had the power to organize and execute a successful call to action effectively. It couldn't bring back the life of Latasha Harlins or convict the thugs who beat up Rodney King, but she galvanized people into action when they were otherwise complacent. It was just the beginning.

Five years later, still in Alabama, Tarana would serve as a youth camp leader. It was there that she forged a relationship with a young Black girl, Heaven. Over the course of that summer, Tarana was a friend, mentor, and safe adult for the twelve-year-old. But, when Heaven revealed that she was the victim of molestation, Tarana became distant and withdrawn. Despite her love for the young girl, her confession triggered memories of her experiences with molestation. "I was not thinking about what I had to give to Heaven—just what I wanted to keep from her," she wrote in her 2021 memoir, *Unbound: My Story of Liberation and the Birth of the Me Too Movement.*

That missed opportunity to connect with Heaven about something so personal would haunt Tarana long after it happened. There were two words she wished she had said to Heaven, that, while it wouldn't have changed her trauma, would have assured her that she wasn't alone: *me too.*

The years and challenges would intertwine, and Tarana continued her community organizing and activism efforts. And the effects of sexual violence continued to appear in the lives of those she loved. Deeper than the hunt for a predator, what incensed her most was that sexual violence, unlike the terrorism that comes from police officers and white supremacy, was far more fluid and understood. Tarana recognized that the threat of sexual violence isn't just that which takes place between cubicles and office hours, but also on school buses among children, in churches among trusted elders, and at dinner tables with family members who choose to violate instead of protect.

By the time Tarana introduced Me Too into the public sphere in 2006, her mission was clear: loosen the tight grip that sexual violence had on Black women and girls by providing safe spaces to discuss, disclose, and have access to vital resources. The integrity-driven determination that drew in a crowd of supporters at Alabama State was the same energy she used to get the word out about Me Too. For years, she would attend panel discussions, rallies, and other spaces that welcomed her to speak on the importance of centering survivors when it comes to sexual violence.

According to the National Black Women's Justice Institute, "nearly 1 in 5 black women are survivors of rape, and 41% of black women experience sexual coercion and other forms of unwanted sexual contact." For every Black woman who reports rape, at least fifteen don't. By facilitating a communal space for Black women and girls to collectively grow forward, heal, and address the impact of their sexual traumas, Tarana was providing a powerful gift to those who were underserved and invalidated.

Over ten years after the Me Too movement, a second wave of Me Too emerged. This time it was led and endorsed by notable white women in Hollywood. This second wave got far more attention and notoriety than the original movement and fostered a global conversation about gender equality, consent, and sexual assault—especially at work. However, the Me Too redux fell short of liberation because it failed to center the marginalized victims.

THE BIG PIECE OF CHICKEN

The first issue with the Me Too redux was that it shifted the objective to the predator. It's always a good day when justice is served. However, with the leaders of the movement's second wave laser-focused on Fortune 500 predators, the likelihood of tangible, equitable justice trickling down to blue-collar work environments was slim to none.

Many men were dethroned from their positions of power, and many more were called out and challenged. However, Harvey Weinstein was the one target that all second-wave Me Too–ers were panini pressed to take down.

For decades, the celebrity producer was known for producing some of Hollywood's most lucrative films, as well as a few Broadway musicals. Behind closed doors, he was a maniacal rapist and sexual predator. More than eighty women would confess to being sexually assaulted by Weinstein. By the time he was charged with rape in 2018, he had already been kicked out of his own production company, as well as the Academy of Motion Picture Arts and Sciences. In 2020, he was found guilty and sentenced to thirty-nine years in prison.

Without question, Harvey Weinstein is a rapist turd who deserves every minute of discomfort that finds him. His conviction would become a major front-facing win for the second-wave movement, especially for actor Rose McGowan, whose stalling career was revitalized through the takedown and subsequent trial of Weinstein. It must have been challenging to face a media and judicial system, both steeped in patriarchal standards and culture, and challenge how it protects men who perpetuate sexual violence.

White women online were quick to reference finally shattering the glass ceiling. The metaphor often describes the moment patriarchal standards are dismantled, opening up to equitable work conditions for women and other marginalized genders. The phrase, while endeared among white women, has long been a term of contention for Black and Brown marginalized genders.

"They shatter the glass because they stood on our backs, and then we're supposed to sweep it up," a friend succinctly described. This is because the power dynamic between white women, Black women, and non-Black women of color has been disproportionately imbalanced for so long, with white supremacy keeping white women at the top at the expense of every other race of women, especially Black women. Just as the rays of light that beamed through the shattered glass of the ceiling shined brightest on white women, so too would the impact of the second wave of Me Too.

AIN'T I A VICTIM TOO?

In 2017, actor Aurora Perrineau filed a police report with the Los Angeles County Sheriff's Department. She confided that, several years prior when she was only seventeen, television writer and producer Murray Miller raped her. It happened one night when Perrineau, who's Black, went back to Murray's apartment, who was thirty-five at the time.

Aurora represented many survivors of sexual violence who spend years wrestling with the trauma in silence, until they're finally prepared to face the impact of their confession. Her career was rising as an actor. And, with a successful actor father, Harold

Perrineau, it must have been hard to walk into that sheriff's office and file a police report. It makes sense why Aurora would wait several years before going public with being raped, as well as why she would feel safe coming out with her experience during a time when Me Too was encouraging survivors to tell their stories and hold their victims accountable. Sadly, Aurora wasn't met with the support and justice that the second wave of the movement appeared to offer. Instead, she was questioned and discarded as being dishonest in her confession.

On the same day that the news broke about Aurora's charges against Murray, actor and producer Lena Dunham, along with the co-showrunner of her then HBO sitcom *Girls*, released a statement that defended Murray and blatantly discredited Aurora's confession. Their statement, which was printed and promoted by *The Hollywood Reporter*, acknowledged that the second wave of Me Too was welcoming in much needed conversations and actions that dismantled rape culture and addressed sexual violence. However, it went on to isolate Aurora's experience, mainly going as far as to say, "While our first instinct is to listen to every woman's story, our insider knowledge of Murray's situation makes us confident that sadly this accusation is one of the 3 percent of assault cases that are misreported every year."

Dunham could have used her influential platform to support a vulnerable victim of sexual assault, but she instead used it to discredit her. A little over a year after publicly denouncing Aurora's experience, she would once again use the media to center her opinion, this time to admit to lying about having "insider information." The admittance of guilt didn't do much to her social standing, but for Black women, the damage had been done and our suspicions proven true; white women wanted to use the intellectual framework and praxis of the original Me Too, but they had no intention of doing right by Black women. The racist-fueled selectiveness white women led with is best described by Rachel Elizabeth Cargle, who coined it "white supremacy in heels."

Without Black and Brown marginalized genders—including those with physical disability and neurodivergence—any collective progress or wins within the second wave benefited only those of the intersection they represented.

TRANS WOMEN ARE WOMEN. PERIOD.

In the two years that Rose McGowan publicly spoke out about being sexually assaulted by Harvey Weinstein, she went from a well-known actor to an overnight activist, author, and influencer. Her social media platforms exploded with new followers and supporters. She became a go-to fixture for all topics regarding Me Too and Harvey Weinstein and would go on to write a memoir and star in an *E! Television* limited series. Unlike other successful movements of the past, the second wave of Me Too relied on white women from Hollywood that provided a level of familiarity matched with credibility. While it may be appealing at face value, the impact of relying on those who lack the experience, integrity, and dedication to lead change for a group of marginalized people truly means that the most vulnerable within that community will experience the harshest of impacts due to said inadequate leadership.

During an event in New York City to promote McGowan's book, *Brave*, activist Andi Weir spoke out in support of trans women, questioning McGowan's intentions on gender inclusion. "Trans women are in men's prisons, and what have you done for them?" she yelled.

"What have *you* done for women?" McGowan shouted back. An aggressive discourse unfolded, with Rose telling Andi to shut up and sit down. Once Weir was escorted out, Rose went on a tirade about not wanting to be labeled cisgender, white, or purple. Her treatment of Weir, along with the refusal to be referred to by the medical term "cisgender," was a telltale of the celebrity's trans-exclusionary radical feminist ideology, aka TERF.

All marginalized genders face increased risk of sexual violence, but for trans women, it's significantly higher. For trans women, the fight for safety doesn't end in predominantly cisgender women-led spaces.

Cisgender women who are threatened by trans women to the point of antagonization are ill-informed about gender identity, but their transphobia further perpetuates violence against trans women and anyone else who identifies outside the binary heteronormative standards. And because transphobia is upheld by white supremacy, openly targeting, misgendering, and attempting to invalidate trans people comes without consequence. Wealthy A-list celebrities like Dave Chappelle and J. K. Rowling regularly use their platforms to target and ridicule trans people and continue to lead thriving careers.

Rose McGowen eventually apologized for the discourse, suggesting that the issue was her poor choice of verbiage and not understanding what cisgender meant. "I'm a woman from Hollywood," she said in an interview. In other words, *I don't know shit about y'all; I'm fighting for me and my friends in The Hills.*

The apology was underwhelming. White women at the forefront of the second wave of Me Too were proving time and again that they had neither the bandwidth nor intention of leading a movement with the same level of integrity as its predecessor. Marginalized genders, specifically Black women and trans women, who were central in the original Me Too movement, had now been received as antagonists.

Gender norms have us in such a tight chokehold that we often decide who will be the victim based on their intersectional currency. A blonde white woman will always reign as the damsel in distress, while the dark-skinned fat woman is deemed too unattractive to be a true victim. And cisgender men are expected to wear their molestation like a badge of honor if their assailant is a woman. Yet, there is no acknowledgment for the Black and Brown queers and trans people most vulnerable to sexual violence. Not every survivor of sexual assault is a woman, and not every sexual predator is a man.

As the second wave of Me Too took off, the gap between marginalized victims, who were all but abandoned, and white women dubbed as heroes only widened. Sex workers, cisgender men, and trans people who were victims of sexual violence were never offered an equitable space to be heard, seen, and supported.

Regardless of personal or moral beliefs, sex work is among America's oldest, most profitable, and most popular industries. It's also one of the most dangerous, largely because sex workers never receive the respect or protection needed. And, like many industries that are reliant on Black and Brown marginalized genders, the sex industry runs from the labor of those who are most vulnerable to sexual violence and murder. People in industries like sex work, who navigate the frontlines of sexual violence, should have been represented in the second wave of Me Too.

By reducing sexual assault to binary gender norms, not only were men not included, but they were also often shamed and invalidated for speaking up. The impact, for cisgender men, often reduced their testimonies to narratives that suggested their sexual experiences were "lucky" or not as serious.

By sticking to a script where the Me Too heroine is a white woman, the antagonist is a white man, and the stage is set in Hollywood, the movement had been reimagined to exclude any and all industries that didn't align with its central characters. For vulnerable employers and genders left out of the conversations, the impact resulted in further perpetuation of heteronormative, patriarchal expectations. And, when it came to race, the damage was highly consequential for Black women and other marginalized genders.

Where the second wave of Me Too stalled, the original movement continues to thrive. Tarana continues expanding on the framework, ensuring that it's gender inclusive, it centers victims, and it starts and ends with healing, safety, and equity.

Because fame was never a motive, she's not the visual activist who appears at every hearing and talk show whenever a sexual assault case begins to trend. However, you can find her in the spaces where the movement is most needed: sometimes that looks like a college campus; other times, it's the set of the *Love and Hip Hop* franchise, where even lace-front edges are snatched by the healing powers of vulnerability, community, and confession, which only the original movement provides.

As for the second wave of the movement, as the hashtag continues to collect dust, many who hoped that it would eventually bridge the gap between victim, community, and healing are still waiting. For all the big convictions and court cases, the second wave has yet to produce tangible results for people—all people.

THERE'S MORE TO ME THAN HIV

◼

by LáDeia Joyce

◼

BLACK AMERICAN WOMAN – SHE/HER – FORTY-THREE YEARS OLD
– MEMPHIS, TENNESSEE

I'll never forget the day I got the phone call that changed my life. It was a Thursday, an unseasonably warm day here in Memphis. I was riding with the windows down, sunroof back, in the middle of rush hour traffic. That call confirmed what I had already been told by my Spirit two days prior: Girl, you got HIV.

As I ended the call, I felt a bit of my soul, my life, my essence slip away. It is often said that HIV is not a death sentence. Lies! In that very moment LáDeia as I knew her died.

Over the previous weekend, I shared with close friends the inconclusive HIV test I had recently taken. I knew they were waiting on an update—one that ended with "negative." I remember emotions pouring over me as I incoherently word dumped via our group chat. It felt like my vocal cords were boxing concrete as the air traveled up from my diaphragm, forcing out the words, "The test came back saying I am HIV positive!"

• • •

Seven years later and I still have no recollection of certain details of the night I got my diagnosis.

With a trembling hand, I picked up my phone and made the call I had been dreading the most. With each ring, a flashback of the last seven years replayed in my broken heart. The man who regularly bared his soul to me and held space for me to bare mine to him. The keeper of my heart, and the bastard who cheated on me. I don't normally leave voicemails, but once I heard that beep, I said everything I needed to say: "Hey, umm, this is LáDeia. I just got the results from the test I told you about last weekend. You know, the one when I told you and you said, 'Don't worry about it; we good.' Well, we're not good! I am indeed HIV positive. You have indeed had unprotected sex with someone who is HIV positive. Because you have, it is imperative that you get fully tested for STDs, including and especially HIV every three months for the next year. Also, contact anyone else your philandering ass been with."

Click.

A torrent storm of emotions started to swirl within me. Ominous clouds gathered on the horizon of my mind. Gale force winds tore at the very fabric of my core. I was swept into an abyss of chaos, darkness, and the unknown. The pain, the anger, the betrayal, and the dismissal merged, creating a tempest within me . . . a storm so fierce, so tumultuous, so violent that even Oya herself would've marveled.

I. Was. Enraged.

I lifted my head toward the moonless sky and wailed with the fervency of a group of prayer warriors during a gully washing session.

I gave no thought to what my neighbors would hear or think. I had to give this sound, and I had to get it up and out. When I had nothing left, I took myself to bed.

The nurse practitioner said I could pick up my test results from the front desk the following morning. How could I suddenly ask a friend, "Hey, you wanna go with me to pick up my HIV test results in the morning?" I didn't have to worry about my friends rejecting me for too long. After reaching out to my homegirl Keisha, she offered to go with me before I could even ask.

"I know you not thinking about going by yourself," she said. She didn't just offer me a ride to the clinic, she gave me support and compassion, which I needed. She let me know that I wasn't alone.

The Price Is Right was playing in the waiting room when I entered the doctor's office. I had so many questions about the newly added three letters to my identity and was convinced that all of them would be answered during this visit. I sincerely believed that those medical professionals would provide me with the information that was missing from the internet.

The walk from the front door to the check-in desk felt like it went on for miles. At first, I couldn't find my voice, but eventually I opened my mouth and spoke. "I'm LáDeia Joyce McNeal, and Nurse Practitioner James left an envelope for me to pick up."

The receptionist broke out a smile and said, "Yes, ma'am. We have them right here." She grabbed a file that was sitting on top of her desk and handed it to me. "Have a great rest of your day and enjoy your weekend." That was it. No information, no details about my next steps, no sympathy. Nothing! Instead, all I got was the large white envelope, which I still have to this day.

Everything within me turned red. I heard red. I saw red. I felt red. I radiated red. I tasted red.

"You mean to tell me nobody is going to sit down with me to explain this shit?" I blacked out. The anger I'd been nursing since finding out about my diagnosis went from a slow burn to a full-fledged raging fire. I started barking at the staff. I demanded that the nurse practitioner who performed my test come up front and immediately. I went on a verbal assault à la Tasmanian Devil style—everybody in my path caught the wrath of this tongue. Staff from the back started to come up front, and they got some too. I know I would have caught a charge if Keisha wasn't there to hold me back. I was dismissed, unheard, not cared for, and I wasn't having it. I wanted everyone in that office to feel my pain that they had just exacerbated with their apathy.

Eventually, a nurse practitioner took us to the counseling room. For the next thirty minutes, a physician fumbled their way through explaining what I should be prepared for. They spoke about different tests and treatments with language that was laced with scientific jargon and a cold bedside manner.

My internal dialogue was all over the place. *LáDeia, how the hell did you end up here? How does somebody like me get HIV? I barely have sex yet get tested every six months and urge everyone around me to do the same! What is this going to look like? What are we going to do? How do we tell my mother?!?! No, God, I can't die like this!!*

It was as if Keisha could read my mind because she started firing off all the questions I'd been asking myself. I watched her go through the documents in that white envelope. She looked the doc square in the eyes and asked, "Where do y'all send the white folks who leave outta here with an HIV diagnosis? Nowhere on any of these lists is there somewhere she can go for care. She came in here with private insurance. Why is she not being treated like it?"

In that counseling room, Keisha's fierce advocacy broke through my layers of confusion and frustration. She demanded answers. It was clear that they were ill-equipped to address the emotional and psychological impact of an HIV diagnosis.

What followed was a journey that was heavy with introspection and shadow work. An HIV diagnosis has an uncanny way of bringing up all your skeletons. At times, I was literally fighting for my life as I fell deep into unpacking emotional boxes.

The molestation.

The daddy issues.

The feelings of inadequacy.

The date rape that that I never spoke about.

The fact that I often dimmed my light to make others comfortable.

The hoarding of money out of fear birthed from traumatic childhood experiences.

That area of abandonment that kept me prickly to keep people from getting too close.

When I wasn't unraveling, I was burying myself in research. I wanted to understand what my new normal was expected to look like. I also needed to find some type of agency, network, initiative, anything that centered Black women. The more I searched, the more I saw the significant imbalances in both representation and resource. It was frustrating, but it only motivated me to stand in the gap.

Fear and stigma had me wrapped tighter than freshly pressed hair slicked back into a ponytail on Easter Sunday. The weight of this scarlet letter felt insurmountable. I became hyperselective about whom I confided in. I held on to a short list of people I disclosed to. These individuals were my trusted tribe, the ones who gave me understanding and compassion. I was blessed to have a small but supportive community of people who knew my whole story, but I still feared that someone would out me.

Navigating this new normal dog-walked me. The complexities of being a Black woman living with HIV was not easy. However, it pushed me to nourish my soul and check the negative voices in my head—my inner critic was so loud! Taking care of myself allowed me to call my power back and stand flat-footed in it, knowing that I deserved all I had poured out on others. Now, let me be real real—it was not all love and light, and it for sure didn't happen overnight.

Embracing this taught me that I'm to share my scars, never my wounds. Wounds exposed leave them unable to heal properly, allowing space and opportunity to bleed. Learning to help and heal those folks you encounter without bleeding all over them, darling, that's a powerful and necessary thing to learn.

While putting into practice lessons learned, in 2017, I created an online profile, albeit secretly, using random handles and no profile picture. Behind private pages, I chronicled my journey with unwavering transparency, pouring my heart out and sharing my experiences, struggles, and triumphs.

My intention was to shift the narrative around how we talk about Black women and HIV. I wanted to be the example, the resource that I had been looking for all along. I used my aliases to challenge stereotypes and tropes that were so prevalent and so wrong in our culture.

My platforms blew up. I forged connections with kindred souls who shared parallel paths. In true Black women fashion, we cultivated a resilient community of encouragement and inspiration, demonstrating that an HIV diagnosis could never confine or constrain our capacity to live boldly.

With my online presence reaching wider horizons, my name was ringing bells, boo! I took the stage at conferences, workshops,

and events, amplifying my advocacy for HIV awareness and education, particularly within the Black community, specifically centering Black women.

Still, behind all the progress was my struggle. Navigating this
illness ain't for the weak. The programs meant to provide aid often
fell woefully short of offering tangible support. More often than
not, I was left to fend for myself in a system that was indifferent to
my quality of life. For all the good I did, I couldn't escape having
to rumble with red tape and bureaucracy to get the simplest of
things done. It is a frustrating dance that drains me to this day.

Many times, I've found myself sitting alone in the driver's seat
idling in a pharmacy drive-thru, tears streaming down my face like
an unyielding downpour, each tear feeling like the weight of a
thousand fears drowning me in uncertainty. I've felt suffocated by
insurance company indifference, a vile and heartless entity that
cares nothing about the life hanging in the balance. In these moments, the fear of dying from HIV complications felt as palpable
as a winter's night shiver that permeates the soul. The reality of
being denied access to the lifesaving medication hovered like a
heavy shadow, refusing to fade away.

* * *

Moments arise where I'm forced to make heart-wrenching
choices between my career aspirations and vital healthcare coverage. "Career vs. coverage," I often say. In the state of Tennessee,
the moment my salary exceeds $48K a year, I could find myself
abruptly cut off from Ryan White coverage. On the other hand,
private insurance can and does fall short, leaving me to shoulder
the burden of uncovered medical expenses, hindering my ability
to access the comprehensive care necessary to manage my condition effectively. The constant struggle to strike a balance between

earning a living and maintaining adequate healthcare coverage has taught me the harsh reality of how financial barriers significantly impact my well-being and quality of life.

In the fall of 2019, I was featured in the first of several paid television advertisements aimed at spreading awareness about HIV treatment. I stood in my living room staring at the fifty-five-inch Vizio on my mantle in complete awe. This Black girl from the pjs of Memphis, Tennessee, who crafted a brand out of an HIV diagnosis, had shown up in such a way that she was on TV — in a commercial starring me.

My notifications started going bananas. At that moment, I felt as if I had reached an apex in what I had set to achieve — shift what people experienced when they saw an HIV-positive Black woman. I was not fully prepared for the bullshit that was about to be unleashed.

For every word of congratulations, admiration, and affirmation I received, there were words so hateful they felt like spewed venom searing my skin and piercing the very depths of my soul. I very quickly learned in real time what society thought about a woman like me who had the nerve to live her life out loud.

People attacked not just my advocacy but my identity. They questioned my intelligence, attempted to diminish my worth, attacked my character and my right to freely exist in the public eye, and it cut deep. It was a vile effort to use my HIV status as a weapon, attempting to shame me back into silence. Stigma, ignorance, and fear had folks in a chokehold as it manifested in every cruel word typed in a comment section. I felt exposed, vulnerable, and defenseless.

After what seemed like thousands of pranayama breaths, I found solace in knowing that my voice and presence ignited conversations that were overdue. I knew for every derogatory troll, there were compassionate and interested hearts watching, learning, and finding comfort and representation in my advocacy.

As time went on, I realized that my existence as a Black woman living with HIV was an act of resistance in itself. I was breaking through barriers and demanding to be seen, heard, and respected. My visibility became a formidable instrument in fighting stigma, defying stereotypes, and dispelling myths. I gave voice to the dismissed and gave face to the overlooked. Like a beacon in the darkness, I knew I wouldn't dim this light for anyone.

At times, the burden of carrying the weight of my advocacy is overwhelming. I am proud of all I've accomplished during this relatively short period, but the toll it has taken on me is undeniable. Mentally, the emotional labor required to navigate both my own healing journey and supporting others in theirs has been draining. Emotionally, the constant exposure to the harsh realities of living with HIV, coupled with the relentless stigma, has left me feeling raw and vulnerable.

I find myself at a crossroads, where my soul yearns for a reprieve, even if temporary. The incessant demands of advocacy work sometimes drown out the soft whispers of my personal aspirations and desires. My deepest longing is to truly manifest and embody the fact that "I'm LáDeia, and there's more to me than HIV."

What happens if and when I walk away? The thought of relinquishing the reins of advocacy fills me with both relief and trepidation. The idea of no longer bearing the weight of being a prominent HIV advocate seems liberating. I could shed the public persona and embrace a life where I am not defined by my diagnosis or activism. I could explore other passions, engage in hobbies, and simply live without the constant pressure of making a difference.

On the other hand, the prospect of stepping back is met with uncertainty. Who do I turn to when the patient LáDeia needs the advocate LáDeia? Advocacy and activism have become intrinsic to my existence, like the air I breathe. It's woven into the fabric of my being, and detaching from it would require untangling a complex web of emotions and experiences.

What I know to be true about my journey with life and advocacy is that finding balance is crucial. It's essential to acknowledge that I am not solely an advocate but a multifaceted individual with dreams, aspirations, and a need for self-care. Embracing my humanity means recognizing that I have limits and that it's okay to seek support and rest.

Advocacy is so much more; it's my ministry. It's the purpose that has ignited a fire within me, pushing me to challenge the norms, defy stigma, and redefine what it means to be a Black woman living openly with HIV. But even within the realm of a calling, there are times when I yearn for the freedom that a life without these responsibilities would bring. The burden of representing a community, of being the face and voice of those who have been silenced, is a weight I carry daily.

Stepping back from advocacy doesn't mean abandoning my cause; rather, it might mean embracing a new role—one that allows me to be an advocate from a place of wholeness. It means learning to reinforce boundaries, knowing when to pause, and understanding that my well-being is not a compromise for the greater good.

I am LáDeia, and there is indeed more to me than HIV. My journey as an advocate will continue, but it will be balanced with the journey of self-discovery and self-care. Together, they form a harmonious symphony, each note contributing to the beautiful melody of a life fully lived. And in this symphony, I find the strength to embrace my vulnerability and celebrate the multifaceted woman I have become.

LáDeia Joyce continues advocating for Black women living with HIV. For more info on her work and how you can support her, follow her on Instagram @ladeiajoyce.

A DRAG DEFERRED

■

"It was the period when the Negro was in vogue."

—LANGSTON HUGHES, *The Big Sea*

S trangest and gaudiest of all Harlem spectacles in the '20s, and
still the strangest and gaudiest, is the annual Hamilton Club
Lodge at Rockland Palace Casino. I once attended as a guest of
A'Lelia Walker. It is the ball where men dress as women and
women dress as men."

The above quote is from Langston Hughes's 1940 autobiography, *The Big Sea*. In just three exquisitely written paragraphs, he
gifts readers a definitive review of the 1920s drag culture in Harlem. His brief yet descriptive views admit that he appeared as the
guest of A'Lelia Walker, the lone child of one of America's first
Black millionaires, Madame C. J. Walker. And the Rockland Palace was known for facilitating high-end events for affluent Black
folks, social events, but most popular, the Hamilton Club Lodge
Ball.

Big Sea is a greater reflection of Hughes's life as a Black man
in Harlem and Paris. It would be easy to read the few paragraphs
about 1920s ball culture and dive into the author's profound re-

flections on race, gender, and politics. But Ricky Tucker, author of *And the Category is . . . : Inside New York's Vogue, House, and Ballroom Community*, breaks down Hughes's insights on ball culture, nearly line for line. In doing so, he proves that the fundamentals of drag culture—the gathering, the fashion, and the shade, were born long before Madonna's version of "Vogue" was introduced to 1990s pop culture.

The idea of a Black man existing outside gender norms during the Jim Crow era was nothing short of a collective rebellion. And a group of gay Black men gathering to dismantle gender norms made the moment a genuine uprising. Black queers curated space and culture exclusively for them, and not as a means of protest but rather the love of drag and the gender identities outside hetero norms. The presence of LGBTQ+ people and culture within the Harlem Renaissance is often overlooked, but it's as relevant today as ever.

By 1967, drag culture in New York City had made its way to the main stage. The girls were nationally organized, well-shaved, and otherwise pageant ready. The 1968 documentary *The Queen* detailed the 1967 Miss All-American Camp Beauty Pageant. In *The Queen*, the pageant is moved to midtown. The doc is a rare glimpse into the world of New York City drag culture, from its fashion to its politics. There is stunning behind-the-scenes footage of drag queens during dress rehearsals and intimate moments of gentlemen discussing everything from childhoods to gender identities. In this way, the documentary serves as a time capsule of the evolution of sexual orientation, gender identity, and how it correlates with drag culture. But, for Black queers, the most prolific moment in *The Queen* occurs in the doc's last ten minutes. It is a brief, game-changing moment in New York drag history that drew racial lines in the sand and served as the breakthrough moment when Black and Latinx Harlem ballroom culture was born.

Crystal LaBeija, a Black drag queen from Uptown, arrived at the Camp Beauty Pageant ready to slay. Crystal was aware of the discrimination that defined and restricted the space for Black and Brown queens in that era. Like many others, the pageant was run by predominantly white men who favored the Andy Warhol waifs and blonde aesthetic of their time. Uptown queens like Crystal represented the more authentic spectrum of the counterculture, including fashion and culture rooted in the pulse of Harlem drag culture, which had been thriving for decades.

Despite Crystal's style and grace at the end of the pageant, the grand prize went to Harlow, an out-of-town queen with a basic makeup job and beat-up wig. She wore a shimmering ocean-blue dress with oversized sleeves that begged to be tailored. Her makeup was, at best, minimal, and she carried herself with a lethargic energy. She would have been a hit if she had been arriving at a costume party as Jeannie from *I Dream of Jeannie*. But, seeing as this was arguably one of the biggest nights of drag culture in a packed audience of queens and allies from across the country, Harlow's pageantry left much to be desired. She couldn't hold a candle to Crystal LaBeija, who showed up ready to win. Donning a wig that was no less than twenty-two inches and sky high, her face was beat for the gods, her waist was snatched, and her presence was fierce. She wore a floor-length white gown with a white feathered stole around her arm and a jeweled headpiece to match.

Shortly after Crystal was announced as a runner-up, sis sauntered off the stage. In a seething read that flipped the entire pageant on its head, Crystal called out the pageant's organizers, the judges, and even Harlow.

From that moment forward, she opted out of competing in predominantly white drag contests. The bitter end inspired her to create a ball that not only catered to the underappreciated Black and Latinx queers north of 110th Street, but one where they, too, could thrive and build within a safe, brave community. In 1972, Crystal and her friend Koko would host their first of many Harlem balls. Ricky Tucker wrote about her divestment from white ballroom culture and subsequent decision to facilitate an event exclusively for Black and Brown queens. "It caused a seismic shift, laying down a cultural foundation that was rooted in protest and thereby unshakable," he wrote. Running off the steam that the Rockland Palace had created decades before, Crystal facilitated space for a new generation of Black and Brown queers who would define drag culture for the world.

NEW YORK CITY IS WRAPPED UP IN LABEIJA

Twenty years later, in 1987, the true pulse of ballroom culture found its way home, back to Harlem. In this era, the queens were younger, more organized, and had a lot more to worry about.

New York City was never "safe" for Black children, but it was especially dangerous in the 1980s. The impact of the crack cocaine epidemic, the murdering and wrongful imprisonment fueled by white supremacists and the New York Police Department, and the AIDS pandemic taunted young Black queers. Many of these kids were fending for themselves on the streets, victims of families who disowned them. Without assistance from family or the government, these children found a home and community within themselves in Harlem ballroom culture. What Crystal LaBeija created as an answer to the white drag world downtown had grown into a fully functional, well-structured community of Black and Latinx queers who provided everything from family structure to room and board to its most marginalized members.

Just as the queens in *The Queen* introduced mainstream culture to the language and nuances of gender identity and sexual orientation, the children of Harlem ball culture would do the same with *Paris Is Burning*. The documentary, which debuted in 1990 and was directed and produced by Jennie Livingston, captured the lifestyles of the Black and Brown men and marginalized genders that embodied the scene. Rather than call themselves queens, they referred to themselves as children. And, while they celebrated their ability to transform into a myriad of characters and illusions, who they aspired to be outside the ball was truly captivating.

Harlem ballroom culture was as centered in the community as it was pageantry, some say even more so. Rather than alliances, there were houses, and instead of leaders, there were mothers. No longer competing with a "me against the world" strategy, the competition was by houses, not just individuals. And, to ensure no exclusion, every participant who walked a ball received a trophy.

By completely divesting from the white norms and standards established by the white ballroom scene, formal wear, auditorium-style seating, and fanfare of the who's who of queer New York, the Harlem children were free to reimagine and innovate the ballroom scene. Left to their own devices, they decided they were all the celebrity and fanfare they needed.

Crystal was absent in *Paris Is Burning* and is no longer known as the mother of House of LaBeija. Instead, the reins had fallen to Pepper LaBeija, a Harlem-based androgynous queer. Pepper and Angie Xtravaganza, mother of House of Xtravaganza, were among several house mothers who took their roles very seriously, providing everything from mentorship to shelter for their house children.

From these children and houses, the global queer culture would be redefined in language, aesthetics, and ethos. It would also serve as strong affirmation that, even in the midst of discrimination, violence, and exclusion from white queers, they would not only survive but, as a collective, thrive. They did this without recognition, support, or protection. They also did it in the face of a global pandemic.

ACT UP

For Peter Staley, it started as a simple cough. And then, random rashes on his face. Soon enough, simple colds that would normally come and go would suddenly leave him feeling weak and severely ill. Eventually, he would find out that he was HIV positive, but much of the information at his disposal was from the street rather than literature or elected officials. Back then, the narrative was that HIV was exclusively for gay people and that those who contracted it got what they "deserved." So, for two years, Peter lived with HIV in secret, telling only his family and closest friends. Until one day, on his way to work downtown, he was handed a flyer. It was from an activist group, AIDS Coalition to Unleash Power, ACT UP. Peter didn't know that ACT UP would become an activist group or that he would become an activist who helped motivate its leading members and change the landscape of activism and social justice.

In 1987, there was still little information and resources regarding HIV/AIDS treatment and even less concern and sympathy. It was considered to be a death sentence, and with good reason. "Everything I read said that I had about two years to live. At most," Peter revealed in the 2012 documentary *How to Survive a Plague*, which chronicles ACT UP's fight for healthcare and humane treatment. While people living with HIV did not have support from the government or the American healthcare system, their strongest weapon was unity. Together, they teamed up and faced off with state and government officials, hospitals, big pharmaceutical companies, and even landlords who evicted people for having HIV/AIDS.

Peter was not a natural-born activist like many young, otherwise healthy men who contracted the virus. Quite the contrary, he was raised in a two-parent household with a well-to-do family and was raised in Berwyn, Pennsylvania. By the time he moved to New York in his early twenties to work on Wall Street, he had already graduated from Oberlin, traveled abroad, and was fully aware that he was gay. What should have been a continuation of his sexual freedom was cut short by his contraction of HIV. In a flash, the life of stability and freedom he envisioned came crashing down, replaced with fears of sudden death and public humiliation. Like many, ACT UP wasn't just a source of social justice but a much-needed community of peers fighting for their lives like him.

ACT UP members had much more in common than those living with HIV. For starters, the majority of them were cisgender white men and women. Also, like Peter, many came from backgrounds with access and privilege that gave them the tools to pursue activism full-time. For example, Larry Kramer, one of the founding members of Gay Men's Health Crisis, was a Yale graduate, critically acclaimed author, and screenwriter. It was well-known that he had profited so much from his award-winning screenplays that he never had to work again. In fact, many ACT UP members were professional artists and well-known throughout New York City. While their privilege doesn't discount their impact or invalidate their efforts, it's worth noting that the societal currency that comes with being white and masculine-presenting cisgender men was an advantage that the children in Harlem were without.

In *Queer and Loathing: Rants and Raves of a Raging AIDS Clone*, writer David B. Feinberg chronicles his relationship with

ACT UP and HIV, not only as an activist but also as a person living with the disease who is acutely aware that he will, indeed, eventually die. For as long as he could, he balanced activism, his health, his career, and his social life. The book is raw and heartbreaking but also eye-opening in the ways that it allows readers to understand the depth of pain and fear that haunt those who are forced to spend what should be the peak of their adulthoods bracing themselves for the end of their lives.

During those pivotal years of ACT UP from 1987–1995, the group faced many challenges and untimely deaths during their fight for justice and adequate healthcare. They would also completely innovate Americans' relationship with activism by taking radical measures to seek equality and change. From taking over the trade floor on Wall Street to planting an inflatable penis on homophobic conservative Jesse Helms's home, the ragtag group of activists would eventually get their demands met, ultimately changing the landscape of healthcare and trial testing, activism, and the relationship between patient, medical professional, and political official.

By 1996, medical advancements had finally discovered the right drug cocktail that would stop the advancement of HIV, changing it from a terminal disease to a chronic condition. Today, people living with HIV can live long and healthy lives, often without fear of transmitting it to others once they are undetected. This is partly due to the relentless activism of ACT UP members and allies in the HIV/AIDS community.

On their own, ACT UP and the Harlem ballroom culture contributed to furthering the rights and opportunities for queers of all races and ethnicities. Without ACT UP, there's a good chance that the HIV/AIDS epidemic would have continued taking lives. And, without the Black and Latinx ballroom culture, queers would be without a praxis of community and survival. But together, both groups redefined the lifestyles, possibilities, and legacy of the global queer community.

Fifty-six years after Crystal LaBeija participated in the All-American Camp Beauty Pageant and for decades after Peter Staley and ACT UP members took over the Wall Street trading floor, the worlds of ballroom culture, activism, and HIV awareness have come full circle. It's also become a major public enemy among American conservatives.

Performers like Broadway and television actor Billy Porter as well as performer and co-host of *Queer Eye* Jonathan Van Ness have made their way into mainstream pop culture while existing as queer, gender fluid, and living with HIV. Though activism is an unshakable presence in their platforms, their existence as artists and truth tellers with fabulous taste precedes them. They serve as testaments of hope to a younger generation of queers who face incredible ridicule, discrimination, and violence.

It's easy to get lost wondering how "strange" Langston Hughes would find today's drag climate, nearly one century after that Harlem ball he wrote about in *Big Sea*. What was once a fashionable competition has evolved into a legitimate community that offers support, resources, and family. Sadly, for all that drag culture has offered, it's under attack more than it's ever been, at least legally speaking.

As of August 2023, twenty American states either have or are attempting to create bans against drag queens and performances. The rhetoric often suggests that performances of drag queens are often lewd and not appropriate for children. But the real intention is the continuation of increasing LGBTQ+ hate laws that have been increasing in the twenty-first century.

On July 29, 2023, a young Black man by the name of O'Shae Sibley was voguing with friends in the parking lot of a Brooklyn gas station. O'Shae was a professional dancer and choreographer and was dancing to Beyonce's *Renaissance* album. After a group of degenerates demanded him to stop dancing, discourse ensued. And then, one of the men stabbed O'Shae, killing him.

No matter the cultural strides made by the children in the ballroom, they are still withheld from the same rights, respect, and safety as others. And many of those children died untimely deaths, if not because of the HIV/AIDS pandemic, because of violence.

It's not enough to simply enjoy queer culture and write that off as tangible support. The drag culture that Americans love to consume through RuPaul's *Drag Race* comes at the expense of human beings who don't often live long enough to reap the accolades of their contribution. Support must come in the form of uplifting, amplifying, and contributing to the grassroots organizations that keep LGBTQ+ communities safe and provided for—especially the Black and Brown–led organizations.

Support LGBTQ+ communities by donating to organizations like The Trevor Project, Gay Men's Health Crisis, and The Marsha P. Johnson Institute.

AFTERWORD

by Dr. Tyffani Monford Dent

B reathe.

I spend part of my time as a psychologist encouraging Black people who exist at the crossroads of marginalized identities to take a moment and just . . . breathe. Oftentimes, we don't know how much we're holding while we survive all the mess that the world has thrown at us. Yet, in this, I realize that I hold my own breath. There's an unconscious part of me that tells me that my exhaling will take up space. Will make less room for them to let out all that they have been unable to release before. Even in writing this afterword, I found myself not taking up space. I'm wired to enter spaces prepared to educate, support, and make space for everyone but myself. It is the nature of my life's work, and, in times like this, how I navigate the world.

Throughout this book, Tamela has taken up space. She has filled it with her pain, her triumphs, her life lessons—in a way that gently insists for all of us to gather and do the same. As I grappled

with the thoughts and memories that flooded my own consciousness in reading this work, I recalled the traumas in my own life —
some I have chosen to share, and some that remain tightly held
within a clenched fist and a wounded heart that has still attempted
to cautiously believe that there are those who want and will protect me at all costs.

I wonder if I should address how easy it is for me to know the
importance of self-care and that such is a duty we have to ourselves while hypocritically not engaging in such. I allow myself to
look inward to the lived experiences of growing up in white spaces
where I was never good enough and at the same time too good to
be valued or, even in my desperation, just left alone. There is
power in our stories, and yet, many of us choose not to tell them.
There is necessity in taking up space, even for those of us who
spent the first part of our lives shrinking and the second half serving as the Blank-I-Don't-Need-Anything mirrors that reflect and
deflect the wants, needs, and desires of everyone else.

So, I breathe. I wonder. How would the world have been different for Tyffani before she was "Dr. Tyffani" if she would have
not only allowed herself to breathe but also to take up space? How
would her world and her experiences have shifted if *Hood Wellness*
was a concept, then? What if a new definition of what it means to
be truly well demanded the telling of my story and the acceptance
that everyone would not understand it, but it was still one that
needed to be told? What if I knew that falls, traumas, bad decisions that felt good, and taking chances were all a part of creating
the person I have become? What if the search for God was truly
searching for Self or simply the attempt to add order to a life that
felt chaotic? What if this book and this idea of doing more than
treading water in the dryness of challenging circumstances and
people had been on my own table when Tyffani was becoming? It

was not, but for my own daughters and all others who are searching to find it, it is here for you. For that, I am grateful.

Everyone deserves to be physically and emotionally well. The concept of *Hood Wellness* is a level of authentically and unapologetically acknowledging our lived experiences that can get in the way of our pursuit of the happiness we are due. It doesn't seek to hide from those traumas and doubts that have plagued us or shaped us, even while knowing that we did not deserve either of them. It is owning the fullness of who we are and knowing that at any time, we should be able to start over. Yet, even in the ability to reset, recognizing that it is a privilege that many do not want to extend to us.

Hood Wellness insists that we find our people. That we know that with whom we surround ourselves can bring joy or can contribute to our despair. It is the awareness that we must show up for one another, and even in the moments of sadness when we lose those who have brought light into our existence — even for a moment — that being in their presence made all the pain worth it. Yet, at the same time, we do not forget that we cannot show up for everyone else and fail to leave something for ourselves. The world will tell us otherwise; we will be trained to believe that our wellness has its foundation in our martyrdom. We will be praised solely for those around us being prioritized. It is the push to not view something as a need when it is our own — but only when it belongs to someone else. *Hood Wellness* snaps back with the understanding that we cannot be for anyone else if we are not being for ourselves. *Hood Wellness* also allows such support to be in the form of the ancestors who prayed for us and in the prayers we make for ourselves. Our spirituality can come in many forms and can include sage, wailing, taking it to the altar, or simply seeing the God(dess) in ourselves.

There is this misconception that healing is pretty. That it is made up of orchestra strings, lit candles, and happy endings that happen before the movie credits roll. Healing is just the opposite. It is hard. It can make one feel as if their soul is being crushed and that we might as well just stay within our unhealthy existence, because at least that difficulty is known. As Tamela reminds us, healing is ugly work. It requires getting down into the depths of our experiences and our souls and seeing all that is there—and trying to make sense of some things that make no sense. Yet, healing is cleansing. Those same tears that we initially found were in our frustration and sorrow suddenly feed the thirst of our beings and water the person we are becoming. Healing allows for therapy, and often demands it. Healing includes seeking new experiences, and occasionally that requires leaving all we know to travel to places unknown (that have been waiting for us). It is a process and not one moment in time. It can require us to circle back and identify what we missed the first time or simply just did not recognize needed our attention. Stumbling is healing.

Even as we work toward our own wellness, we also know the power in sharing it. We bring others with us. We expand the community and teach the lessons we have learned along the way. Our challenges become vicarious learning for others. Our transparency opens the door for others to do the same. Within our journey toward wellness, we engage in activism and advocacy to make the road less rocky for the next person—while also knowing that such work will require us to intentionally be mindful to not let it pull us back under.

Hood Wellness is community. It is safety. It is knowing that not everyone has the same resources but helping them find joy in the ways they can. *Hood Wellness* is manifesting your amazing emotionally and physically healthy future—in whatever ways work for you. It is not owning guilt that does not belong to you from individual perpetrators or simply trying to survive in a world that never wanted you to in the first place. It is recognizing when you have internalized misogynoir and other harmful societal messages and working every damn day to eradicate them. *Hood Wellness* is showing up in all the ways you want to and making space to celebrate others doing the same.

In *Hood Wellness*, we have begun to explore what it means to own our stories—all of them—and to radically love on ourselves and on those who fully see us.

May we all one day be hood well.

Breathe.

ACKNOWLEDGMENTS

This book has been the greatest community I have ever been a part of. Thank you to everyone who laid hands on this, who held my hand through this, who loved me through this.

Thank you, Holly Raines, for the invaluable gift of your time and your voice. Thank you, Marco Rodrigues and Dylan. And, to the contributors and writers who have been so selfless with your lives—Joshua Dixon, Simone Gordon, Kit Fenrir Amreik, LáDeia Joyce, and Shevone Torres—this book is nothing without you.

From October 2019–October 2021, I would not have survived without communal support, financial, emotional, and otherwise. Thank you to the following individuals, groups, and organizations: The Black Fairy Godmother, The Black Feminist Project, Layla Saad, Done for Didi, Lisa Barlow, Jennifer Allison, Dana Lubin Garcia, and Cathy Loup. Thank you for advocating for me to have resources that I could not have lived without. The only reason why this book exists is because of your support.

Brenda Gordon and Tyra Yvette Gordon, thank you for every thing and every time. Thank you for guiding me and holding me and teaching me and helping me start over, again and again. This body of work is a reflection of the love and intention you've poured into me the past forty-two years of my life.

Tanya Denise Fields. My nigga. All the words in the world could not convey how grateful I am be in community with you. You changed my life. Literally. Thank you for investing in me. Thank you for patiently teaching me, through action, what community looks like when we lead with love and boundaries. May we celebrate this, always.

Dr. Tyffani Monford Dent, thank you for taking up space. And for always being a safe space for us. Your love takes no days off. I'm moved by your words and changed by your influence.

Abiola Abrams, thank you so much for your mentorship. From giving me space on your stage in 2010 to sharing your gems of wisdom and the power of your support, you really show up! Fourteen years later, I still look up to you with dreamy eyes, inspired by all the ways I get to be, simply because I've seen you embody it first. Thank you, sis.

Sandy Broadus, thank you for always protecting me, always speaking love over me. I didn't start believing I could do this until you kept telling me I could. I love you.

EbonyJanice. EbonyJanice! Before I ever met you, before you ever knew who I was, my life was shifted by your words. I've said it before, and I'll say it again: you have the strongest command of Self that I've ever seen in a human. Thank you for affirming me with your friendship and elevating me with the framework you blessed us with in *All the Black Girls Are Activists*. You keep me perpetually impressed, my nigga. Thank you. Love you.

To my editor, Neva. You showed up on time and understood the assignment. Thank you for gathering me. V. Ruiz, thank you for advocating for this work! Thank you for teaching about this business in ways I've never had the opportunity to learn. You are a gift. Juliet Diaz, I love you, prima. Your support and empathy have walked with me through some challenging times, and I am so grateful to you. Thank you.

Thank you to the good folks at Simon & Schuster. Your support and enthusiasm in *Hood Wellness* is deeply appreciated.

Danny Rodriguez, thank you so much for being in community with me. You are the soulmate I've always dreamed of, and your ability to be so consistent in how you love and show up in the world forever moves me. I think I want to have your baby.

Brighid Ghosio, thank you, bestie.

To A. E. Rooks, thank you so very much for being a friend, confidant, mentor in this wild book business, and life coach.

To my immediates: Tyrone, Terrell, Charmaine, thank you for loving me from the bottom. Loving me through hardships and conflict. Thank you for never giving up on me. And, to my sweet baby angels: Somalia, Najee, Naasir, Jaier, Jamaeri, Little Terrell, Missani, Lexi, Aubrey, and Bella. And Daddy. Thank you. You're my forever hero.

To my friend, my sister, my publish-sis, Rebekah Borucki. Thank you so much for believing in me and in *Hood Wellness*. Your support in this turned what would have been a pamphlet into a living, breathing community with pages. When they see *Hood Wellness*, they see you. It's a blessing to create, grow, learn from, and get to love you. Our challenges have only made us stronger, and, after all these years, our intention is unwavering. I love that for us.

In memory of Aunt Maryan, Ma, Papa, Tio Pepito, Debra, Cheron Carnarvon, Tiar'a Rowland, Ethel Waters, Hattie McDaniel, Louise Beavers, Latasha Harlins, David E. Feinberg, Jeremiah Reeves, Holly Raines, Mrs. Perez, Nancy Green, Pepper LaBeija, Crystal LaBeija, Angie Xtravaganza, Larry Kramer, William Ford, Yusuf Hawkins, Erica Garner.

And to anyone who took the time to read this, you deserve more and better. Nobody's going to give it to you, so you gotta snatch that shit. Take it and make it yours. I'm rooting for you.

BIBLIOGRAPHY

INTRODUCTION

DeBerry, Jarvis. 2020. *I Feel to Believe: Collected Columns*, September 24, 2020.

MY NECK, MY BACK

Doyle, Glennon. 2021. "Beauty: How did we get trapped in the cage and how do we break free?" We Can Do Hard Things Podcast, Episode 18, August 17, 2021. https://momastery.com/blog/episode-18/.

Jiminez, Ileana. 2010. "The master narrative." feministteacher.com, April 10, 2010. https://feministteacher.com/2010/04/13/exposing-the-master-narrative-teaching-toni-morrisons-the-bluest-eye/.

Johnson, Martin. 2006. "No Butts About It." *The National Post*, January 18, 2006. Seth Rosenthal on X: "like you have gotta be fuckin kidding me (this is '06, so a little later than I just said)." Twitter, July 1, 2022, 10:55 a.m. https://t.co/LGY3WkIIwf.

Whitlock, Jason. 2009. "Serena Could Be the Best Ever, But . . ." FOX Sports on MSN (archive.org), July 19, 2009. https://web.archive.org/web/20090709162516/http:/msn.foxsports.com/tennis/story/9757816/Serena-could-be-the-best-ever,-but-.

CAN I HATE YOUR ORDER?

Fowler, Kate. 2021. "Bartender Reveals How Customers Treat Her Differently Since Gaining Weight." Newsweek.com, June 22, 2021.

https://www.newsweek.com/cassidy-lane-tiktok-bartending-service-industry-pretty-privilege-experience-video-1603028.

Indeed.com. 2023. Server salary in New York, NY. https://www.indeed.com/career/server/salaries/New-York–NY.

Popken, Ben. 2014. "Report: 80% of waitresses report being sexually harassed." Today.com, October 7, 2014. https://www.today.com/money/report-80-waitresses-report-being-sexually-harassed-2d80199724.

BEG BORROW HEAL

Gilbert, Elizabeth. 2006. *Eat Pray Love.*

GUMMY BITCH

Statista.com. 2022. "41 million Americans wear dentures." June 23, 2022. https://www.statista.com/statistics/275484/us-households-usage-of-dentures/.

LAST MAMMY STANDING

Bogle, Donald. 2001. *Primetime Blues: African Americans on Network Television. New York Times* on the web. https://archive.nytimes.com/www.nytimes.com/books/first/b/bogle-blues.html?scp=6&sq=ethel%2520waters&st=cse.

Dresser, Norine. 1999. "A Grave Policy." *Los Angeles Times.* https://www.latimes.com/archives/la-xpm-1999-oct-16-me-22878-story.html.

Eaton, Isabel. 1899. "Special Report on Negro Domestic Service." Nyhistory.org. https://wams.nyhistory.org/industry-and-empire/labor-and-industry/black-domestic-workers/#resource.

Elliot, Nancy Miller. 1995. *Buck Clayton's Jazz World*, page 81. November 27, 1995.

Jackson, Carl. *Hattie: The Life of Hattie McDaniel*, pp. 107, 30.

Lance, Steve. 1996. *Written Out of Television: A TV Lover's Guide to Cast Changes, 1945–1994*. Madison Books, page 22, May 7, 1996.

Massie, Victoria M. 2016. "The First Black Oscar Winner Fought Segregated Housing in Los Angeles—and Won." Vox.com, February 24, 2016. https://www.vox.com/2016/2/24/11105204/hattie-mcdaniel-housing-oscars.

Mears, Hadley. 2018. "The Thrill of Sugar Hill." Lacurbed.com, February 22, 2018. https://la.curbed.com/2018/2/22/16979700/west-adams-history-segregation-housing-covenants.

Waters, Ethel, and Charles Samuel. *His Eye Is on the Sparrow: An Autobiography*, pp. 1, 17.

THE STAKES IS HIGH

Ford, Yance. 2017. *Strong Island*. Directed and Produced by Yance Ford. https://www.imdb.com/title/tt5873150/.

Kappstatter, Bob. 2017. "The Story of Bernard Goetz, The Subway Vigilante." *The Daily News*, August 14, 2017. https://www.nydailynews.com/new-york/story-bernhard-goetz-subway-vigilante-article-1.815968.

Sheidlower, Noah. 2020. "The Controversial History of Levittown, America's First Suburb." *Untapped New York*. https://untappedcities.com/2020/07/31/the-controversial-history-of-levittown-americas-first-suburb/.

THE SOUTH'S GOT SOMETHIN' TO SAY

Pew Research Center. 2023. "Facts about the US Black Population." Pew Research Center fact sheet, March 2, 2023. https://www.pewresearch.org/social-trends/fact-sheet/facts-about-the-us-black-population.

THE SWEETEST SUNDAY EVER KNOWN

Cargle, Rachel Elizabeth. 2023. *A Renaissance of Our Own: A Memoir and Manifesto of Reimagining.* Random House, May 16, 2023.

Kaur, Harmeet. 2018. "Kanye West Just Said that 400 Years of Slavery Was a Choice." CNN, May 4, 2018. https://www.cnn.com/2018/05/01/entertainment/kanye-west-slavery-choice-trnd/index.html.

The Official CROWN Act (thecrownact.com). https://www.thecrownact.com/.

Seghal, Parul. 2019. "White Women Were Avid Slave Owners, A New Book Shows." *The New York Times*, February 26, 2019. https://www.nytimes.com/2019/02/26/books/review-they-were-her-property-white-women-slave-owners-stephanie-jones-rogers.html.

The Whitney Plantation. https://www.whitneyplantation.org.

BUSTIN' NUTS IN AN ANTIABORTION STATE

National Partnership for Women and Families. 2018. "Black Women's Maternal Health: A Multifaceted Approach to Addressing Persistent and Dire Health Disparities," April 2018. https://nationalpartnership.org/report/black-womens-maternal-health.

Owermohle, Sarah. 2022. "Why Louisiana's Maternal Mortality Rates Are So High." *Politico*, May 19, 2022. https://www.politico.com/news/2022/05/19/why-louisianas-maternal-mortality-rates-are-so-high-00033832.

FOR BLACK GIRLS UNSHIFTING . . .

Harris, Tamara Winfrey. 2020. *The Sisters are Alright: Changing the Broken Narrative of Black Women in America.* Berrett-Koehler Publishers, October 12, 2020.

Harris-Perry, Melissa. 2013. *Sister Citizen: Shame, Stereotypes, and Black Women in America.* Yale University Press, March 26, 2013.

Jones, Charisse, and Kumea Shorter-Gooden. 2004. *Shifting: The Double Lives of Black Women in America.* Harper Perennial, July 24, 2004.

Lorde, Audre. 2007. *Sister Outsider: Essays and Speeches.* Crossing Press, August 1, 2007.

Welteroth, Elaine. 2019. *More Than Enough: Claiming Space for Who You Are (No Matter What They Say).* Viking, June 11, 2019.

ME TOO . . . BUT WHO ALL GONE BE THERE?

PART I: SHOUT-OUT TO CLAUDETTE COLVIN

Adler, Margot. 2009. "Before Rosa Parks, There Was Claudette Colvin." NPR, March 15, 2009. https://www.npr.org/2009/03/15/101719889/before-rosa-parks-there-was-claudette-colvin.

Blumelaw.net. 2021. Motion to Seal, Expunge, and Destroy Juvenile Records. https://www.blumelaw.net/wp-content/uploads/2021/10/Claudette-Colvin-Expungement-Motion-Affidavit.pdf.

Gray, Jeremy. 2015. "The Execution of Jeremiah Reeves: Alabama Teen's Death Sentence Helped Drive the Civil Rights Movement." Alabama.com, February 4, 2015. https://www.al.com/news/2015/02/the_execution_of_jeremiah_reev.html.

Laughland, Oliver. 2021. "Claudette Colvin: The Woman Who Refused to Give Up Her Bus Seat – Nine Months Before Rosa Parks." *The Guardian*, February 25, 2021. https://www.theguardian. com/society/2021/feb/25/claudette-colvin-the-woman-who-refused-to-give-up-her-bus-seat-nine-months-before-rosa-parks.

Williams, Rachel. 2021. "Civil Rights Pioneer Claudette Colvin on What It Takes to be an Activist." Oprahdaily.com. https://www. oprahdaily.com/life/a36632202/claudette-colvin-civil-rights-activist-interview/.

Younge, Gary. 2000. "She Would Not be Moved." *The Guardian*, December 15, 2000. https://www.theguardian.com/ theguardian/2000/dec/16/weekend7.weekend12.

PART II: ME WHO?

Burke, Tarana. 2021. *Unbound: My Story of Liberation and the Birth of the Me Too Movement*. Flatiron Books, September 14, 2021.

Burns, Katelyn. 2018. "Rose McGowan Broke Down in a Transphobic Rage." *them*, February 2, 2018. https://www.them.us/ story/rose-mcgowan-broke-down-in-a-transphobic-rage-last-night.

Cargle, Rachel E. 2018. "When Feminism Is White Supremacy in Heels." *Harper's Bazaar*, August 16, 2018. https://www. harpersbazaar.com/culture/politics/a22717725/what-is-toxic-white-feminism/.

Donnelly, Matt, and Tim Malloy. 2017. "'Girls' writer Murray Miller Accused of Raping Underage Actress, Aurora Perrineau (Exclusive)." *The Wrap*, January 17, 2017. https://www.thewrap. com/girls-murray-miller-aurora-perrineau-harold-perrineau-lost-oz/.

Pedersen, Erik. 2017. "Actress Accuses 'Girls' EP Murray Miller Of Sexual Assault; Showrunners Lena Dunham & Jenni Konner Defend Him — Update." *Deadline*, November 17, 2017. https://

deadline.com/2017/11/girls-producer-sexual-assault-murray-miller-aurora-perrineau-1202211274/.

A DRAG DEFERRED

Feinberg, David B. 1994. "Queer and Loathing: Rants and Raves of a Raging AIDS Clone." *Viking Adult*, November 22, 1994.

France, David. 2012. *How to Survive a Plague*. https://www.imdb.com/title/tt2124803.

Gay Men's Health Crisis. https://www.gmhc.org.

Livingston, Jennie. 1990. *Paris Is Burning*. https://www.imdb.com/title/tt0100332/?ref_=fn_al_tt_1.

The Marsha P. Johnson Institute. https://www.marshap.org.

Prater, Nia. 2023. "What We Know About the Killing of O'Shae Sibley." *Intelligencer*, August 11, 2023. https://nymag.com/intelligencer/2023/08/what-we-know-about-the-killing-of-oshae-sibley.html.

Simon, Frank. 1968. *The Queen*. https://www.imdb.com/title/tt0063477/.

The Trevor Project. https://www.thetrevorproject.org.

Tucker, Ricky. 2021. *And the Category Is . . . Inside New York's Vogue, House, and Ballroom Community*, page 50. Beacon Press.